SOUTH ASIA: A SHORT HISTORY

South Asia
A Short History

Second Edition

Hugh Tinker

UNIVERSITY OF HAWAII PRESS
HONOLULU

Published in the United States by
University of Hawaii Press
2840 Kolowalu Street
Honolulu, Hawaii 96822

Published in the United Kingdom by
The Macmillan Press Ltd
Houndmills, Basingstoke, Hampshire RG21 2XS
and London

First edition 1966 by Pall Mall Press and Frederick A. Praeger

Printed in Hong Kong

Library of Congress Cataloging-in-Publication Data
Tinker, Hugh.
    South Asia : a short history / Hugh Tinker.—2nd ed.
       p. cm.
    Bibliography: p.
    Includes index.
    ISBN 0–8248–1287–5 (paperback)
    ISBN 0–8248–1289–1 (hardcover)
    1. South Asia—History.   I. Title.
DS340.T56   1990
954—dc20   89–5099
                      CIP

For Clement Hugh Tinker (1893–1963)
in affectionate memory.
And for his great-grandson, Merlin,
with affectionate hope.

Contents

List of Maps

Preface

The South Asia which this book will explore is made up of the present-day countries Pakistan, India, Bangladesh, Burma and Ceylon (Sri Lanka).[1] They have much in common; all find their origins in the ancient Indic civilisation. They formed the British Empire bloc in the Indian Ocean which was the heart of that worldwide empire. Yet also they have been conscious of regional and cultural differences. Throughout history, these differences and divergences worked against an overall unified outlook. In the 1980s the differences often appear more important than what is held in common. Yet, despite confrontation and conflict, South Asia has shared too much, particularly in the century and a half after 1800, for neighbours to be seen as complete outsiders, beyond the circle of familiarity.

The problems inherent in taking a historical view which will attempt a synthesis of this vast region have disinclined historians to accept the task, though many have taken 'the subcontinent' as their stage. When this work first appeared the standard histories mainly dated from before the advent of independence – the multi-volume *Cambridge History of India* and the volume known to so many students as Moreland and Chatterjee (1936). In the intervening years historical surveys have been published incorporating the great body of research and writing which appeared in the 1960s and 1970s. Probably the best-known works are by Stanley Wolpert (1977), D. P. Singhal (1983) and Judith Brown (1985). Full references are given in the reading list at the end.) These writers have adopted different criteria: Judith Brown is concerned only with the period after British rule started and Wolpert places most emphasis on the modern period while Singhal deals most fully with India before the British conquest. Each of them begins with the subcontinent as the setting, and each has some difficulty in dealing with the period after 1947 inasmuch as their stage contracts to the area which now forms the Republic of India with only incidental references to Pakistan and Bangladesh.

---

[1] The name Ceylon has been retained in this book although since 1972 the island is officially called Sri Lanka. Its name has altered oftentimes. In Sanskrit it was *Lanka*, simply 'an island'. Mariners from the Arabian seas knew it as *Serendip* (hence, serendipity). In Pali it was *Sihalan*, shorted to *Silan*, that is Ceylon, and this was common usage from the thirteenth century AD.

The present work remains the only one to deal with all South Asia, past and contemporary.

A revision made after two decades is a risky business: inevitably the author's outlook must change. Yet, rereading these pages after so many years they still appear convincing, for the most part. There were some errors, and the appearance of the *Cambridge Economic History of India* has tested some conclusions and revealed inadequacies. The text has been revised wherever this was essential, but the overall presentation – very different from any adopted elsewhere – is preserved.

Because the general reader, or the student embarking on more detailed work later, will require to be informed about the immediate past, the chapter previously headed 'Two Decades of Independence' has been replaced by two entirely rewritten chapters and the last twenty years have been brought into focus. A final assessment of the post-independence period is still not possible: one's conclusions must remain tentative.

However, they too come within the overall conceptual framework which ought now to be stated explicitly. One definition of history is the 'continuous methodical record of public events' (*Concise Oxford Dictionary*). This book is, by that definition, not history. Its purpose is to try to bring South Asia to life in the mind of the reader: South Asia, throughout the ages, in the great cycle of empires, and in the unnoticed existence of the villages. The history of South Asia has been presented mainly as a record of public personages, whether in the chronicles of its own historians, or in the accounts of European scholars, be they men of action or men of the study. *Tarikh*, the Arabic term for history, also means 'dates', and there is no lack of chronological narratives, which place in order those rulers, events, laws and decisions of governments, which provide the ostensible framework of history. Yet, more than of any other great culture, it is true to say of South Asia that the key to understanding lies in the infrastructure of society, tradition, custom, religion, ideas, rather than in the formal pattern of historical events. This book attempts to bring together outward form and inner motive in order to arrive at an interpretation of a great civilisation.

The term 'South Asia' is recent, and is far from receiving universal acceptance. To the north, the Himalaya is by no means an impenetrable barrier, but it represents a fairly distinct demarcation line between cultures, and areas of political influence. To the south, the Indian Ocean (a more apt description than President Sukarno's would-be 'Indonesian Ocean') is one of the great seaways of the world, open to the traffic of Romans, Arabs, Chinese, Portuguese and all the later European intruders. To east and west, although there are formidable barriers by land – bare mountain and mighty river – what we call South Asia blends and blurs into neighbouring sub-continental regions. Where, then, does South East Asia begin? Assam and eastern Bengal must surely be accounted parts of South East Asia. Yet Indian influence throughout the ages has seeped over into Burma, and what used to be called 'Further India'. To the west, the land of the Indus, Sind, has for centuries inclined towards the Islamic culture of the Middle East; while the Punjab has been a moving frontier, with the boundaries of India sometimes running through Kabul, sometimes pushed nearly to Delhi. Of course the same is true of Europe, whose eastern frontier stood in one moment of time at Constantinople, in another at Vienna. Yet to assert that South Asia possessed the same overall cultural unity as European Christendom is to strain the analogy. It was really only during a century of British rule that South Asia became a totality for administration and trade: and even then regional differences remained more significant than the superficial unity.

Today, there is certainly a challenge to the different political units of the area to discover a greater sense of unity. Where, before 1942, the Union Jack flew relatively undisturbed, today there are separated, and still diverging, states and peoples. Starting in the east, from Burma, we cross Bangladesh, with Assam and the NEFA united to India by a slender sliver of territory. Besides the sixteen linguistic states of the Indian Union, there is to the north, Nepal, an independent state, and to the south, Ceylon. Kashmir remains an international focus of dispute, before Pakistan is reached, and Afghanistan, once a British satellite, now very conscious of its independent position amid international rivalries. Most histories are content to deal with the Indian heartland, and to treat the near neighbours only as factors in India's border relations. By concentrating upon broad themes, rather than upon individual topics, this work strives to present a balanced picture of South Asia as a whole, without ignoring the nuances of difference within its varied parts. Generalisations are notoriously misleading, and so the effort is made to illuminate the broad theme by detailed illustrations, including the contributions of leaders and pioneers among its peoples.

From the days of classical Greece, Europeans have believed that the lands of the Erythraean Sea (the Indian Ocean) were realms of wisdom and of gold. In our own days, Western thinking about South Asia has been debased into regarding it as an area of poverty, of 'under-development'. Yet this was and is one of the great mother-lands of our world culture. The civilisation which Toynbee called Indic is a spring of life which offers refreshment such as nowhere else can be found. Jawaharlal Nehru observed that India's 'peculiar quality is absorption, synthesis'. It was not surprising that Peaceful Co-Existence found its most convinced supporters in India. For long periods of time, rival religions and cultures have co-existed in South Asia. Mutual tolerance, cross fertilisation and interaction have marked relations between communities. Time and again, this peaceful co-existence has been rudely terminated, as leaders of one community have sought to dominate and obliterate their rivals. In almost every instance, the attempt to impose a unified system of thought, or of government, has shattered the loose but workable harmony of co-existence, and has led to the fragmentation of the Indic world. Then, laboriously, the different communities have rediscovered some new formula for mutual association.

Westward, South Asia is flanked by the Middle Eastern world of Islam. Despite manifold internal divisions, the Islamic world presents an almost uniformly hostile face to those who would challenge or infiltrate. To the north-east lies China, perhaps the most monolithic cultural and political system anywhere; self-sufficient, and suspicious of all outsiders. In absolute contrast, South Asia is open to every movement and pressure of the outside world: in this respect it compares with neighbouring maritime South East Asia.

Though today South Asia has discarded the unity of British rule, and its new nation-states often regard each other with virulent suspicion, still they are linked together willy-nilly by a mutual sharing of peoples and religions. None of the new states is culturally self-sufficient or undifferentiated. India, the homeland of 700 million people in the 1980s contains almost three-quarters of the inhabitants of South Asia. Bangladesh has a population of 90 million and Pakistan about 85 million. Of the remaining states, Burma has an estimated 35–40 million, Ceylon about 15 million and Nepal much the same number. The little mountain kingdom Bhutan has about 1·6 million souls. If the impression that India is Hindu is accepted, with Pakistan and Bangladesh predominantly Muslim, while Burma and Ceylon are regarded as Buddhist, then there seems to be a pattern of sharply differentiated countries and cultures. But it must be remembered that *Indian* Muslims number 60 million – far more than in any of the countries of the Near and Middle East – while there are many millions of Christians, Sikhs, Buddhists and Animists among the minorities. Bangladesh, even after the great exodus of 1947 and subsequently in 1970, has 14·5 million Hindus together with small communities of Buddhists, Christians and Animists. Ceylon, predominantly Buddhist, has three million Hindus dwelling in the north and elsewhere, with important communities of Christians and Muslims. Burma, where about three-quarters of the population are Buddhists, has sizeable minorities of Christians and Animists. There were over one million Indians in Burma down to 1942, mainly Hindu: about half fled before the Japanese, and after independence many were expelled in 1962; but the Indian legacy is still important. In Nepal and Bhutan Buddhists and Hindus are almost evenly balanced. And so we see in each South Asian country a cultural tapestry, even if one particular religious value is dominant, with the other religions interwoven. Elsewhere the pattern is repeated in a different form, with another dominant element.

Each nation reproduces a similar language patchwork in which the different elements recur in differing proportions (Map 1.) The Indian

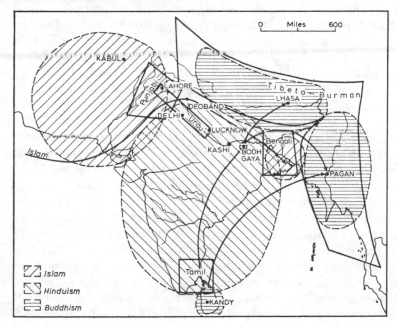

Map 1. Ties of race and religion.

constitution (Eighth Schedule) recognises fourteen tongues as 'the languages of India'. Hindi has become the official language, while Sanskrit – the root language of the sacred Hindu books – and Urdu, 'the language of the camp', are also of an all-India character. The remaining eleven languages are regional in their spread; seven belong to the Indo-Aryan family (Assamese, Bengali, Gujarati, Kashmiri, Marathi, Oriya, Punjabi) while four are Dravidian languages (Kannada, Malayalam, Tamil, Telugu). Pakistan shares all its main languages with India; Urdu is the official language of Pakistan, while Bengali is the language of the predominant mass of the Bangladesh population. The main regional language of Pakistan is Punjabi, while Kashmiri is also spoken. The other main languages include Sindhi (Indo-Aryan) and Pashtu and Baluchi which belong to the neighbouring Iranian family of languages: there is even a small area in the west where a Dravidian tongue, Brahui, is spoken. Sinhalese, the mother tongue of three-quarters of the people of Ceylon, belongs to the Indo-Aryan family; almost all the rest speak the Dravidian Tamil. Burma stands somewhat outside the main area of South Asia; nevertheless, there are important linguistic affinities. Pali, the sacred language of Buddhism, and the source of many words in Burmese, was spoken two thousand years ago in south Bihar in India and derives from Sanskrit. Burmese belongs to the Tibeto-Burman family, as do most of the 140 languages of Burma: these include Jinghpaw, Chin, and Naga (all extensively spoken on the India-Pakistan side of the dividing hills) together with Kuki and Khasi, of the same family. The Tibeto-Burman family embraces the indigenous languages of Bhutan and Sikkim (Lepcha) and of Nepal (Newari) as well as some Indian hill dialects.

Similar links can be established in the arts: in music, dancing, drama, painting and sculpture. There are, of course, manifold subcultures throughout Southern Asia, and it would be absurd to pretend that people of one region are able to communicate and to feel their connection with others separated by great distance, by geographical barriers, and by national frontiers. And yet there are noticeable similarities between, let us say, the way of life of the paddy lands and villages of east Bengal, Burma and Ceylon. Also, there are equally striking contrasts with the way of life of the paddy lands and villages of China, or even of Vietnam.

The history of South Asia cannot be demarcated in terms of decisive events or dominant policies or protocol. It has to be seen like the mighty rivers, the source of life for so many of the peoples of

South Asia. We cannot hope to understand Indus and Ganges and Brahmaputra just by attempting to make a survey of their course from source to mouth: we have to try to perceive them in all their majesty and variety and mystery.

The history of South Asia also cannot be adequately evoked by concentrating upon the central events and the dynastic history of rulers: it has to be seen as a panorama of peoples. The special quality of South Asian history was well understood by Jawaharlal Nehru, who observed in his *Discovery of India* that its story resembled 'Some ancient palimpsest on which layer upon layer of thought and reveries has been inscribed, and yet no succeeding layer had completely hidden or erased what has been written previously. All of them exist together in our conscious and subconscious selves, though we may not be aware of them, and they have gone to build up the complete, mysterious personality of India.'

Surely Nehru was right, and the conventional division of history in South Asia into the so-called Hindu period, Muslim period, and British period is quite artificial and indeed misleading? Perhaps we may do better if we try to see South Asian history in terms of a classical period, a medieval period, and the modern period. But we shall have to remember that these categories blend and blur into each other. Thus, although it can be argued that the modern age began in the port cities of Bombay, Madras, Calcutta and Colombo as far back as AD 1700, and these cities had acquired most of the characteristics of modern Western society by the early years of the nineteenth century (a professional and mercantile middle class, institutions of self-government, a free press, schools and colleges), the middle ages continued to hold their sway in the remoter Indian provinces (such as the Punjab) until the middle of the nineteenth century; in Burma down to about 1900; and in some Indian princely states down to 1947.

Although, no doubt, it is trite to describe society and government in South Asia before the entry of the West as static, still it is true to suggest that the great tradition held to the same course through the centuries. This work is designed to show how, even under the stress of disintegration following upon over-enforced centralisation, the tradition remained.

Sardar K. M. Panikkar suggests in his influential *Asia and Western Dominance* that a new pattern was created with what he calls the 'Vasco Da Gama epoch'. But the arrival of da Gama's Portuguese squadron off Calicut in 1498 did not transform the world of South Asia. There was a new pattern in sea-power and sea-trade (though the change was by no means as complete as was once supposed) but the interior continental life of South Asia continued on its course. It was not until the nineteenth century was well advanced that Western influence began to change the lives of the ordinary people, and to supplant the traditional systems of government and social order. The island of Ceylon is something of an exception. From the end of the sixteenth century, Portuguese and Catholic influence was predominant in the coastal areas. Yet even Ceylon's case shows that it was only in the maritime connection that Europe played a vital role in Asia before 1800. The nineteenth century saw the advance guard of South Asia, the middle class, emerge under Western influence; together with the introduction of a skeleton or nervous system throughout the whole length of South Asia – communications, and the beginnings of industrialisation – to form the foundation for the revolution of the twentieth century. Now, under our own gaze, the ordinary people of Asia are undergoing the process which used to be called 'Westernisation' but is now perhaps more aptly termed 'Modernisation'. The slow, almost imperceptible development of past ages has been caught up by a frenzied stampede of change today: change which may be instant and immediate in one area (for example, national politics) but which may still be slow and uncertain elsewhere (as in many aspects of society and economics).

This, then, is the justification for an arrangement whereby as much space is devoted to the events of the last century and a half, as to all the centuries which came before. This allocation does not imply any kind of judgement upon the relative importance of the modern or medieval periods: that would be presumptuous.

Many of the historians of South Asia would challenge such a balance between ancient and modern times. It is the prevailing mode among Indian historians to look to the remote past for the origins of almost all of the institutions of contemporary India. There is much to be said for this point of view. The present author will only observe that in writing this book he has thought it not a good idea to duplicate the approaches of other writers, whether Asian, European or American. In planning this book, the author constantly had in mind a passage by Marc Bloch, that great French historian who was executed by the Nazis. In *The Historian's Craft*, Marc Bloch tells us: 'Misunderstanding of the present is the inevitable consequence of ignorance of the past. But a man may wear himself out just as fruitlessly in seeking to understand the past, if he is totally ignorant of the present.' This is very much the purpose of this study. First, let us try to understand the revolution of today, against that interaction of East and West which began, so to speak, yesterday. And then perhaps we shall begin to be aware of the continuing tradition, the great tradition, from which the peoples of South Asia derive so much of their unique quality.

In a lecture which Sir Keith Hancock delivered at London University Senate House, 'Smuts and the Shift of World Power', he closed with a pellucid phrase: 'The living past remains my study'. It is the purpose of this book to show the reader that, in South Asia, the living past still pervades the present.

HUGH TINKER

1 The Great Cycle of History

Migration, the grand theme of man's history almost everywhere, is the key to any understanding of the great cycle of South Asian history (Map 2). But a reader whose perception of the word 'migration' is shaped by the experience of North America must try to understand a very different kind of process in South Asia. Instead of a surging movement across a great continent, completed within little more than a century, we have to conceive of waves and eddies of migration continuing for over three thousand years. And instead of an attempt at total assimilation – the 'melting pot' philosophy of the United States until recent years, which included even the final integration of the American Black into the body politic – we have to grasp the implications of the 'palimpsest' nature of South Asia. The early migrants may be partially absorbed by later migrants. Their language, beliefs, customs, even ethnic features may be moulded by the latecomers; but much of the original structure remains; submerged, perhaps, but not dissolved. Each successive wave has displayed certain dominant characteristics, but all attempts at 'cultural imperialism' have failed to overcome the earlier elements. Certain invaders deliberately kept apart from those they had conquered: such was the policy of the Aryans, three thousand years ago, and of the English, during the last two hundred years. Yet, time and again, South Asia has witnessed the conquest of the conquerors: though very often this reversal has taken many centuries to make itself felt.

Only the earliest of the immigrants have suffered the fate of the North American Indian: extinction, or preservation as a minute fossil group. The first known race to inhabit South Asia were the little people known as Negrito. The main Negrito remnants are found in the Philippines, while the Semang of the Malay peninsula still survive in remote spots. The only survivors in South Asia are the Mincopies of the Andaman Islands. Less than five feet tall, the Andamanese aboriginals still pursue a semi-nomadic existence, hunting, and following the earliest form of shifting cultivation. This technique, sometimes called 'slash and burn', consists in cutting down a section of jungle, burning it off, raising a few crops until the soil is exhausted,

1

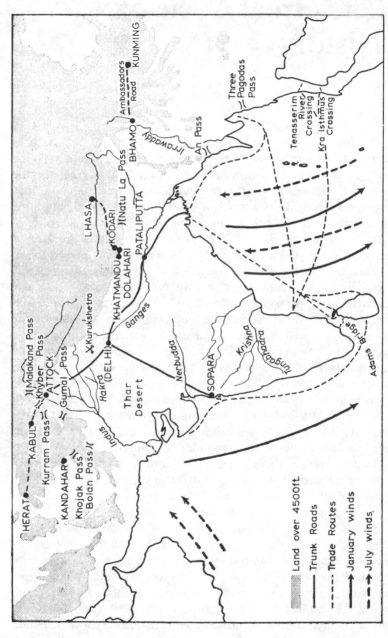

Map 2. Migration, invasion and trade routes.

and then seeking a new site. This form of existence, it will be understood, necessitates migration. It has been followed by other primitive peoples in South Asia.

What became of the Negritoid throughout Southern Asia? Did they flee before men of higher stature? And who came after them? Were they the Veddoid group, of whom some thousands survive today? Among these survivors there are the Sakai of Malaya and the Veddah of Ceylon, as well as scattered tribes in South India, such as Puliars, Mundavars, and Nairs. Their stature is slight (just above five feet) and they are still semi-nomadic. Many of these tribes have interbred with later peoples, whether on a basis of slavery, or conquest. It may be that the Veddoid immigrants were preceded by Mongoloid tribes, the precursors of the Tibeto-Burman peoples. The Naga of the Assam–Burma border, and the Wa of the Shan hills are regarded as autochthonous. These Mongoloid peoples, the farthest-reaching of the greatest racial group on earth, scattered out along the foothills of the Himalaya, where they could carry on their shifting cultivation while keeping above the malarial valleys where they did not thrive.

Evidence of the Mongoloid strain is visible in many of the peoples of north-east India. As a dominant race, the Mongoloid did not penetrate beyond Burma, Assam, and the Himalayan hill states, of which Tibet and Nepal are the most important. The early Mongoloid groups were followed, and sometimes supplanted by later migrants who had absorbed superior techniques (perhaps from contact with the Chinese) and who evolved superior types of political organisation. The first civilisation in Burma was that of the Pyu: they encountered the Mon, coming in from the Menam valley. The Pyu disappeared and the Mon gave ground when the Burmese descended into Burma about the eighth century AD. They were followed by branches of the great Tai race who established themselves in Burma as the Shans, and as the Ahom rulers of Assam.

The regions of Mongoloid penetration, where South Asia marches with East and South East Asia, have remained cultural frontiers of the Indic world. What we may call 'maritime' South Asia – the peninsula and Ceylon – has been civilised by what is usually called the Dravidian people. The Sanskrit term *Dravida* was originally applied to the South Indian kingdom of Conjeveram, and then extended to the country of the Tamil-speakers, or even more widely to all those who speak the non-Aryan languages of South India. From this comes a crude distinction between the dark-skinned Dravidians and the

light-skinned Indo-Aryans. But the 'Dravidians' represent at least
two great waves of immigration. The first main group belong to the
Veddoid or Australoid race; of small stature, with wavy or curly hair,
long head, broad flat nose and fleshy lips. The second group is
identified with the 'Mediterranean' type, with taller stature, a more
prominent, narrow nose, a lower cranial vault, and a fuller growth of
hair. A variant on the 'Mediterranean' type is of Phoenician appearance, with a long, convex nose. There is evidence to show that
speakers of the Dravidian tongue inhabited north-west India in
ancient times: one pocket of Dravidian-speakers remains in the
Brahui dialect of Baluchistan. But the Dravidians came under
pressure, and gradually retreated south, following the arrival of the
Indo-Aryan immigrants some time before (or perhaps after) 1000 BC.

Surmise has placed the original homeland of the Indo-Aryan folk
in the north German plains and in the Arctic circle (according to the
nationalist leader, B. G. Tilak) but most scholars believe the Aryans
to have originated between the Danube and the Oxus. Once again,
this people are identified not with a racial type (the blond Nordic of
Nazi fantasy) but with a language. Sanskrit emerged in a literary form
with the hymns of the *Rig Veda*, a work composed over many
centuries, but completed (the scholars are almost unanimous) before
the creation of the first Greek classical epic, the *Iliad*. The Aryans
seem to have encountered the Dravidians in their city-culture in the
Indus valley; to have destroyed their forts and ruined their cities and
to have imposed their own social system upon India north of the
Vindhya hills. Leaving behind the thin soil of the Punjab, they
pressed into the fertile Ganges plains, settling the rich agricultural
region between the Himalayan foothills and the broad Ganges. Here
they built their centres of power, of learning and religion: Ajodhya,
Prayaga (later, Allahabad), Kashi (Banaras). With the settlement of
the Ganges plains, Indic civilisation begins to assume an appearance
of stasis. The free-ranging Aryan spirit becomes dominated by the
environment: subject to the annual rhythm of the cold season, the hot
season, and the monsoon; reassured by the stately flow of Mother
Ganges; fascinated by the distant grandeur of the eternal snows of
Himalaya.

During early encounters with the Dravidians, the Aryans appear to
have intermarried and come to terms with the existing peoples. This
easy-going attitude did not last. Once settled in the Gangetic plains,
the 'white' Aryans evolved an elaborate ritual to keep themselves
apart from the dark masses, the *dasa*. From this division was to

emerge the caste system, conducted according to the ordinances of the priestly Brahmins.[1] Because the Aryans in the Punjab did not embrace the full caste ritual, they were looked on with hostility by the peoples of the Gangetic plain, *Aryavarta*. The river Saraswati was regarded as the boundary between the pure and the impure Aryans. The Hindu epics urged men not to dwell in Punjab: the *Mahabharata* says 'Let no Aryan dwell there even for two days.'

In the Middle Land, *madhya-desa*, the Hindus were able to practise their belief in racial purity. But north-west India continued to be a highway for immigration – or invasion, as it now appears to be. Out of central Asia came successive waves of nomad peoples who are sometimes linked with the Aryans and sometimes with the Mongol wanderers from the northern steppes. Those called Scythians, or Sakas, poured into Punjab about 600 BC and their descendants form distinct tribes, such as the Ghakkars, to this day. Some believe that the Jats, who form one-fifth of the Punjab population, are Scythians. There are legends that the Buddha came of Scythian stock, while the ancient kings of Burma traced their origins to the Sakya tribe, who are supposed to have produced Maha Thamata, the first king of mankind. After the Scythians came the Greeks, whose conquering leader, Alexander, is still regarded all over Asia as the greatest king of all. Greek settlements grew up in the north-west. And just as individual British soldiers married Indian girls and settled down, so Greek warriors dropped behind in the long marches by the banks of the Indus, and were welcomed for their physique and fair skin. Today, in a village in the Salt Range Mountains of northern Punjab, a village boy will often appear with fair hair and steel-blue eyes and a corn-coloured complexion.

The predominant west-to-east rhythm of northern India was reversed by the rise to power of Candragupta Maurya and his grandson Asoka (Map 3). Candragupta came from the northern country, perhaps from Gandhara. Was he from a Greek warrior family? Or was he a Vaisya, a member of the middling, cultivator caste? And what is the significance of the lowly origin assigned to the Mauryas (like that of Jesus Christ, the carpenter's son) compared to the divine or magical origins claimed for almost every other Indian hero of antiquity? The Mauryan empire pushed back the frontiers of India through the Khyber Pass to the mountains of the Hindu Kush

---

[1] The four *varnas* or 'limbs' of society were the Brahmins (priests), Kshattriyas (warriors), Vaisyas (cultivators, traders), and Sudras (servants).

6

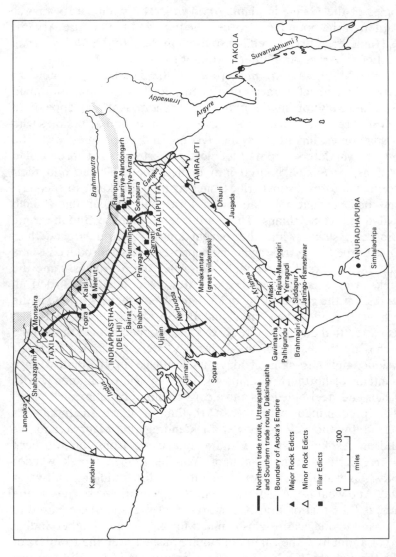

Map 3. Asoka's Empire, *c.* 250 BC

Northern trade route, Uttarapatha
and Southern trade route, Daksinapatha
Boundary of Asoka's Empire

Major Rock Edicts
Minor Rock Edicts
Pillar Edicts

TAKOLA
Suvarnabhumi ?

Irrawaddy

Argyre

Brahmaputra

Rampurwa
Lauriya-Nandongarh
Lauriya-Araraj
Sohgaura
Ganges
PATALIPUTTA
Rumminde
Sarnath
Prayaga
Bairat
Bhabru
Ujjain
Nerbudda
Meerut
Topra
Kalsi
INDRAPRASTHA
(DELHI)

TAMRALPTI
Dhauli
Jaugada

Mahakantara
(great wilderness)
Krishna

Maski
Rajula-Maudogiri
Yerragudi
Siddapur
Jatingo-Rameshwar
Gavimatha
Palhigundu
Brahmagiri

ANURADHAPURA
Simhaladvipa

Monsehra
Shahbazgarhi
TAXILA
Lampaka
Indus
Girnar
Sopara
Kandahar

0   300
miles

(often called the 'Hindu Slayer'). Beyond this vast realm – the greatest empire in Asia, Europe, or Africa in its day – missionaries and emissaries went forth to spread the compassionate creed of the Lord Buddha which Asoka accepted and spread among his people.

For the first time, the whole of South Asia, and beyond, was brought under the influence of one unified political and religious system: and as was to happen so many times again, the great achievement was followed almost at once by dismemberment. It was as though the effort of unification overstrained the resources of rulers and ruled, and precipitated a reaction, an acquiescence in division. It may be that a kind of geographical-political 'fault' or fracture was already appearing between the Indus system of the north-west and the Gangetic system of the Middle Land. At Asoka's death, the Mauryan empire was divided into two. The division may have been for administrative convenience, or it may represent the outcome of a struggle for power. The western provinces, including those beyond the Khyber Pass, were governed from Ujjain and went to Kunnala, son of Asoka; the main, eastern provinces fell to Asoka's grandson and remained under the rule of Pataliputta, the former capital. Within a few generations, the Maurya dynasty disappears from history.

To the west, another irruption appeared, that of the Kushans, an 'Aryan' group from the mountains of Turkistan, the country of the Oxus. This grim highland has been the nursery of invaders throughout history. North, south, east and west they have followed the track of conquest. The Kushan Empire stretched away to the oases of Central Asia: its grip descended upon northern India as far as the holy city of Kashi (Banaras). The capital was located near modern Peshawar. Kanishka, the most important of the Kushan emperors, tried to attract to himself some of the glory of Asoka, as universal emperor and *Rajarsi* (that is, a ruler who is also a sage) by patronising Buddhism. His empire was no more permanent than Asoka's: within a hundred years it had crumbled away.

The problem which was to confront the rulers of northern India from ancient times to the present day had now emerged: where to attempt to establish a frontier? The obvious place might seem to be the Indus River; but rivers have never lasted long as frontiers, and the Indus has hardly ever been the effective boundary of India. One reason is that the Khyber Pass, just a few miles beyond, is the high road of the invaders of India. A solution which has been attempted from the time of Asoka, onward to the 'Frontier Policy' of Lord

Lytton in the nineteenth century, has been to establish a 'scientific frontier', running from Kabul to Kandahar giving lateral communication along the interior line of the frontier and providing shelter behind a defensive screen of hills, while firmly holding the passes. The danger of this solution is that it commits the paramount power in India to maintaining standing armies beyond the passes, absorbing a disproportionate amount of the imperial military and financial resources. Moreover, India is constantly sucked into the politics of central Asia.

The rulers of northern India have frequently adopted an interior solution to this frontier dilemma. Recognising that Punjab represents a hornet's nest of pugnacious peoples lying across the track of any would-be invader, they have drawn back behind this no-man's land to the vital corridor just north-west of Delhi. Here the outlying ranges of the Himalaya – the Siwaliks – and the Great Indian Desert – the Thar – compel any invader to advance along a single route. Here the invader is at the end of a tenuous line of communication, while the Indian defender has at his back all the resources and reserves of the most populous region of India. Here, throughout history, the rulers of northern India have made their stand. According to the *Mahabharata*, this was the ancient Kurukshetra, or Field of the Kurus. Here the legendary battle between the Pandavas and the Kauravas waged for eighteen days: it was the first of many on this field.

Upon the ruins of the Mauryans, a new Indian empire rose up at Pataliputta, that of the Guptas. The first of the dynasty emerged in AD 320, and thereafter Gupta authority was established right across the northern plains to Kurukshetra. Under Ċandra Gupta II (*c.* 375–415)[1] the foreign grip over western India was loosened. Ujjain was recaptured, and the whole country to the mouths of the Indus brought under direct rule. The north-west was compelled to recognise Gupta suzerainty, though an interior policy of defence was followed. In the north-east sub-Himalayan hills, little states such as Nepala and Kamarupa (in Assam) also became feudatories, while the southern kings were brought into a relationship of respectful recognition.

Once again, invaders from the north-west erupted into India. The

---

[1] Note that throughout this book, dates given in brackets after rulers are regnal dates. Dates of other persons given in brackets indicate the life-span.

Huns or Huna seem to have been a branch of that nomadic race which terrorised Europe. The Huns had the strength to defeat their Indian adversaries, but not the ability to organise a vassal state. Gupta authority dwindled away, but another Gangetic kingdom arose with its capital at Kanauj, under the rule of Harsa (AD 606–47). His sway was acknowledged from the Indus to Bengal, but Harsa exercised authority through an infrastructure of local rulers. The empire did not survive his death, and the familiar pattern of fragmentation followed (Map 4). Bengal settled into a separate existence under the Pala dynasty, still practising in a degenerate form the principles of Buddhist kingship instituted by Asoka. In northern India, the initiative passed to kings of the Gurjara clan. The Gurjaras appear to be a Scythian tribe, originally known as Yuchi; they were originally serpent-worshippers but were accepted into the broad fold of Hinduism. Like the Jats, their caste status is somewhat ambiguous. The Gurjaras or Gujars remained a nomadic people, grazing their horses and their cattle far and wide. One branch of the Gujars settled in Gujarat; the main body followed a semi-pastoral life amid the wastes of the Punjab, but the Gurjara-Pratiharas emerged from the wastelands to found a kingdom in the Gangetic plain. This, again, had a feudal type of structure and lacked any central organisation to give the monarchy backbone.

The last defenders of Hindu power in northern India were the clans of Rajputs. These were the offspring of ruling families (many in number because of extended polygamy) in the barren lands on the verge of the Thar desert. These rulers had wrested the fertile oasis-like areas of cultivated land from their aboriginal owners and assumed the style of Rajputs or Sons of Rulers (*raja putra*). The Rajput clans were divided, broadly, into three groups: those claiming descent from Rama to the Sun, or from Krishna to the Moon, and those claiming to be born of fire. The origin claimed by the third branch, the *Agni-Kula*, symbolised their transformation from Scythian outsiders into Aryan insiders. The Rajputs assumed the mantle of the Kshattriyas; warfare was their occupation. The 'fire-born' Rajputs were the Powar, Parihar, Solanki, and Chauhan clans. When, at the beginning of the eleventh century, invaders began to appear beyond the Khyber, the Rajputs rallied to repel them. But despite their valour, they lacked organisation and cohesion, and they failed to halt the invader. The Chauhans had emerged as leaders of the Rajputs, and among them the bravest was Prithvi Raj of Ajmir,

10

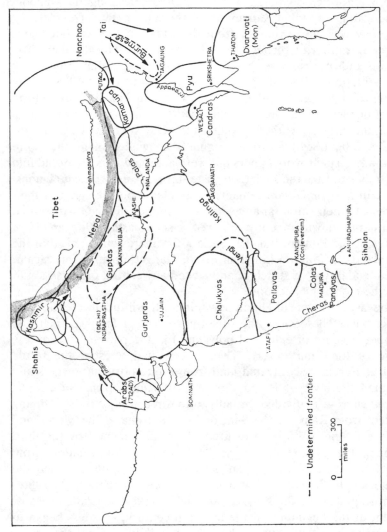

Map 4. Twilight of the Hindu states, *c.* AD 700.

Nanchao

Tai

Burmese

Putao

Kamrupa

Tagaung

Irrawaddy

Pyu

Srikshetra

Thaton

Dvaravati (Mon)

Wesali

Candras

Tibet

Brahmaputra

Palas

Nalanda

Jagganath

Kalinga

Nepal

Kashi

Guptas

Kanyakubja

Anuradhapura

Sihalan

Kancipura (Conjeveram)

Vengi

Kashmir

Shahis

Gurjaras

Ujjain

Chalukyas

Pallavas

Colas

Madura

Cheras

Pandyas

(Delhi) Indraprastha

Indus

Arabs (712 AD)

Somnath

Atafi

- - - Undetermined frontier

0   300

miles

who was also Lord of Delhi. He raised a mighty army and took his stand upon the historic battlefield of Kurukshetra at a place called Tarain or Taraori. The invaders were beaten back at this first battle of Tarain in AD 1191. The following year, another invading army appeared at Tarain, said to number in its ranks 120,000 horsemen, swiftly moving mounted archers. The Chauhan host had no reply to this novel style of battle; their speciality was the hand to hand encounter; they were slain in their thousands in three days of battle and northern India stood open to the will of the invaders: the Tartars and Afghans, soldiers of Islam.

The preoccupation of northern India with the invaders from the hills and steppes of Central Asia had almost no repercussions upon the peninsula, south of the Vindhya hills. There is a dualism in Indian history; the northern defensive landward watch against invaders from beyond the mountains, with emphasis upon military organisation and power; and in the south, a reaching out across the ocean, occasionally in warlike terms, but more generally to trade and provide services. Sometimes the outward-looking spirit dominates the whole sub-continent (as in Asoka's reign), more often the northern obsession with the interior and defence embraced the south; but for long periods the two attitudes co-existed separately. The penetration of the priestly dominant caste and the priestly language, Sanskrit, took much longer to develop in the south. In consequence, the Dravidian vernacular languages acquired a literary tradition long before the languages of the north. Tamil attained something like its present form soon after Asoka's day; Kannada and Telugu emerged a few centuries later, with Malayalam as the last to achieve an independent literary form. Among the Tamil speakers, there were three main rulers, the Pandyas of the extreme south, the Colas of the Coroman-del coast (Coromandel is, properly, Cola mandalam), and the Cheras or Keralas of Malabar: it was here that Malayalam developed out of Tamil as a separate language. South India possessed those wonders which the kings of many lands desired – ivory, apes and peacocks, precious stones and costly spices. Traders came from far Arabia and China, and Tamil merchants voyaged across the seas. Many Tamils traded with nearby Ceylon, and began to exercise political influence in the island. From the third century BC onward, Tamils began to force their way to the throne of Ceylon: in the fifth century AD, rulers of the Pandyan line occupied the throne. The transmission of the great cultural tradition of the north into the lands of the south was furthered by the Pallava dynasty which emerged about AD 325 to the north of Coromandel. They appear to have been outsiders, and the name of the dynasty means 'brigand' in Tamil. Established at Kanchi or Conjeveram, the centre of learning and religion, their capital was a meeting place of religions – Hindu, Jain and Buddhist, while north Indian literary modes were introduced. Administrative and political concepts were also absorbed from the Gupta empire. The intermediary role of the Pallavas came to an end when they were overwhelmed by the Cola power about AD 900.

The picture changed with the rise of the Colas in the tenth century, reaching a climax with Rajaraja the Great (AD 985–1018) who conquered all South India and extended his hold over Ceylon (Map 5). Under his son, Rajendra (1018–35) the Cola power reached out to threaten the empire of Srivijaya in Java and Sumatra. The Colas were great administrators and great temple builders: they extended irrigation schemes on a vast scale, and laid out their cities on spacious lines. And yet, within two centuries, their great achievement had disintegrated. The Colas were expelled from Ceylon in 1070, and their frontier districts were lost soon after. The Tamil south as a whole was threatened in the fourteenth century by the pressure of emergent Muslim states in the Deccan. The Pandyan state was destroyed in 1334. Meanwhile, Tamil power was reasserted in the extreme north of Ceylon, and from about 1300 the kingdom of Jaffna was established, and was to maintain a separate existence for 300 years.

The dualism of the Indian sub-continent was reproduced on a reduced scale in Burma, as between the enclosed, interior character of the north and the centre, and the outward awareness of the south. The first civilised society in Burma, that of the Pyu and the Mon, was focused upon the south. The capital, Srikshetra (Old Prome) was an Indian-style sacred city with circular walls, simulating the universe. The culture was after the Indian pattern, and the script borrowed from south India. This society was overthrown by the Burmese, invading from the north. In their early days, the Burmese were inward-looking and defensive in their attitudes, but as the dynasty of Pagan was consolidated in central Burma, the Burmese kings began to look outwards. Under Anawratha (1044–77) and his son, by an Indian queen, Kyanzittha (1084–1112), the Court looked to India and Ceylon again. The magnificent temples built during this period reproduced the south Indian style of architecture, with its high, terraced towers, covered in exterior carvings, the north Indian style, with inner worship halls, and grille-type windows, Sinhalese and

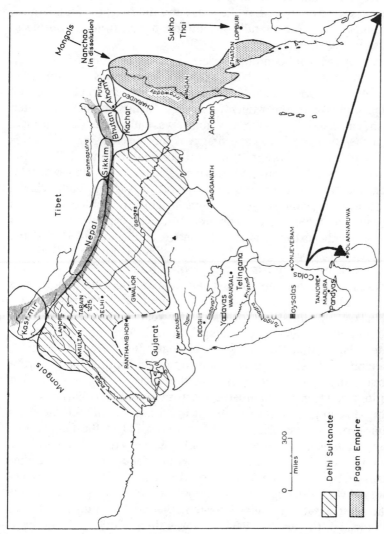

Map 5. External invasion and conquest, *c.* 1250.

13

Chinese features in carving and ceramics, and a purely Burmese adaptation of the solid stupa or shrine in the characteristic 'hand-bell' shape of the *dagoba*. It has been established that Indian craftsmen worked upon some of the temples, and it seems probable that other foreigners were employed by the kings and the religious foundations. But almost always the overall conception emerges from the Burmese-Mon synthesis of this age.

When the Mongol conquerors seized power in China, Burma felt the repercussions of their ability to thrust their armies over immense distances and through country thought of as impenetrable. The first big encounter with the Mongols, or the Tartars as they are often known, came in 1277: to the Mongols it was only a frontier skirmish, but to the Burmese it was the first real foreign invasion. Ten years later, the Mongols swept down into central Burma, led by the grandson of Kubla Khan, and occupied Pagan. When Pagan disintegrated and Burma relapsed into a cockpit of warring feudal chiefs, the outward-looking spirit was almost entirely submerged by a narrow, racial chauvinism. The first Burmese capital had been at Tagaung in the extreme north; the move to Pagan had shifted the political centre of gravity back towards the delta and the sea – where it had been established in the days of Srikshetra. Now, the Shan overlords moved the capital northward again; their first choice was Pinya (1312) in Sagaing district, near to the *ledwin*, the rice-granary of Kyaukse, or 'stone weir' district. Fifty years later, the Shan ruler, Thadominbya drained the swamps around Ava, and shifted the Golden Palace and the royal city to that site where the capital – Ratanapura, 'the city of gems' – was to remain for the greater part of Burma's subsequent history. It was the decisive step towards that isolationism which has stamped the Burmese national character.

The Muslim invasions of northern India had begun with the Arab conquest of the coastal areas of Sind in AD 711 in the floodtide of expansion which followed the death of the Holy Prophet. The annexation of Sind, from the sea, was not followed by any further enterprise in India: the barrier of the Thar desert was enough, combined with a strong maritime opposition from the piratical chiefs of the west coast. The next invasion, that of Mahmud of Ghazni, came through the Khyber Pass, and was the prelude to centuries of pressure from Iran and Central Asia. The first independent Sultan of Delhi was Iletmish (1211–36). Among the many contenders he subdued was Taj al-din Yildiz, who established a kingdom in Punjab, and who met Iletmish in the historic corridor of Kurukshetra in a third battle of Tarain in 1215. The rule of Turks and Afghans which was established in northern India from the time of Iletmish down to its submergence in the Mughal Empire under Akbar was almost wholly Indian in its scope.[1] The efforts of the sultans were directed to enforcing their authority over the princes and people of India. The Muslim establishment was continually reinforced by immigrants; Persians, and Afghans, and Turks from beyond the Oxus. All these newcomers were adventurers: they were attracted by stories of the careers open to men of talent in the Courts of Hindustan. In general, the Persians were men of the pen; Afghans and Turks, men of the sword. From Iran came a succession of skilful officials, scribes and scholars, and men of science: out of the mountains of Central Asia came the low-browed, hard-riding, hard-fighting men who raised up, and brought down the Sultans of Delhi. The Persians introduced their beautiful language into India – it has been called the Italian of the East, so melodious and poetic it is. Because the Persians filled so many administrative and diplomatic posts, Persian became the language of government; fulfilling this role for many years after the British became the ruling power, and still cultivated today by Indians (both Hindu and Muslim) who belong to official families. Alongside Persian there grew up the *Zaban-i-Urdu*: Turki for 'Language of the Camp'. Urdu (as it soon became known) was a military lingua-franca. Its grammar came from Sanskrit, its vocabulary from Indian tongues, Persian, and Turki, and its script from Arabic. Urdu did not remain a mere medium for soldiers' use: it was taken up by poets and historians, and soon attained an accepted literary status.

The attempts of the Sultans to unite India under their rule came near to success with the reign of Muhammad bin Tughlak (1325–51). He drove ever onward until only the extreme south lay beyond his sway. His dominions were organised into twenty-three provinces, under governors who were his subordinates: only the Rajput princes succeeded in retaining their independence in their strongholds far away beyond waterless deserts. Tughlak strained the resources of his empire to breaking point. He transferred his capital, with all its thousands of inhabitants, from Delhi down to the Deccan to Deogir, renamed Daulatabad. He launched fantastic military expeditions: to conquer Khurasan beyond the Oxus, and to invade China through the Himalaya. All this frenzied activity weakened the state, and

---

[1] There were five Turko-Afghan dynasties, known as the Slave Dynasty, the Khilji Dynasty, the Tughlak Dynasty, the Sayyid Dynasty, and the Lodi Dynasty.

under Tughlak's feeble successors, his all-India empire began to disintegrate. Into this power-vacuum swept the Mongol invader.

Different branches of the Mongols had long hovered beyond the protecting barrier of the intervening mountains as the unseen threat to India. Chengiz Khan overcame the Turks in their homeland in the time of Iletmish: but there were no repercussions over the Indus. Mongol invasions into Punjab began in 1297; they were repulsed, but the Mongols came again. Not until a hundred years later did Timur the Pitiless cross the Indus (1398) and descend upon Delhi. The utter horror of his massacre of hundreds of thousands of spectators, bystanders in the high game of power politics, has no parallel except Hitler's systematic extermination of the Polish and Jewish peoples in our own day. Like an army of locusts, Timur's horde rode back across the Indus, leaving ruin behind them.

During the next two centuries, Delhi remained to symbolise the imperial idea, but its empire had vanished. One satirist spoke of the empire as stretching all the way from Delhi to Palam (the nearby village which now gives its name to Delhi's international airport). One after another, would-be kings rode to Delhi to seek the throne. So many failed in the attempt that a popular saying arose, *Hanuz Dilli dur ast*, 'It's a long way to Delhi'. It is said that a soothsayer accompanied one pretender, and when consulted each evening reiterated these words. When the army was only one day's march from the capital, the claimant jeered at the oracle: but he was killed next day beneath the city walls. The throne was occupied from 1451 by a dynasty of Lodi Afghans. The best of these was Sher Shah (1529–45) who temporarily restored the empire. He fought his way to power against a challenge from Babur, a descendant of Timur on his father's side, and of Chengiz Khan among his mother's ancestors. Babur was like his forebears in leading a roamer's life. Ejected from his homeland, he made his headquarters at Kabul, where emissaries from India invited him to intervene in Hindustan. Babur advanced upon Delhi, and once again the corridor of Kurukshetra saw the clash of invader and defender. At Panipat, in 1526, Babur proved himself the master. Babur's army made free with the riches of Delhi and Agra: to Babur's son Humayun went the immense diamond, the *Koh-i-noor*, or Mountain of Light, which was to undergo many adventures before finding its way into the crown of the British sovereign. But these triumphs did not give Babur rule over Hindustan. For the remaining four years of his life, he fought continuously. When his end came in 1530, at the age of 46, it is said that he accepted death in order to save his desperately-ill son Humayun: Babur is said to have walked around his son's couch, and taken his sickness upon himself. A legend only, perhaps, but in accord with the chivalrous, adventurous man who left a vivid autobiography, the *Babur-Nama*, and founded the line of the Mughal emperors of India: some warm and generous, some cold and vengeful, but all men with a sense of style, a sense of greatness. With Babur began that Mughal love of India: a foreigner's love of a land that was fair and bountiful in comparison with the ancestral steppes and deserts. This love was epitomised in the Mughal passion for designing artificial gardens in which streams and waterfalls and murmuring trees were combined in a pattern of delight. With their ancestral memories of the parched wastes of Central Asia, the Mughals never tired of flowing water. Harshness and softness; these were the elements they loved to juxtapose and contrast. The Mughals were artists in the art of living: and in the art of death. Babur's body was interred in a garden at Kabul. Humayun's tomb was erected on the outskirts of Delhi, in the first of those magnificent mausoleums whereby the Mughals raised monumental death to the level of poetry.

Events in northern India had only occasional impact upon the kingdoms of the peninsula. The Deccan and the western seaboard came under the rule of Muslims who arrived as foreigners but who mostly responded to the 'melting pot' cultural atmosphere. In the extreme south, Hinduism retained its hold upon every facet of the scene. From 1347 to 1490, most of the Deccan was included in the Bahmani kingdom: the dynasty claiming descent from Bahman the Persian. There was a strange dualism in this kingdom, a tension between the native ruling class and foreign adventurers from Arabia, Persia, Afghanistan, and East Africa. We may see many echoes of Hindu traditions in government and ceremony. The Bahmani kings were mighty builders, and their fortresses dominate many isolated hills and defiles to this day. When the Bahmani kingdom crumbled under Mughal pressure, the former governors of provinces made a bid for independence. The governor of Bijapur, who stood forth as king in 1489, was a Georgian slave, who became a Shiah Muslim, and added to his cosmopolitan capacity for adaptation by marrying a Maratha lady and making Marathi the language of government in his state. Under his successors, Brahmins were appointed to official positions, while Christians – Portuguese and others – were given encouragement. Bijapur eventually succumbed in 1686 to the dual pressure of the militant Hindu power of the Marathas and the fanatical hatred of Alamgir, or Aurangzeb; the last of the all-powerful Mughals.

Meanwhile, in the Tamil south, a great Hindu kingdom rose and fell. 'The City of Victory', Vijayanagar, was founded in 1336 on the banks of the river Tungabhadra as a bastion of Hinduism against the expanding Muslim power of the Bahmanids. The city was sustained by the fertile area between two rivers known as the Raichur Doab.[1] Wealth also came from mines, containing precious stones: the Koh-i-noor is supposed to have originated in Vijayanagar. The kingdom reached its zenith under Krishna Deva Raya (1509–29) who recreated the symbolism of the sacred city revolving around the god-king. Under Krishna Deva Raya the boundaries of the kingdom were advanced northward, but forty years later Vijayanagar came to an end. The alliance of the Muslim rulers of the Deccan defeated the Hindus in the battle of Talikota (1565), decided by the advantage of artillery manned by Turkish mercenaries. However, the overthrow of Vijayanagar did not signify the total collapse of Hindu rule through-out India. In the extreme south, the Rajas of Cochin and Travancore retained a little more than nominal independence, while the Rajput princes could not be dispossessed of their remote desert cities by any number of Muslim military expeditions. Similarly, in far-away Assam, the Ahom rulers of Thai origin were Hinduised in the seventeenth century, and resisted all attempts by the Muslim gov-ernors of Bengal to penetrate the jungles which protected their valley; while the Hindu Rajas of Manipur, Cooch, and Cachar also survived beyond the reach of Muslim power.[2] The theory of a 'Hindu Period' followed by a 'Muslim Period' in Indian history is only applicable to the north-west and the Gangetic plains. When we view Indian history in the round, we see that Hindu and Muslim power flowed side by side, and occasionally intermingled. Even on the central stage of Indian history, the fall of Vijayanagar was followed only a hundred years later by the rise of the Marathas. But meanwhile the Mughal Empire was to achieve what only Asoka had achieved before (with the exception of Muhammad bin Tughlak's fleeting attainment) – the unification of India under one law.

The period from 1200 to 1500 in Ceylon was one of almost

---

[1] Just as Panch-ab or Punjab means 'Five Waters' or rivers, so Do-ab means 'Two Waters'; but the term is commonly applied to all riverine lands.

[2] These tribal chiefs were assimilated into the Hindu caste structure in the seven-teenth and eighteenth centuries. The Naga ruler of Manipur was accepted as a Kshattriya.

uninterrupted decline, in terms of the nation. The sequence we have followed in India – collapse of central power, followed by the emergence of local governors claiming an independent role – was followed in Ceylon. The rulers began a dangerous fashion when they began to hire mercenaries from south India to fight their battles for them. Vijayanagar was only the foremost of the south Indian states which interfered in the politics and life of the island. Ceylon even suffered the curious fate of a Chinese invasion or landing by one of the great fleets of junks which the Ming emperors despatched into the southern seas. But the main causes of Ceylon's decay seem to have been internal: the collapse of the great irrigated system of cultivation, and the inability of the political and social structure to embark upon rejuvenation and reform when required. Amid the decline, the greatness of Sinhalese culture was symbolised by the cult of the Tooth of the Buddha. This relic was enshrined in a temple at Kandy in 1286, and was a supreme object of veneration of the whole Buddhist world. Presents from Burma were frequently offered at the shrine, and in 1555 the king Bayinnaung (1551–81) sent craftsmen to beautify the holy place. Subsequently, the Portuguese captured what was alleged to be the Tooth and ground it to powder, while Bayinnaung secured yet another Tooth, said to be the authentic relic, and lodged this in a pagoda at Pegu; yet the temple guardians at Kandy continued to insist that the veritable Tooth had never left its ancient shrine, to guarantee the continuance of the Sinhalese race and religion.

Bayinnaung inherited the throne of a united Burma from Tabin-shwehti (1531–50) who had stepped into something like a power vacuum, following the collapse of Shan power in the north. He assaulted the Mon city, Pegu, and began the attempt – which was to obsess all subsequent Burmese rulers – to subdue the other states which surrounded Burma. Tabinshwehti's reign ended (like so many others in Burma) with a kind of madness taking control of the king. From greatness he descended into debauchery. Bayinnaung had to carry out the task of unification all over again. Having taken Pegu, he went on to subdue the Shan princes, great and small. He established Burmese control over the Shans far to the north and the west, compelling them to render tribute to him, and to serve him in his wars. Then he went on to conquer Ayuthia (1569). Along with other rulers, the king of Ayuthia was permitted to maintain a miniature Court in a Burmese captivity. Bayinnaung made his capital at Pegu, in the delta, naming the twenty gates of the city after his vassal states: Chiengmai, Tenasserim, Hsenwi, Ayuthia, and the rest. Throughout his vassal territories he erected pagodas, with inscriptions recording that Bayinnaung was their king. Besides his dealings with Ceylon, he sent a mission to Mughal India. Burma was once again a member of the Asian international community, but this greatness did not long outlast Bayinnaung's death. In 1600, Pegu was pillaged and burnt, during a double invasion of Burma from Ayuthia in the east and Arakan from the west. Bayinnaung's palace was consumed by flames. Bayinnaung's successors returned to Ava, where they made their capital; his grandson, Anaukpetlun (1605–28) succeeded in reuniting the kingdom, but only by constant marching and warfare. The story of those times becomes a monotonous repetition of accounts of raids and sieges. The Burmese kings declined in vigour and command: after 1648, no king took the field in person for more than a century. By the 1730s, the Manipuris were raiding down central Burma, grazing their wiry little ponies under the walls of Ava city. Finally, the Mons rose against their Burmese overlords, and having restored their own independence in the south, under their able king Binnya Dala (1747–57) they marched upon the Burmese heartland and in 1752 the Mons occupied Ava. The Burmese were required to drink the water of allegiance to Binnya Dala. Most of them acquiesced in their defeat; but in a far-off market town called Moksobomyo, 'the town of the hunter-chief', a few held out behind their bamboo stockade.

The Arakanese kingdom which pressed so hard against the flank of Burma was another Janus-like polity, now facing this way, now that, according to the prevailing push and pull of superior power; similar to the kingdoms of the Deccan, oscillating between the northern and southern attractions, between Muslim and Hindu influence; similar to the kingdom of Jaffna, sometimes associated with peninsular Tamil and Malabar forces, sometimes with the Sinhalese influence of the island.

Arakan received the message of the Lord Buddha earlier than inland Burma, because of its sea communications with the ports of the Bay of Bengal. The Mahamuni image, north of Mrohaung, was the oldest Buddhist shrine in Burma. During the Pagan empire, attempts were made to carry away the image, but all failed. The Pagan kings had to be content with restoring and beautifying the shrine. From the eighth to the tenth century, the kings adopted Brahmanical rituals, and their coins were issued in the Sanskritic (Nagai) script. Thenceforward, Theravada Buddhism predominated. In 1404, the Burmese ousted the Arakanese king, who fled to

Bengal, and took service with the king of Gaur. He returned to Arakan with Muslim troops, and was reinstated in 1430. His Muslim followers erected the Sandihkan mosque at Mrohaung, and his successors, although still Buddhists, adopted names and titles in the Muslim style, and struck medallions or coins in Persian-Arabic script. Chittagong was occupied in 1459, and Arakan preyed upon the delta towns of eastern Bengal. The most bizarre episode in Arakanese history was the flight of the unsuccessful contender for the Mughal Empire to Mrohaung in 1660. Shuja, brother of Alamgir, arrived with a retinue of courtiers and a marvellous treasure. The king (Sandathu-damma, 1652–84) kept Prince Shuja against his will, and asked for his daughter in marriage. Shuja, in despair, plotted to overthrow the king, but he failed, and was driven into the jungle where he died. His supporters continued in the service of the kings of Arakan, and remain a separate group to this day.

The Mughal Empire in India flourished for a century and a half under four monarchs only: Akbar (1556–1605), Jahangir (1605–27), Shahjahan (1627–58) and Alamgir or Aurangzeb (1658–1707). All these monarchs are known not by their personal names but by titles which signify their world-wide governance. Jahangir was the son of a Rajput princess; so was Shahjahan, and this made him three-quarters Hindu by blood, though not in outlook. The first three great Mughals were men who gloried in self-indulgence; but their genius raised wine and women to the level of inspiration. Akbar was, like Peter the Great of Russia, illiterate. Thrust into responsibility as a boy, he had an amazing capacity for sure decision and instant action. Akbar contended for the imperial city, Delhi, and for Hindustan upon the battlefield of Panipat where his grandfather had fought. In 1556 his forces confronted those of Hemu, the Hindu general of the fading Sultan of Delhi. The second battle of Panipat was probably the most decisive encounter in Indian history. Akbar raised the Mughal position from that of the most important of many Muslim states in India to that of the paramount power over all India. His conquests did not subjugate the Deccan and the south, but he created an administration and an imperial elite of high officers, the *mansabdars*, to carry through his work. Akbar was able to think in larger terms than those of race, and he endeavoured to make the Rajputs, and other influential Hindus his coadjutors. True, his regime remained predominantly foreign: three-quarters of his high officials came from outside India. But he tried to do everything to make Mughal rule acceptable to his subjects. Jahangir, his son, secured the throne after intriguing against his father and his father's faithful servants. Jahangir was a gifted writer and painter and artist of nature. But his reign was not edifying, and before he died (not far from the Vale of Kashmir which he so loved) Jahangir's sons had begun to struggle for the succession. Shahjahan secured his title to the throne by putting to death all other male claimants. This emperor's claim to greatness rests mainly upon his superb building achievements. It was he who raised the Old Delhi we still know (its formal name was Shahjahanabad) with its great mosque and its red fort with the inscription: 'If there be a heaven upon earth, it is here, it is here, it is here.' Shahjahan's masterpiece was, of course, the Taj Mahal, erected as a memorial to his much-loved wife. Once again, the succession was anticipated by a lining-up of forces, throughout the empire behind the various contenders. Shahjahan had four sons. After the liberal religious policies of the first two Mughal emperors, he had reverted to Islamic orthodoxy; but his eldest son, Dara Shukoh, was of a philosophical, ecumenical cast of mind: his enemies said that he drank both 'spirituous' and 'spiritual' wine. The second son, Shuja, was governor of Bengal; and it was he whose life ended in the Arakan jungle. The third son was Aurangzeb, nicknamed by his brothers 'the Mullah', the Religious One. Despite his unorthodoxy, Shahjahan loved his eldest son, and kept him by his side. The others were sent off to govern important provinces; and in the case of Aurangzeb, to command the forces fighting on the frontier of the empire in the Deccan. In 1657, Shahjahan became seriously ill: the sons decided to move. In Bengal, Shuja proclaimed himself emperor, while the fourth son, Murad, did the same in Gujarat. The morose Aurangzeb did not declare himself, but advanced towards the capital with his hardened troops and his hard-hitting artillery. Dara Shukoh moved to oppose his advance, supported by the Rajputs, his allies against the bigoted champion of Islam. The two sides met at Samugarh, about eight miles east of Agra, in June 1658. Firepower and generalship decided the day: Dara Shukoh was compelled to flee. Aurangzeb advanced upon Agra and took the failing Shahjahan prisoner; the deposed emperor lingered on, a captive in his own royal palace, gazing across the Jumna to the Taj Mahal, the tomb of his beloved, until he died in 1666. Aurangzeb assumed the title of Alamgir, the World Shaker, and proceeded to deal with his brothers. The miserable Dara was driven to the utmost boundaries of the empire. He was betrayed, and handed over to Alamgir, who paraded him through the streets of Delhi amid the wailing of the people; he was murdered in prison in August 1659.

Akbar had established a firm northern frontier beyond the Kabul–Kandahar line, but he had been content to move cautiously south of the River Narbudda into the Deccan. His successors began to probe into hostile country – into the far valleys of Assam and down into south India. Alamgir, whose first appointment was that of Viceroy of the Deccan, became obsessed with conquering the south. His principal enemy was Sivaji, a Maratha chieftain, sprung from the sinewy, spare people of the mountainous Ghat country which runs down the western rim of the peninsula. Sivaji was contemptuously dismissed as 'the Mountain Rat' by Alamgir; but he was more like a mongoose fighting a swollen python. From inaccessible hill forts, his mounted followers struck across rugged country at great speed, eluding the cumbersome Mughal armies. For over twenty years, Alamgir's forces campaigned against the Marathas and the other southern rulers. When the end came for Alamgir in his eighty-ninth year, he died at Ahmadnagar, in the Ghat country, still trying to subdue his enemies. Nominally, the Mughal Empire now enclosed all the lands gained by Asoka and Tughlak; only the extreme southern tip of India remained independent. But already, by Alamgir's death, beside the Marathas, organised in a loose confederacy of chiefs, the Rajputs and the Jats were in open revolt. Now, as before, the great officials of the empire began to behave like sovereign princes; the governor or Subahdar of the Deccan set up a quasi-independent Court at Hyderabad; the Subahdar of Bengal went his own way at Murshidabad; while the Nawab Wazir or Lord Chamberlain of the empire took for himself the rich territory of Oudh. Once again, invaders poured through the north-western passes. The forward frontier gave way to the interior frontier, the Kurukshetra line. Nadir Shah, the emperor of Persia, occupied Kandahar, Kabul, and Lahore. The Mughal forces were arrayed against Nadir Shah near Karnal, just north of Delhi, but they were cut to pieces. The Persian monarch stripped the imperial treasury of all its accumulated wealth – the estimates vary between £20 millions and £120 millions – and bore away the peacock throne, alone valued at over £2 millions. After the Persians came the Afghans, with invasion upon invasion. In 1760, the Marathas – whose conquests stretched from sea to sea – occupied Delhi and set up their own nominee as emperor. The following January, the Afghan monarch arrived to contest their coup. For a third time, the historic field of Panipat was to provide the stage for the clash between the foreign attacker and the native defender. Once again, the foreigner won, and the Maratha power was – for a time – brought down to the dust. The third battle of Panipat was virtually the end of the Mughal Empire. Puppet rulers were still given the empty title of Ruler of the World, but the real struggle for supremacy was decided elsewhere.

The Maratha power was to revive, and dominate western and central India. In the cockpit of the Punjab, the grip of the Afghans was wrenched away by the Sikhs, who thrust back the frontier of India to Peshawar and the approaches to the Khyber. The Gurkhas of Nepal carved out a sub-montane Himalayan empire which stretched from Darjeeling to Simla. The succession states of the Mughal Empire – the courts of Hyderabad, Oudh and Murshidabad – imitated the Mughal magnificence. In the extreme south, a soldier of fortune, Hyder Ali, and his son Tipu Sultan, established a Muslim state in Mysore and the maritime lands of Malabar. None of these rulers was strong enough to make a bid for supreme control; each was compelled to conclude alliances in order to be safe against predatory neighbours. Indian politics had become an enormous game of chess, in which only the most skilled player could calculate the consequences of any move. Unfortunately, the play was augmented by the addition of two pieces – only pawns, the others thought – the French and the British. But before the game was over, pawn had become sovereign, and the other pieces lay toppled beside the board.

On a smaller scale, and at an earlier date, the rulers of Ceylon had sought to play a similar game, and had suffered a similar fate. The eclipse of Burma came about not because the native rulers sought to involve the West in their affairs, but for the opposite reason: because they tried too strenuously to keep the West out.

The Mon advance into Upper Burma was challenged by a squire from the town of the hunter chief; but a squire with the blood-royal in his veins, and the courage of a lion in his heart. Alaungpaya, as he was later called ('the Future Buddha'), reigned only for eight years (1752–60) during which time he reconquered Lower Burma, and then set out on that campaign irresistible to all Burmese heroes – the subjection of Ayuthia. While himself laying a cannon against the city walls of Ayuthia, he was injured by the weapon's exploding and died on the return march to Burma. G. E. Harvey, the historian of Burma, records this epitaph: 'Men are remembered by the years they use, not by the years they last.' Alaungpaya's successors carried the frontiers further forward. Independent Arakan was liquidated in 1785; Tavoy, Tenasserim, and the Shan princes were reduced to subservience. And then the Burmese began expanding into India;

Manipur was conquered, and after several campaigns (which the Burmese nicknamed 'The Creeper-Cutting Wars') Assam came under the Burmese hegemony in 1819. These westward encroachments made the Burmese the neighbours of the British in Bengal, and there were border raids and counter-raids. The British despatched envoys to Ava, but neither king nor court was prepared to take very seriously the emissaries of what was after all a mere trading company. In 1824, the Burmese general Bandula, the victor of the Assam campaigns, was ordered to march upon Calcutta and bind the British Viceroy in chains (considerately made of gold). This ill-considered move was to lead, after a further sixty years, to the extinguishment of the Burmese kingdom. Most of the kings, living in isolation at the successive capitals of Ava, Amarapura, and Mandalay, attempted to deal with the British threat by ignoring it, by shutting it out. But the last king, Thibaw Min, adopted the disastrous policy of seeking to take a pawn from the West – he invited in the French. Awaiting only a suitable moment, the British forces then advanced to eliminate this potential French bastion which would threaten British India.

It may seem casuistical to argue that, on the one hand the rulers of South Asia contributed to their downfall by involving the West in their internal affairs, while on the other they incurred the same fate by attempting to shut the West out. This interpretation is set down in explanation, not in justification. In the situation which emerged when the West intervened in Asia, the unstable equilibrium which had for so long produced something like a network of state and inter-state relations was adequate no longer.

South Asia is provided with what appears to be a perfect set of 'natural' national and international frontiers. But we have seen how ineffective these were throughout the ages. Northern India was sometimes associated with Central Asia, sometimes isolated from its affairs. The Deccan was sometimes subordinate to Delhi, more often quite separate. Northern Ceylon was sometimes yoked with the Tamil south of India, sometimes a part of the politics of the island. Arakan now looked towards Bengal, now towards the interior of Burma. Burma was sometimes associated with the outlook of Ceylon and maritime South Asia, and yet was mainly concerned in coping with the Tai (Shan) communities spread out around the hills enclosing the Irrawaddy and Chindwin Valleys and plains.

Geography does not provide a ready-made solution to the problems of national and international stability in South Asia. Neither did economic development create a framework of overall stability. The greater part of the population subsisted within an agricultural pattern in which the village was the main unit. Trade did evolve a wider pattern; but any evolution towards a national or international system in which the economically dominant elements – the entrepreneurs – would emerge as a stabilising yet dynamic force, was stultified by the negative attitudes of those who governed. Government has provided the basic framework in Western Europe and North America: the skeleton, the communications system, which gives shape and movement to most aspects of life. Government in South Asia, however, remained a superstructure without an infrastructure. It is most apt that the symbol of authority in South Asia is the umbrella. The umbrella is held aloft: it shields and protects, but it is not an instrument for bringing together the little people toiling in their fields, and the big people, sitting in their halls of audience. In Ceylon and Burma, government remained to the end of the old regimes as a means whereby the king could express his sacred and awful splendour. In northern India, the Muslim invaders invented the idea of administration: of a system articulated so that the apex and base were part of the same machine, responsive and responsible to the will of those called upon to govern. Yet this machinery of administration was not transmuted into the mechanism of responsible government (as in Western Europe) because the Sultans and the Mughal emperors remained 'Strangers in India'; they did not succeed in identifying their regimes with the outlook of the governed.

The main influence in shaping the outlook of the ordinary people was that of religion: using this term to mean not just an ethic, or a philosophy, but meaning a way of life. Hinduism, Buddhism and Islam can be projected as ideological religions in the accepted Western sense; but for the ordinary people they provide not a set of ideas but a design for living – for living not in some ideal, hypothetical world, but for living in their own dwellings and fields, among their own folk, and among all the changes and chances of everyday life. Throughout the ages in South Asia, men have been aware of the potential dynamism of religion. Some have tried to 'mobilise' religion, as it were, for the betterment of mankind. Others have sought to manipulate religion for their own purposes. Out of this manipulation has come the perversion of religion, which has become a force driving men apart. The first major example was the Aryan concept of caste, of the immutable division of mankind into higher and lower, clean and unclean. Then came the Buddha's mission of reconciliation and liberation, followed by the counter-attack of the Brahmin priesthood, which exiled Buddhism to Ceylon and Burma. The brotherhood of man was preached by medieval Hindu visionaries, and by the religion of fraternal equality, Islam. Yet the introduction of Islam into India was to give rise to the most potent of the divisions which have split asunder the peoples of South Asia. After Akbar had attempted to liberalise Islam, and bring together the different religious confessions within one 'House of Worship', as he called it, his great-grandson deliberately emphasised the unique superiority of the creed of Muhammad, and drove the militant Hindu races into revolt.

The great cycle of history in South Asia demonstrates an extraordinary continuity. There was ebb and flow, as we have seen, but at no time was there any great break with the past (such as the fall of Constantinople to the Turks) or any great challenge to the past (such as the enforced modernisation of the Russians, in the eighteenth century, and again at the Revolution). Yet one is compelled to question whether traditional South Asia had any further capacity for self-renewal. It appears that the Sinhalese pyramid of government began to crumble about the twelfth century, and was thereafter doomed to decay, whether or not external forces hastened the process. The Burmese monarchy, though demonstrating a remarkable capacity for survival, did not develop any dynamic difference which would enable the kings to establish their rule upon foundations firmer than their own individual capacity to reign. Even the Mughal Empire, with its magnificent monuments and its mighty power, was condemned to undergo something like a political earthquake every time an emperor began to lose control; and except for the happy accident that four able rulers were thrown up in succession – and survived the hazards of an era of disease and sudden death – this empire could not have lasted so long.

If the political systems of South Asia appear to have become exhausted over a period of two thousand years, the dynamism of its social organisation and religious and moral thought continued to show resilience and rejuvenation. This dynamism included a capacity for syncretism and harmony – 'absorption, synthesis'.[1] When South Asia was compelled to give way to Europe on the political plane, this social and religious resilience remained, to bear the peoples of South Asia along, until in the fulness of time political power was restored.

---

[1] The great Darwinian controversy over evolution and natural selection, which rocked Christians in the West, hardly raised a ripple on the surface of Hinduism, Buddhism or Islam: they were able to absorb this revolutionary theory without any need for re-evaluation of doctrine.

2 The Economic Life of the People

The winning of the land is always the first drama in the history of every country: and the one which is least well documented. The transfer from a semi-nomadic pattern of shifting cultivation to a settled system of farming based upon the husbanding of water is the greatest economic revolution in Southern Asia. Shifting cultivation would support only one crop annually. The scattered fields would be sited on the hillside. The valley lands, covered in heavy jungle, were left to the wild beasts; tiger, lion and elephant. Shifting cultivation could support only a sparse population, and there was no surplus for trade. The changeover to settled cultivation was no sudden process. While the more enterprising communities adopted the improved technique, others clung to the old way. Those outside of the main areas of population continued with shifting cultivation for centuries: some of the aboriginal tribes still practise 'slash and burn' even today. Among the important factors of change, were the growth of knowledge of irrigation techniques, the use of iron tools, and the yoking of cattle for agricultural processes. In northern India, these changes may tentatively be ascribed to the period between 800–600 BC. During these centuries the fertile land of the Ganges valley was colonised. It may be that human settlement helped to change the climatic balance in northern India, by deforestation, and erosion of the soil. At some period, north-western India became increasingly arid. Some rivers dried up, and even disappeared: the strangest example is the former mighty river Hakra, which flowed through what is now the desert of Bahawalpur. All that now remains is its tributary, the Ghaggar, which disappears into the Thar Desert: the Hakra ceased to exist in the eighteenth century. Climatic change may have been the cause of the disappearance of the ancient cities of the Indus valley, rather than the pillage of the invading Aryans. Because we cannot speak with certainty about the climate of ancient India, we cannot describe the distribution of crops with certainty. But it seems reasonable to suggest that the people of north-west India were wheat-eaters, while almost all the remaining inhabitants of Southern Asia were rice-eaters.

Settlement and cultivation in Ceylon first developed in the so-called 'dry zone' around Anuradhapura some time after 400 BC. At first the settlers followed the method of shifting, dry cultivation of rice, but at an early stage they began to employ the technique of growing paddy in 'nurseries' or seed-beds, and then planting the young shoots in flooded fields. There was an elaborate development of irrigation techniques by means of 'tanks' or reservoirs.[1] The technique was to build a dam across a broad valley, or else to build up a more extended retaining wall in U-shape. The tank might be directly supplied by a river or stream flowing into the reservoir; or in more elaborate systems a diversionary channel would draw water from a distant river to maintain the reservoir. With water supplied from tanks, at least two paddy crops could be raised each year. After many centuries of tank-building in Ceylon (as in south India also) political instability led to their falling into decay. Gradually, the central zone of the island went out of cultivation. It seems probable that this process of collapse was accelerated by the tanks having become vast breeding grounds for the anophelese mosquito which spread malaria throughout the population. It would seem that, having deforested the central area and completely changed the water-table by damming and diverting rivers, the Ceylonese unwittingly played a large part in creating the dry zone. Once the highly organised irrigation system began to break down, climatic change began to be felt. Even the course of the monsoon might be affected: certainly the capacity of the flora and fauna to reproduce the former balance of nature was destroyed. And so central Ceylon was given over to jungle for many hundreds of years.

Something like this sequence occurred in central Burma. The whole of south and central Burma was settled by the Pyu (a vanished race) and the Mons, who developed the techniques of artificial irrigation. When the Burmese thrust down into their future homeland they may have learnt something of wet-rice cultivation from the Chinese, but more likely they took over the technique – as they took over the land – from the Mons. Their first main area of occupation about AD 800, was the 'Eleven Villages' of Kyaukse ('stone-weir') district. Khamlu, one of the eleven villages, continued to be left to the Mons. The Burmese then fanned out and down the Irrawaddy

---

[1] Tank is found in Indian languages in various forms (*tank'h, tanka, tanku*). Like so many technical terms, its derivation is disputed; some deriving it from Sanskrit – *tadaga, tataka*, 'a pond or pool', and some from Portuguese, *tanque*, for an artificial sheet of water, with stone banking.

valley, creating areas known as *tuik* or enclosures. On reaching Minhla, they seem to have called a halt. The Burmese carefully demarcated the land with boundary pillars, and created a complex system of maintenance and use of weirs and canals. The centre of their culture was the region to the south of Mount Popa, the Olympus of Burmese mythology. Here grew up the great city of Pagan. Then, a complex system of dykes, weirs and sluices allowed the thirsty land to provide two or three crops a year in what was a dry area with about 45 inches of rain a year. Increasingly, the produce of the land was donated by king and laity to the great temples which were erected for miles around the city walls. This diversion of resources weakened the kingdom, and Pagan was in no state to resist the Mongol invasion. There was no sudden collapse, but as with Roman London a gradual decay. With the collapse of most of the irrigation system, central Burma declined and to this day remains semi-desert. There is an old Burmese proverb: *kyaung-la, ywa-sha; ywa-lok, ya-hsok*: 'Cultivation yields way to men, and men yield way to monks' (or the fields are swallowed up by the town, and the town is swallowed up by the wilderness, where only monks remain). Today, the age-old city of Ava lies abandoned to the jungle; but the chanting of the monks is still heard from the ancient monastery to which they cling.

Even before the people of South Asia adopted the plough, agriculture was based upon the use of domestic animals. Throughout the wetter areas, the water buffalo was in most common use; elsewhere bullocks or oxen were employed, while in the parched north-west the camel was adapted to agriculture. Because a yoke of oxen is such a basic element in agriculture, units of measurement are often derived from the oxen's labour: for example, in Burma, the area which a yoke of oxen can cultivate in a morning's work is a common unit of measurement. Draught cattle were first used for harrowing, for drawing water from wells or streams, for haulage, and later for ploughing, after the invention of the plough.

Besides the main crops of rice (or wheat in the north of India) the peasant cultivated millets, for food and fodder, pulses, beans, sesamum (or sesame) for oil, sugar-cane, and cotton. In south India, Ceylon and Burma palm trees were extensively grown: different varieties produced coconuts and copra, and toddy for fermentation. Most peasants liked to have an orchard, for shade as well as fruit, and the mango was widely cultivated.

In early times in India the Sudras, the class not entitled to the sacred thread, seem to have existed as the bondsmen of the three

higher *varnas*. The Sudras tilled the soil as helots, toiling for the ruler
or for the religious foundations (temples, monasteries, seminaries) to
whom extensive grants of land were given. Alongside these labourers, there were free farmers, peasants, who seem to have enjoyed
much the same status as the yeomen or freemen did in medieval
England. Gradually, from the Gupta period onward, the status of the
two classes seems to have moved towards a common level. Some of
the Sudras acquired customary rights, which gave them a portion of
land to till as peasants (others remained landless labourers) while the
old peasantry found their position deteriorating into something not
far removed from serfdom. From the second century AD, the mass of
the rural population became liable to forced labour; to act as porters
for government officials and landlords, and to toil on public works.
Taxation became more severe and manifold, with levies imposed by
officials and landlords upon every kind of occasion. Then subinfeuda-
tion increased: between the peasant and his ruler, several layers of
middle-men or middle masters were interposed. Something like a
feudal system prevailed. In Ceylon and Burma, the cultivator always
enjoyed a good standing in the community: better, for example, than
that of the fisherman or boatman.

The rural economy was simple and local. As irrigated cultivation
expanded, a surplus above that needed for subsistence was achieved.
A large part of this surplus was demanded by the ruler as tribute, or
rent (the distinction was blurred). Quite a sizeable proportion of the
remainder would go in religious offerings, to priests, monks, shrines,
or temples. Some would remain to be exchanged for agricultural and
domestic necessities. A market system existed in most areas. Often
goods would be taken to a local market town; sometimes the market
would revolve around a traditional circuit, as the 'Five Day Markets'
still do in Burma. Certain villages of skilled crafts grew up: a village
of weavers, or potters, or metalworkers. These would draw their
customers to them. Then, many Indian villages built up their own,
internal group of craftsmen. Every village would have its barber, and
most would have workers in leather, iron, and wood. The old Indian
village community is often described as 'self sufficient'. So it was, in
many ways; but a neighbourhood economy of interrelated villages
gradually extended in areas such as the Ganges valley where population became more intensive. However, even in this area there were
great tracts of jungle and wasteland to separate rural communities
from each other.

The village community in India, and to some extent in Ceylon, became increasingly enmeshed in a web of traditional custom, authority and obligation:

> God made them, high or lowly,
> And order'd their estate.

Although King and Court in Burma were aloof, semi-divine, the mass of the population were commoners, divided into two main classes. In Pagan times some, the *asan*, were free, though mainly engaged in hereditary occupations (the great majority cultivators). Others were bonded, serfs called *kywan*; some serving the crown, others the monasteries. These different categories dwelt apart. The villagers co-operated for their defence. Old Burma had a social tradition known as *dahmya*, 'swordblades', which virtually licensed the young bloods to fight and roam; so village defence was a constant priority. On the social plane there was a tradition of co-operation: for example in raising the main parts of a new house (for custom required the roof to be on before sunset, after work had begun in the morning). But in economic affairs, especially in agriculture, the individual and the family were more free in Burma than in the rigidly organised village society of India. However, throughout South Asia there were rules to be followed. Nobody could build a house except of a prescribed style and size, in accordance with his status. Dress, also, was closely prescribed. The lowest castes in India and Ceylon, both men and women, were forbidden to cover the upper part of the body; neither could they eat or drink from vessels made of metal – only earthenware must be used. Low caste men must not sit upon a horse (in Ceylon, the lowly might not sit on a stool), indeed the lowest of all might not use the same pathways as their betters. The use of wells and watering places was strictly controlled; the lowest castes had to draw their water from ponds, often after the cattle had drunk. Some of these injunctions were ordained by royal decree; but most of this sumptuary code was made up of local custom.

Because of their isolation, few villages were linked with the central power. From the time of the Mauryan Empire in north India, there were royal highways. The chief route was the highway which connected the north-west with the eastern Gangetic plain; this ran from Taxila, near the Indus to Pataliputta, and was extended to the eastern seaport of Tamralipti (not far from the modern Calcutta). There is evidence that this road was kept safe by imperial police detachments. There were staging-posts and resting-places and the road was shaded by great trees. Hundreds of years later, the Muslim emperors re-established this great highway, after it had fallen into disrepair, while at the beginning of the nineteenth century the British rebuilt the Grand Trunk Road, as it was now called, from Calcutta to Peshawar. The purpose of this trunk highway – in Mauryan, Mughal, and modern times – was to facilitate imperial communications, to provide for the passage of troops, and only incidentally to assist commercial and passenger traffic. Trade and travel were mainly carried on the great rivers, both of India and of Burma. The Irrawaddy was supplied with regular boat services, and travel downstream was quite rapid.

International trade grew up in the Indian Ocean before the Christian era. The Arabs have been credited with first learning to navigate across the ocean, using the prevailing monsoon winds: but Greek, Egyptian and Levantine sailing masters were using the technique from the first century AD, to reach India, while Indian vessels were making direct sailings to the Malay peninsula, and the Malays were sailing westward. The Indian traders called Malaysia *Suvarnadvipa*, the land of Gold; the name *Karpuradvipa* or Camphor Land was probably applied by them to western Borneo, while *Takkola*, the land of Cardamom, was another destination.[1] The rise of the Roman Empire, with its demands for oriental luxuries, stimulated this trade. It may be that the spreading of Buddhism in India helped to free merchants from restrictions against crossing the Black Waters which Hindu belief insisted rendered the traveller unclean. Some of this trade was connected with the Bengal port of Tamralipti, but more lasting connections were built up with south India and the Coromandel coast, leading, in the ninth and tenth centuries AD, to dominance over the coasts of Malaysia by the south Indian Cola power.

A flourishing ship-building industry developed to support this maritime trade, mainly based on the west coast of India. Shipbuilding also developed in Pegu and other ports of south Burma; Burmese teak being the best for this purpose. Pegu traders also joined in the commerce of South East Asia. One example of the international nature of trade in Asia is the widespread use of common measurements. The most remarkable is the weight known in India as the *maund*, or properly, *man*. Its origins are unknown, but in ancient

---

[1] The location of these early cities and states in South East Asia is entirely hypothetical. Some early writers also speak of *Suvarnabhumi*, which is probably the coast of Burma, south from the Gulf of Martaban, while *Takola* also means an 'Emporium' or 'Market' and probably applies to Thaton on that coast.

Babylon the *mana* represented one-eightieth part of a talent. It appears subsequently as the ancient Egyptian *mna*, the Hebrew *maneh*, and the Roman *mina*. The *man* was taken to India by the Arabs, no later than the eighth or ninth century AD. Its weight varies: the standard is 82 lb. In Ceylon, the equivalent to the *man* is the *amuna*; measurement of weight and quantity. Another international weight which tells us something about trade patterns is the *viss*, from Tamil *pisa*. It weighs about 3 lb. The *viss* is a common weight in south India and Burma, though in Burmese *pisa* has become *peiktha*.

Coinage was known in India and Ceylon from early times, but was not widely circulated. The striking of a coin, with name and superscription, was one of the principal marks of kingship, and was jealously guarded. In the times of the great empires, there was a uniform system of coinage; but when petty rulers were appearing on every hand, seeking to substantiate their claims by issuing coins, the currency became uncertain and often debased. Among coins in use, the greatest antiquity must be given to the *karsha*, originally a copper coin or weight, which originates in post-Vedic times. *Karsha* is the original of Sinhalese *kasi*, a coin in general, and for the English 'cash'. Among coins of high value, was the *hun* or *pagoda*, a gold coin circulating in south India. The standard Indian coin, the rupee (Sanskrit, *rupya*, 'wrought silver') was introduced by Sher Shah in 1542, as a silver coin. The rupee is still the principal coin in India, Pakistan and Ceylon. In Muslim times it was linked to the gold *mohur* (10 rupees=1 mohur). Coins were current in the Indian-influenced kingdom of Arakan in the west of Burma, but there was no coinage issued by the kings of Burma until the very end of the last dynasty. A medium of exchange existed among merchants in the *tical* (old Mon) or *kyat*, a weight in silver equivalent to 1¼ rupees in value. In independent Burma the *kyat* has taken the place of the rupee.

It does not seem that trade formed the basis for any great urban culture in South Asia, as certainly happened in Europe. The great cities owed their being to government or to religion. Kashi (Banaras) was a religious centre from Vedic times. Pataliputta, Ujjain, and Taxila were the most important centres of government under the Mauryas; in addition, Taxila, on the threshold of the ancient Greek civilisation, was a great home of scholars.[1]

In order to supply the courts, armies, and temples of these cities,

---

[1] Burmese culture is full of Indian echoes, half-submerged memories of Indian classical models. The Burmese word for 'university, college' is *takkatho*, derived from Taxila (properly Takshasila).

craftsmen and merchants were attracted to them. The various trades and professions established themselves in one section or ward of the city: such as the famous Chandni Chowk, the Street of the Silversmiths, in Old Delhi. In ancient India as in medieval Europe, the various trades and crafts became organised in powerful guilds. These acquired a strong hereditary character, and imposed strict regulations upon techniques of manufacture and upon prices. The guilds had a recognised status; they were internally autonomous, and their leaders dealt directly with the government official in charge of the city. Gradually, different cities acquired a special reputation for certain products which were regarded as the most superior throughout India.

Ceylon and Burma followed the Indian urban pattern; though with the smaller size of these countries, the capital was dominant and unique to an extent not known in India. Although there were other towns, the seats of governors, or the site of temples, these were overgrown villages: the scale and layout of dwellings was on village lines, the rural economy filtered right into the centre of the town, and all the ties of the townsfolk ran out into the countryside, making them (sociologically) villagers who happened to be living in a more densely populated area. The capital in Ceylon and in Burma did have an urban atmosphere. The city wall set a boundary on the urban limits, and the intramural buildings had an urban style. There was a congregation of bankers, merchants, officials, scholars, whose outlook was urban, while the palace-city within the capital was a pageant of high manners which constantly served to demonstrate the aloof, elevated character of the court. Yet beyond the walls of the official city, the rural character of society was reasserted. Most of the craftsmen lived in the suburbs (unlike the Indian concentration under the city guilds) and stretching away beside the roads which led to the capital there were colonies of weavers, or silversmiths, or stonemasons, following the pattern of craft villages which was general.

Over the centuries, it is not easy to discern any trends which created great changes in the South Asian pattern, comparable to the rise of the urban bourgeoisie in medieval Europe. Some hint of a social struggle may be discerned in the emergence in south India of a great division between the castes; with the cultivators supporting the Brahmins in the alignment of the 'Right Hand' castes, while the craftsmen challenged Brahmin supremacy through a 'Left Hand' association. There are many instances of struggles and fights between the Right and Left Hand factions: the Pariahs usually spear-headed the Right Hand alliance, playing the drums, while the Left Hand stalwarts were the *Panchalars* (the 'Five Classes'), the stonemasons and metal-workers, and the *Pallars*, the leather-workers. During the centuries before the Muslim invasions, the general trend in India was towards greater stratification and rigidity; any kind of social or economic mobility became difficult. As in medieval Europe, there was an idea of an absolute, fixed fund or pool of wealth and labour; if one man worked too hard, he would thereby diminish the amount of work available to his fellows. Therefore, the guilds and castes strictly regulated the output of their members. Much the same applied to wealth. Any merchant who accumulated riches knew that he was liable to have these sequestrated by the king on his death. All this worked against any great changes in society, and in particular against the rise of a capitalist class.

It appears probable that this extreme stratification of Indian society contributed to the ease with which the Muslim invaders swept across northern India, for only those of the warrior caste were expected to stand up and oppose them. The Muslim conquest did not have immediate social and economic results, though among the earliest groups to accept the faith of the invader were several of the craftsmen castes: it might be possible that, baulked in their challenge to the Brahmins and the cultivators, they chose this means of raising their status.

As Muslim rule was consolidated in north India, so economic life was enlarged, rather than developed, by the empires of the Turkish sultans and the Mughals. To an even greater extent, the imperial court was the great regulator. The Muslim rulers were builders on the grand scale. Successive capitals were created. 'Old Delhi' was built by Kutb-ud-Din (d. 1210), the second city was Siri, and the third Tughlakabad (founded 1321). The fourth and fifth cities (Jahanpannah, 1327, and Firozabad, 1354) were established by Tughlak's heirs. The sixth city, Shahjahanabad, was the ultimate capital of the Mughals. In addition, the capital was also set up at Daulatabad in the Deccan, Lahore, Agra, Fathpur Sikri, and Allahabad. Each foundation of a capital produced a spate of buildings: palaces, mosques, forts. This gave employment to masons, architects and craftsmen, and encouraged the elaboration of new techniques and styles: but it also threw a great strain upon the masses whose tribute paid for these buildings. The royal treasury can be imagined less as a reserve bank than as an oriental Fort Knox. It was the tradition that the ruler did not draw upon the accumulated wealth of his predecessors: he amassed his own store of gold. This tradition was followed not only by the imperial rulers, but also by lesser princes, so that even up to the present day there are said to be remote fortresses in the Rajput principalities where, under the guard of hereditary keepers, are stored the jewels and bullion of an ancient day. The Muslim rulers draw a huge income from the operation of state monopolies. Frequently the ruler would permit none but his own agents to engage in trade: even in such staple products as food grains. Sometimes the state would farm out its monopolies to merchants or lords, when they would enjoy the exclusive right to buy and sell a commodity in return for a subvention to the state. Under the Mughals, the state set up as industrialist: there were factories called *Karkhanas*, where armies of workmen produced manufactures for the court and the army. The regulation of trade by tolls and taxes upon the sale and movement of goods was uniformly imposed.

Under this dominance by the state, the merchants might grow rich but could not achieve that power and influence which the urban bourgeoisie of Italy and the Low Countries acquired in Renaissance Europe. The merchant could not build a great town residence because of the strict sumptuary regulations. He could not acquire a landed estate, because all land was (theoretically) the possession of the state. Under the later Mughals there was discrimination against Hindu merchants who were required to pay customs duties on their goods at 5 per cent, while their Muslim rivals were mulcted only $2\frac{1}{2}$ per cent. This does not seem to have greatly affected the predominance of the Hindu merchants.

There was little the wealthy merchant could do, behind the doors of his cramped, gloomy ancestral home, other than count his riches, and perhaps bequeath his wealth to a temple or some other charity. Certain castes took the lead in the acquisition of wealth. Bankers from the remote Rajput land of Marwar spread their business empire right across the subcontinent. Among these Marwari clans of business men, the Agarwals and the Khatris acquired a name for enterprise, but the great bankers and moneylenders were the Seths and Mahajans. One Jagat Seth was given this sobriquet (meaning 'banker to the world') by a Mughal emperor after organising a massive purchase and distribution of foodgrains.

The mechanism of banking and exchange was certainly developed as far as in Europe. The *hundi* or bill of exchange was negotiable throughout India, or in the marts of Persia and South East Asia. A complicated and sensitive money market existed, to cater for the many kinds of coinage in circulation in India. The financial system functioned, in an era of slow communications, only because the money-lenders and money-exchangers belonged to known castes and clans. The 'brotherhood' of an individual banker would know very well how his credit stood, and would trust him accordingly. Because the banking world of India was conducted on lines of interior information, bankers attached the highest importance to being known for trust or credit-worthiness. The confidence-trickster was unknown in the world of Indian medieval commerce.

Within the main limits of the Muslim Empire, the merchants had to walk warily and humbly; but on the borders of the empire they were less dependent. The west coast of India, especially Gujarat, was held loosely by the emperors of Delhi. At Surat, the mercantile community was the equal of the officials. The merchants included, beside the Hindus, Parsis from Persia, Jains, and Bohras, a Muslim trading community. Virji Vora (Bohra) was almost like the merchant princes of Italy. He controlled the wholesale market, virtually fixing prices and quantities. He monopolised the coastal or 'country' trade of the west coast. He had branches in Ahmadabad, Agra, Burhanpur and Golconda. When the European trading companies appeared, they had to do business through Virji Vora like everyone else. A similar merchant prince had his headquarters at Pulicat in south India. This was a Chettiar, known as Malaya: possibly an indication of his overseas trading interests. Malaya had to be courted by the European merchants who traded on the Coromandel coast, and he acted as banker to them. Thus it was that in Surat and other port-towns, something like an equal alliance between the ruler and the merchant aristocracy grew up. Elsewhere in India the merchants were the underlings.

In general the trading castes were quite separate from the castes of craftsmen. Denied the opportunity to go in for merchandising, the Indian artisan could not hope to expand his business, as so many enterprising mechanics were to do in Europe and North America. Yet Indian manufacturers enjoyed an international reputation for their quality. The muslins of Dacca, the calicoes of Malabar, were the main exports to the West. Gold and silver cloths, brocades, and embroideries were exported to Persia and Turkey. Jewellery, silverware, ivory, were luxury products, manufactured for a small, select market. Small-scale production was the rule, though cotton textiles were organised in areas of high production like Bengal on a system of 'out-workers' who received their raw material from an entrepreneur, processed the cotton into the finished product, and then returned the goods to the entrepreneur, being paid on piece rates.

The Mughals were essentially an urban element, and their influence upon the life and economy of the countryside was small. The great change introduced by Akbar was the revenue settlement carried out by his Finance Minister, Raja Todar Mal. This made no alterations in landed rights: like the similar Domesday survey in England, it professed to determine what the existing rights and obligations were, and fixed these for hundreds of years, thus giving the peasantry some kind of security. Akbar ordered that the land tax should be paid not in kind but in cash. This, also, merely regularised a practice which had begun before, but the change worked to the disadvantage of the farmers. In the old days, when the grain crop was harvested, it was brought to the village threshing-floor, and was divided up according to custom: so much to the ruler, so much to the village menials and artisans, and the rest to the cultivators. But with the substitution of a money demand, the emphasis was placed upon gathering up this sum, without too much consideration for the internal rights of the village folk. As the practice of letting out the collection of the land tax to revenue farmers increased, so the old village customs and connections were subjugated to the control of the revenue farmer or his local agent. As these *zamindars* or land managers increased the area of their control, so under the later Mughals they assumed the powers of princes rather than of mere landlords.

It does not seem that the obligation to pay taxes in cash led to a monetised economy. Within the village, the old economy based upon subsistence, services, and payment in kind largely continued. There were few innovations in agricultural methods. Muslim rulers built a limited number of canals and aqueducts, mainly in the neighbourhood of Delhi. The 'Persian Wheel', a method of lifting water from a deep well by an endless chain of buckets or pots, operated by a simple mechanism turned by an ox or camel, was probably introduced into northern India by incoming Muslims. This was the most ingenious method of water-lifting: most well-irrigation was done by simply hauling up leather bladders of water.

One feature of Indian rural life which only becomes well-documented from the Mughal period onward was the constant threat of famine. There are references to famines as early as Mauryan times, but it is only in the accounts of sixteenth-century European travellers that the subject is first fully treated. It is clear that, outside Bengal, the whole of India was liable to famine. Years of major famines were

1540, 1555, 1596, 1630–31, and 1669–70. Most of these occurred when the Mughal Empire was stable and at peace. The collapse of the empire led to even more widespread dearth, disease, and death. During these famines, the normal conventions and restraints which held together rural society were abandoned. Parents sold their children, men and women sold themselves into slavery; even canni-balism was accepted. Ralph Fitch in his account of his 'wonderful travailes' (as Richard Hakluyt called them) found much at which to marvel: but he also found in his journey down the Gangetic plains in 1586 'few villages but almost all wilderness, with many buffes [buffalo], swine and deer, grass longer than a man, and very many tigers'.

Under the later Sinhalese kings, the economy of Ceylon declined and contracted. This was partly because commerce was taken over by foreigners, especially after the Portuguese and then the Dutch extended their grip over the maritime provinces, and partly because any kind of development of an indigenous merchant class was checked by the system of royal service, *rajakariya*. Under this system, all agriculturalists, craftsmen, and traders were obliged to devote a proportion of their effort to the service of the state. Some of the more skilled and specialised crafts were required to serve the king and court. For example, the potter caste was required to send quotas of men to the capital to work for three months in every year for the king. During this period, their only remuneration was to receive rations. The different royal departments of service were designed to provide a specific service – weavers, washermen, drummers, etc. When a function ceased to be useful, the members of that service might be required to discharge some new function: thus, the depart-ment of archers (*dunukara*) was in time given the entirely new function of supplying the royal stores with the spice turmeric. Even the foreigners were liable to *rajakariya*. From about the thirteenth century AD, foreign trade was in the hands of 'Moors', that is Arabs and Indian Muslims, together with the Chettiars, the bankers of south India. These foreigners were obliged to give three months' service every year (like the Sinhalese) and the Moors who monopol-ised trade with the coast in salt and grain were required to provide free transport facilities for all royal requirements, and also to pay taxes in salt and fish. In return for these gratuitous services, all they received was the right to reside in the king's dominions. We have seen that in India the court was the main stimulus to trade and industry and to the development of a monetised economy. Because in latter-day Ceylon the court functioned on this *rajakariya* basis, it served to stifle any such expansion. Even in the provinces, the people were tied to the system, as all the officials 'ate' the harvest of the peasants, and all public works were built and maintained by the labour and materials compulsorily given by the people.

The decline of Ceylon began as early as the tenth century. The zenith of Sinhalese civilisation is often depicted in the twelfth century: but already there was evidence of economic paralysis in the debasement of the currency and the disappearance of the standard gold coin, the *masuran*. Some authorities see a cause for the decline of the economy in the absorption of resources in a twelfth-century passion for the construction of colossal temples, or *stupas*. 'The golden monastery is shining but the stomach is empty' is a saying current in Burma: but equally applicable to Ceylon. Whatever the cause, there was a contraction in the commerce of Ceylon. By the fourteenth century, the denomination of *masuran* was copper, not gold: in the eighteenth century, the only gold coin in use was the Indian *pagoda*. The circulation of specie was minute: a British official calculated that the total revenue in gold and silver of the last king of Kandy was no more than £1,500 per annum.

This static economy was able to support few manufactures: calico, silver and iron products, carvings, all for local consumption. Agriculture was mainly on a subsistence basis; as the marvellous irrigation works of an earlier day clogged into ruin, so tillage contracted, and the peasant moved on to new sites in the jungle, often lapsing into the 'slash and burn' cultivation of primitive times. All around the mountains of the central provinces of the Kandyan kingdom great forests closed in. The jungle was the safest barrier to the intrusion of the European invaders from the lowlands, and so the dark foliage of the tall jungle trees was left to grow in profusion to shut out the unwelcome world of the Westerners.

Burma, like Ceylon, experienced economic decline after the collapse of the Pagan kingdom. When the colossal Mingalazedi (Royal Auspicious Pagoda) was being built, 1274–80, a prophetic rumour spread abroad: 'The pagoda is finished and the great country ruined.' To avoid the fulfilment of the prophecy, the king discontinued work; but he was persuaded to complete the building. A few years later, the Mongols invaded Upper Burma, and the Pagan civilisation flickered out. Trade and the arts and crafts only revived on a limited scale in the Mon kingdom of Pegu in the fifteenth century. Thereafter, a modest entrepôt trade grew up, with merchants coming from China, South East Asia and the West, to exchange their cargoes (pepper, camphor, porcelain, opium) for Burmese products: rubies from the north, lac, wax, ivory, horn, lead, tin, and the great storage jars for which Pegu was celebrated. When the Burmese power revived, Pegu was attacked and reduced.

The later kings of Burma, the Konbaung line, made Ava in the north the centre of the kingdom's trade and wealth. As in Ceylon, a system of service tenure was developed. Social organisation was functional, rather than territorial or on class lines. Part of the population was liable to pay taxes, the *athi*, and part to render personal service, the *ahmudan*. Among the latter, many were military men, but some belonged to hereditary groups giving personal service to the state: these included the palace cooks and the palace sweepers. Unlike Ceylon, this liability seems to have been limited to those who remained near the capital. A man who migrated to distant parts could evade his obligations. All trade and production were subject to royal monopoly. The rubies from the mines of Mogok, the 'earth-oil' or petroleum of Yenangyaung: almost every extractive or manufacturing process must give of its best to the king. The king could sell any trade to a monopolist; who, in return for tribute paid to the king, enjoyed exclusive trade in a given commodity – such as teak. Even the marketing of vegetables in the bazaar of the capital city was given to a monopolist by Bodawpaya (1782–1819). In consequence trade was stagnant. In addition, Bodawpaya plunged into a megalomaniac programme of temple building, and in the Mingun Pagoda raised up what is calculated to be the hugest mass of solid brickwork in the world: about six million cubic feet of bricks. By such extravagance, the kings consumed the wealth of Burma. The last king but one, Mindon Min (1853–78) made a steady effort to rebuild the economy. He instituted a coinage, and introduced a tax levy, on a money basis which replaced the service system. The governors no longer 'ate' their provinces, but received salaries, paid from the royal treasury. Mindon tried to rationalise the monopolies. He (or his agents) directly traded in staple commodities, such as rice, cotton, sugar. He granted licences for other exports: the most important being teak. He purchased river steamers, and planned factories: but none entered into production. The last king of all, Thibaw Min (1878–85) was unable to collect the taxes, so he fell back on state lotteries and upon sales taxes in the environs of the capital. Once again (mainly because of the service system) no indigenous mercantile class grew up in Burma. Almost all trade, wholesale and retail, was in the hands of foreigners – mainly Chinese – together with Indians and Armenians, except for the petty trade of the market place. It appears to be an age-old feature of Burmese life (one upon which the earliest travellers comment) that women have always dominated the market-stall trade. A considerable element of social amenity enters into this trade: Burmese women enjoy the gaiety of the market, the opportunity to display their charm and wit. But a very penetrating business shrewdness underlies their dealings, and there are cases of Burmese women who have built up sizeable businesses. But in old Burma the restricted nature of local trade prevented them from getting very far.

Agriculture in Burma hinged upon the productive capacity of the irrigated districts to the north and west of Ava and upon areas in the delta of Lower Burma. During the wars of the eighteenth century, large areas in the delta were denuded of population and relapsed into jungle. Because of the lack of a large-scale market demand, subsistence agriculture remained the rule. In the dry zone of central Burma the rains were insufficient, but in most of the agricultural areas there was no fear of a drought, as so often in India. There were famines in Burma, and these seem to have been caused by pests, such as rats, descending upon the standing crop. There was terrible destruction by monstrous rats in 1596, but the worst disaster was the *maha-thayawgyi* or Great Famine of 1812, when people were reduced to grubbing up jungle plants, and entire villages were deserted by their people who wandered around searching for scraps to eat. There were supposed to be central grain depots for such famines, but most kings were more concerned to keep their own granaries in the capital as security against any cessation of regular supplies.

This survey has revealed a world in which, before the advent of the Europeans, trade and industry remained an adjunct to government and institutional religion throughout South Asia. We see in India most of the facilities present for a commercial development such as could lead to the growth of industry: a network of banking and other business organisation, secured by a business community of known integrity, and a network of arts and crafts comprising skilled artisans also systematically organised according to recognised standards. All that was required in India was a superstructure of government adjusted to a capitalist economy, and improved access to markets. Even in India, this potential for commercial and industrial growth was only a tiny segment of the economy: the vast majority of the population remained wedded to a traditional system of agriculture. In

Ceylon and Burma, no prospect of any kind of 'take off' could be expected in the economy because the system had worked to prevent the emergence of any commercial class, and had even discouraged more than a limited development of arts and crafts. Such trade as existed was almost entirely in the hands of foreigners: and it might be expected that the development of commerce or industry in the future would be left to foreign enterprise, whether Asian or European.

Perhaps this survey of the conditions of life in ancient and medieval times has appeared to draw an unattractive picture. Life was insecure, in the sense that the ordinary peasant or artisan had little or no control over the forces which motivated his existence. Yet there was a certain security in the severely limited capacity of the state to intervene in his affairs. As we shall see in the next chapter, the systems of government in South Asia were absolute and all-powerful in theory. Yet, because of poor communications and slender organisation, the state was compelled to leave the mass of the population to themselves. A village might expect to be left alone the whole year through, apart from the visit of the tax-gatherer: apart from the dreadful visitation of an army on the march. The whole year through, the village folk lived their days, according to custom and religion and the accepted relations of one group with another. The days were lightened by the festivals, by visits to or from the fair or the market, and by great events such as a pilgrimage to a holy place. Because this was an unlettered society, we have no direct evidence of their feelings. We do have their folk tales and legends. They represent a world that was strange, uncertain, dangerous perhaps – but not squalid or ugly.

3 Government and the Social Order

According to the legends of India and Burma, the first king of all was Manu: 'For when these creatures being without a king, through fear dispersed in all directions, the Lord created a king for the protection of this whole creation, taking for that purpose eternal particles of Indra, of the Wind, of Yama, of the Sun, of Fire, of Varuna, of the Moon, and of the Lord of Wealth (Kubera). Because a king has been formed of particles of those lords of the gods, he therefore surpasses all created beings in lustre. . . .'

The Laws of Manu were not composed until the early years of the Christian era, when Hindu kingship was fully evolved. The early Aryan rulers were tribal chiefs. Their claim to rule came from the blood of the leading family which flowed in their veins. They were acclaimed by the clans and demonstrated their kingship by prowess in battle, and judgement in council. Only the strong could rule: and a blind man, or one suffering from deformity was excluded from the succession. During the Buddha's day the little kingdoms of north India still retained a tribal character.

We may surmise that in a nomadic or semi-nomadic society, such as that of the Aryans during their days of roaming, or later among the migratory Burmese, and later still among the Muslim invaders from Central Asia, decisions were taken by the leaders alone. When people are on the move, there can be no time for the slow working of the processes of consultation and decision-forming among the community at large. Among the migrants, if there was a dispute over women or cattle there must be rapid adjudication by a chief before one or both of the parties wanted to move on. But when the community became stabilised and settled, then there was time for people to build up recognised customs and traditions, which could be applied to any matter in dispute. Then, rather than refer the case to an autocratic arbiter, it would be decided by the 'brotherhood' (*biradari* or *bhaiband*). This brotherhood was most often composed of the senior members of the caste or tribe; but there is some evidence to show that in south India such tribunals were composed of

45

representative members of the different castes residing in the same village or market town. Because of the difficulty of settling disputes or reaching decisions within the wide context of the brotherhood, affairs were often entrusted to an inner council, known as the *panchayat*, or Council of Five. Five was a sacred, magical number (*Panchmen parameswar*: 'God is in the Five'), but in practice the panchayat might be larger or smaller than that number.

As the nomadic peoples settled, principalities and powers exerted dominion over them. Trade routes, rivers, and other advantages helped to determine which grew strong. The first power to make extensive claims was Maghada which arose in the sixth century BC. Already rulers were claiming superlative attributes, but the Maghada kings were of lowly origin and their lineage was linked with the *naga* or snake, to which was attributed mysterious qualities. Maghadan conquest stretched along the Ganges plain, east and west. Attracted by stories of Maghadan wealth, Alexander of Macedon, who had conquered Persia with ease, marched through the mountain passes and across the Indus river. He was opposed by the king of the Purus, known to the Classical West as Porus. Despite their war elephants, the Indian host were defeated. The passage across the Punjab rivers, the principal invasion route of all time, lay open. Alexander's soldiers were weary; they would not go any further. He was compelled to lead them down the Indus to the sea, and thence he returned to Persia, leaving his general to rule over the Indus borderland.

Despite the brevity of his stay (327–325 BC), Alexander – Iskander, or Sikander as he is known in Asia – was remembered in legend as the ruler over all, the universal emperor, which now became the pattern of kingship. This universal empire was achieved in India by the Maurya dynasty. Their capital was established at Pataliputta in Bihar (on the site of Patna); and as was to be the custom throughout South Asia, kingdom, capital, and king were all known by the selfsame name. During the Mauryan period, as control spread across northern India, a pyramid system of government developed, while a theory of politics was elaborated in the work known as *Arthashastra* or 'Treatise on Polity', ascribed (though this is much in dispute) to Kautilya, a minister of the king. When Mauryan rule had spread down over central India, the throne passed to Asoka about 274 BC. To his subjects Asoka was known as *Devanampiya* or 'beloved of the gods', but for his rank and title he was content to be called Raja or ruler.[1] Later, the title of raja was assumed by princelings, landlords, even officials; and kings called themselves 'great ruler', maharaja. In the same way, although Chengiz and Timur, the mighty Mongol conquerors, were known simply as Khan, this title has been devalued until the common soldiers of the Muslim rulers called themselves Khan. The point to be remembered is that the first emperor of all India held sway before the mystique of monarchy had been fully developed. Just as the conversion of the Emperor Constantine was a great turning point in Europe, so the adoption of Buddhism by Asoka was a major event in South Asia. It is probable that Asoka was devout: it is supposed that he took vows as a *bhikku* or monk. Following the Buddhist practice, it would be possible for him to withdraw from the world for a while, and then resume his kingship. Tradition firmly asserts that the third Buddhist ecumenical council took place at Pataliputta about 240 BC, under his patronage. This council launched Buddhism as an international movement, the great seminal influence which has transformed Central and South East Asia. From Asokan Buddhism emerged the concept of *çakravartin*, the 'wheel-turning monarch', the universal lord of righteousness. Fundamental beliefs in this system are the twin concepts of *dharma* and *karma*. *Dharma* (Pali, *Dhamma*) the teaching, the law, has religious and social as well as political implications. It is the moral standard – the 'truth and beauty' of our Western ethic. All have their duties and obligations to discharge, but the ruler has the supreme task of maintaining harmony among his subjects by upholding the *dharma* of all while providing an example through fulfilling his own *dharma*. Here is one of the significant differences between the political fundamentals of East and West. Western man insists that the prime factor is the establishment and assertion of rights; the Asian replies that a true relation between the individual and community is created by the recognition of obligations. Since Vedic times, Indian rulers were known as *Dharta-vrata*, 'Upholder of the Sacred Law', but for Buddhist kings this function became even more explicit: in later times, in Burma the monarch was 'Lord of the Great Law', *Mintayagyi Paya*, and in Ceylon 'Sun of the Spotless Law', *Vimala Dharma Surya*.

---

[1] *Raja* is one of the great Indo-European root words. In India it has taken various forms, such as *Rai*, *Rao*, *Rana*, *Rawal*, and in south India *Raya*. This form, *Raya*, is close to the Spanish, *Rey* (king), but other European forms are also related, while even the *Regents* of some American universities are distant connections of South Asian royalty.

Like *dharma*, *karma* was a concept received from Hindu belief
which was given a higher power by Buddhism. *Karma* represents the
consequences of one's actions during life which determines one's
existence during the next cycle of rebirth. The endless cycle of birth
and rebirth – the wheel of life to which man is chained, according to
Hinduism – can be resolved according to Buddhist teaching by
following the Noble Eightfold Path. Along the path to enlightenment, the prince is very near to the goal. The Lord Buddha was, of
course, the Sakya prince Siddartha; while in the incarnation immediately before, he had lived as Prince Wesantara. Some sort of
equation emerges: because the man who would be king must acquire
great merit, therefore the man who is king must have acquired great
merit. As a coming Buddha, the Buddhist ruler sheds the aura of his
righteousness over his people. The king is the exponent and protector
of the law, *Dharma*, and of the Five Moral Precepts. He is the
protector and promoter of the Buddhist Order, the *Sangha*, and of
the *bhikkus* or monks who are its members.

Asoka demonstrated the royal protective power by causing pillars
to be erected in all parts of his empire: at Peshawar, in Kathiawar, on
the Nepal frontier, in Orissa and Mysore, edicts engraved upon rock
or carved upon high pillars proclaimed the Asokan code, *dharma*, or
rule of righteousness. Besides directions for right conduct, there were
prohibitions on cruelty and slaughter of living creatures, and directions for social harmony and order. As with other great moral and
ethical leaders, the example of Asoka was not enough. His people did
not fully carry out Lord Buddha's teaching, and the Mauryan Empire
gradually disintegrated. But the ideal of *çakravartin*, the universal
lord of righteousness, remained; the avowed goal of every little
princeling and contender for power.[1]

When the next great dynasty emerged in India, the Guptas,
Buddhism had fallen away from its former predominance and
Brahmin influence was paramount. As the caste of priests and
scribes, the Brahmins were not altogether adapted to assuming the
office of king. For kingship is power, and one of the most significant
aspects of governance in India is the concept of *dandaniti*. *Danda*,
literally 'the rod', or chastisement, was necessary in order to maintain

---

[1] The *çakravartin* was symbolised by 'the seven jewels': seven symbols of power.
These were: the wheel of universal power, the goddess of fortune, the queen, the
crown prince, the minister, the imperial elephant, and the horse. Some or all of these
symbols were associated with kingship throughout South and South East Asia.
Sometimes the wheel appeared as the umbrella.

order. 'It is danda and danda alone which, only when exercised by the king with impartiality and in proportion to guilt, either over his son or his enemy, maintains both this world and the next'; so says the *Arthashastra*. This treatise goes on to analyse in detail the methods whereby force is exploited as an extension of statecraft. A whole chapter is devoted to showing how profit (*artha*) may be derived from warfare. Clearly, the Brahmins could not take on the role of a warrior king: but they could absorb the authority of kingship by so surrounding the royal person with their protocol that nobody else could approach the king except through the mediation of the Brahmins.

Their technique was to elevate the king beyond the reach of the multitude as a god is elevated, and to evolve elaborate ceremonial which isolated the king and overawed the people. They appear to have borrowed their unifying system from Sumeria, in the ancient Middle East. The Sumerian rulers erected a style of temple known as Ziggurat or Mountain of God. These were supposed to represent the universe, earth and heaven, through their successive levels or terraces (the Tower of Babel was a Ziggurat). According to Brahmanic – and Buddhist – belief, a magical mountain, Mount Meru, forms the axis of the universe. Its summit is the abode of the war-god Indra, god of the East. The two religions differ in detail, but both agree in conceiving of a circular universe, with Mount Meru as its apex, of lower continents where spirits and men abide, and of encircling oceans. Employing the idea of the microcosm, this universal symbolism was reproduced in the symbolism of the sacred capital city, with the palace upraised in the centre, representing Meru; with the city around, and the moat beyond, representing surrounding oceans. The city gates, facing north, south, east and west, represented the cardinal points. Finally, the king, seated upon his throne, represented the universal ruler, *çakravartin*, and the lord of the heavens, Indra.

Throughout his reign, the ruler depended upon the priests to carry out the sacred ritual which would confirm his legitimacy as a sacred king. First came the coronation, when the principal ceremony was the *muda abhiseka*. This rite symbolised the rebirth of the ruler as divinely dedicated to ruling his people. There was a ceremonial pouring of water over the king's head, to the accompaniment of prayers of purification and dedication. As the people vowed their loyalty, so the king vowed in return to govern justly, to give protection, and to support religion. Some have seen in this ceremony a form of contract between king and people. The king was equipped with symbolic paraphernalia: the white umbrella, the royal elephant, queens principal, and queens lesser. Thereafter, the celebration of the annual festivals, such as the Spring Festival and the Rain Festival, were led by the king and court. The birth and coming of age of the king's heirs were public events – all celebrated through the medium of the Brahmin priests, or *purohitas*.

When there was no strict law of succession, the choice of an heir-apparent was of key importance. Usually the king would name an elder son as his heir; but where the sons were small, the king not young and the times dangerous, it would be wiser to choose a brother not a son. Once chosen the *Yuva Raja*, as he was called, was associated with governing. He would be given the office of commander in chief (the key to power when the old king died). Sometimes the *Yuva Raja* (the name, literally, means 'lord of the east') would be regarded as the second, junior king. This extension of his role was more fully developed in Burma, Siam, and the countries of South East Asia.

The king was assisted by a council of ministers. This council – in which the Brahmins were the dominant element – always made up its membership according to a number of astrological significance: twelve was sometimes favoured, but eight was the number recommended in the Vedic *Mahabharata*. A minister was entitled *mantri*, which is derived from *mantra*, 'a secret formula of magical power'. The essence of the *mantri*'s position was secrecy; the preservation of the secrets of kingship, with a touch of magical power. Because the Brahmins alone preserved knowledge of the scriptures, the epics, and the law codes of ancient Hinduism, they could preserve their privileged role in the court and in the state. The judges and royal officials throughout the land were mainly Brahmins.

This elaborate court protocol was absorbed by Sinhalese royalty. The *purohita* played a key part in Sinhalese court life, and most probably Brahmins from India fulfilled this role. Similarly, as a Burmese state was established, the ritual was copied; perhaps via Ceylon, sometimes via little Indian frontier states like Manipur, and sometimes by direct invitation to north Indian Brahmins to take office under the Burmese kings. In the same way, Indian Brahmins were called to the courts of Cambodia and Java. Perhaps because they were more isolated as foreigners in South East Asia, the Brahmins sought to identify kingship even more closely with their exalted priestly office. In south India, the temples support hundreds of women as *deva-dasis* or 'slaves of the Godhead'. The *deva-dasis* were regarded as married to the God: besides their duties as dancing girls, they had intercourse with the God through his minions, the priests. In South East Asia, these fertility rites became more elaborate, with the divine king being required to maintain the prosperity of the realm through ritual sexual intercourse. The symbolism of the universe reproduced in the capital city also became infinitely elaborate, attaining its apogee in the sacred city of Angkor Thom, *Nagara Dham*, 'the great capital'.

As the realm expanded, so the problem of royal control over the outer provinces became more difficult. This problem was most acute for the vast empires of north India, but the kingdoms of Ceylon and Burma also found the royal power overstretched. An obvious device was to appoint a royal son or brother as viceroy of some distant or valuable province. But all too often such an appointment gave the royal governor the idea of using his delegated power to raise forces to seize the throne. It was usual, therefore, to require any viceroy of position to leave his family to reside at the court of the king, where they remained as hostages for good behaviour. Sometimes, the king would select as his governors men of no rank or foreigners, believing that they would be less likely to aspire to the throne. The king would ensure that he was informed about what was happening in all the corners of the realm by employment of an army of spies, confidential agents, and news-writers to send a constant flow of information to the capital. Of course, such men can be bought, and so the king would proceed as frequently as possible on tours through his dominions. He would be accompanied by a great retinue of officials and soldiers, and his capital would be symbolically recreated in the layout of the camp. Unless the king was especially secure, such absences from the capital might afford the opportunity for a usurper to seize the city and the royal palace: and such was the belief in the prestige of the capital that, once installed on the throne, the usurper could expect to be recognised by the multitude as lawful king. The Hindu kings and emperors of India, and their counterparts in Ceylon and Burma never devised adequate machinery to ensure the unity of the realm; and division and disruption were always to be feared in the outer provinces.

The Guptas evolved an imperial administrative structure of provinces and districts which was copied by the Pallava rulers of south India, and from them by the Sinhalese kings. But these administrative hierarchies were far from being like the rigid imperial framework of a later age, and were subject to stresses and pressures from below as well as from above. In some of the princely states of Rajputana the aboriginal inhabitants, the Bhils, were fond of saying 'The Rajputs are the lords of the state, but the Bhils are the lords of the soil.' When the premier Rajput prince, the Maharana of Udaipur, was enthroned, he was first anointed with the mark of sovereignty, the *tika*, by a Bhil. A striking parallel to this custom is found in the extreme east of Burma where, at the coronation of the *Saopha* (prince) of Kengtung, aboriginal Wa tribesmen first seat themselves on the throne, before giving way to the Shan (Tai) prince. The infrastructure of the empires and kingdoms of South Asia was a web of local authority and local custom. The Aryan kings had been at the head of a number of clans, internally organised and responsible to their own leaders. The Aryans in their conquests encountered many tribes and clans whom they left to their old ways. Up and down India there were local chieftains, great and small, whose leadership over their own people was recognised by the overlord. A similar network of chiefs and head men emerged in Ceylon. The apparatus of government dovetailed into the village system. The complex network of reservoirs and canals developed under the kings of Ceylon during the ten centuries up to AD 1000 required elaborate controls, both for maintenance of the irrigation works and over the use of water by all. At the level of the village community, a network of tribunals was established to supervise the use of water by their members, and also to ensure that the customary rights of the village were not eroded by neighbours claiming more than their recognised share of water. The *gansabha* (or *gansabhawa*, as it is usually transliterated), the village council, was established in a more systematic manner than the Indian *panchayat*, and besides its responsibilities in the irrigation field, it adjudicated in disputes and attended to other village affairs. The *gansabha* had a recognised place at the base of the administrative pyramid, and endured the vicissitudes of power struggles at the higher levels of government.

In Burma, in addition to recognised tribal and territorial chiefs, there were the chiefs of 'regiments' of yeomen (the *ahmudan*) loosely associated in peacetime in their farmsteads, but banded together in war as archers, spearmen, horse-soldiers or warboatmen. These local allegiances were founded upon relationships of mutual obligation between leaders and led. The state had to allow for these local loyalties in its governance.

In return for protection, the maintenance of law and order, the South Asian ruler required from his subjects a share of their produce.

Mostly they were agriculturalists, who gave a share of their crops; but the labourer would give his labour and the craftsman of his skill. What we now call taxation was known in India, Ceylon and Burma as 'eating': governors were 'eaters of provinces'. The king was entitled to a proportion of the produce – often one-sixth was demanded, but it might be one-quarter. The mass of the people knew nothing of a money economy, and so their share was given in kind, and stored in the royal granaries. In addition, traders were mulcted for their share of taxation by an elaborate system of dues and tolls. In principle, all commerce and trade came under the king (just as all land belonged to the king) and so all transactions had to pay a percentage to the state. Tolls and customs (known in ancient India as *sulka*) came to about one-twentieth of the value of trade. These levies were gathered in every market town and at junctions on roads and rivers. These tolls, together with the produce of the land, were levied and supervised by the department of the Treasury (*kosa*), one of the principal organs of the government, along with the army and justiciary. The Treasury was also usually in the hands of the Brahmins.

Underneath, the 'lords of the soil' lived out their lives mainly oblivious to the activities of the government. The ordinary people kept away from the trammels of the state so far as possible. In the Punjab (where they speak out frankly) they advised: 'Never stand behind a horse or in front of an official'; while of the style of justice in olden days, the Punjabis said: 'He who gains his point pays his *shukhr'ana* [present of thanks]; he who is cast pays his *jurmana* [penalty]': meaning that both sides lose in an appeal to royal authority. The world of the village functioned entirely on its own. The liability to pay land-revenue, and to give labour service when required by the state was recognised; but apart from a vague sense of the king's protective power, the countryfolk recked little of the state. The settlement of disputes, the protection of the community, the provision of amenities: these were evolved within village society, or not at all. In time of war, the village people would be involved, willy-nilly; conscripted to fight or to provide supplies, or else looted, killed, or enslaved by the invader. Amid the calamities of flood, fire, pestilence and famine, war was the worst calamity. But it had to be endured in the same inevitable, immutable way. The countryman expected no say in these matters. His great aim was to be left alone by the state.

When northern India became a battle-ground of Muslim conquest, village society reacted variously to the 'Time of Troubles'. Where the people were able to resist, as in Punjab, local independence was strengthened. The villages were fortified, the people stood together, and were able to maintain their traditions and their rights. But where nature or economic weakness left the people defenceless, as in many parts of Bengal, their old institutions were destroyed and the rural folk became little better than bondsmen to their oppressors.

The Muslim invasions injected a new element into government and society: that of foreign domination. The Aryans had embraced India as their own homeland. The Muslims always remained, in a sense 'Strangers in India'. Every Muslim foot-soldier thought of himself as one of the rulers and quoted the old saying 'What was gained by the sword must be kept by the sword.' There was a military flavour about all departments of government.

Yet the peculiarly Indian capacity for absorption and synthesis began to work upon the Muslim invaders, with their alien religion and their harsh, Central Asian outlook. As early as the year 1300, the Turki conquerors were marrying Indian girls, while Hindu converts were being assimilated into the ruling elite. The first of the Sultans of Delhi to attain an imperial hold over north India, Ala al-Din Khalji (1296–1315), treated defeated Hindu rulers with conciliation, and married their daughters. His principal general was a converted Hindu (Malik Kafur). He was content to leave the Hindu kingdoms of the south in a tributary relationship with Delhi.

None of the Sultans of Delhi succeeded in establishing a dynasty to rule for any length of time. Rulers were nominated by army leaders, or fought their own way to power. The Delhi Sultans were compelled by circumstances to be content with a military paramountcy in northern India. Their resources were insufficient to reduce the Rajput princes or the kingdoms of the south. The mass of the population were left to their customary situations in the social framework. The Muslim impact was mainly confined to the capital and the administrative centres of the provinces. The Sultans' governors were military officers, and civil government was continually declining into semi-independent military rule. At the very end of the Sultanate period, Sher Shah (1529–45) introduced reforms which were to provide the foundations for the much more stable administrative system of the Mughal Empire. Sher Shah was able to eliminate much of the patchwork, local character of the web of government and to create a more unified system. He divided his empire into 47 divisions, each called a *Sarkar* (government). These were subdivided into about 113,000 basic revenue units, the old Hindu *Pargana*. Each

Sarkar was headed by a military supervisor (*Shiqdar-i-Shiqdaran*) and a civil head (*Munsif-i-Munsifan*).

The political theory of the Delhi Sultans provided a kind of mirror-image of Hindu and Buddhist theory. The Sultan was chosen by God to be his servant. He was required to govern according to the teaching of the Quran and the Shari'a. The Muslim historians who recorded the reigns of the Sultans adopted an equation which in practice followed the pattern of Buddhist doctrine on kingship (or for that matter, the Chinese concept of the Mandate of Heaven). The ruler who governs according to the Will of Allah will enjoy Allah's blessing and will flourish: therefore the ruler who is successful must enjoy Allah's blessing and must therefore be a pious Muslim, governing according to the Quran and the Shari'a. Islamic practice required a ruler to give protection to his non-Islamic or infidel subjects; but they would be treated as *dhimmis*, second-class, which meant they must pay a special tax, *jizaya*. It is probable that few Sultans deemed it politic to enforce the *jizaya* tax.

The first and greatest of the Mughal emperors, Akbar (1561–1605), put Islamic theory aside and attempted to bring about a fusion of Hindu and Muslim forces. He attempted to evolve a religion in which all men could join: the *Din-i-Ilahi* or *Tauhid-i-Ilahi* (Divine Monotheism). Akbar revived much of the semi-divine pomp of the Hindu kings. Along with the Muslim festivals, the emperor would celebrate Hindu festivals such as *Holi*, the Spring Festival, and *Diwali* in the Fall. He borrowed the old Hindu royal custom of having himself weighed on these occasions against his own weight in grain, coral and gold. These offerings were then distributed to the multitude. From time to time the Emperor would hold a public darbar, for his leading subjects, while on festival occasions he would appear at a special balcony of the palace so that the populace might take *darshan*: that is, receive grace from the light of the royal countenance. Mostly, however, the Emperor was surrounded by the inner court and it was in the Private Hall of Audience (*Diwan-i-Khas*) that the magnificent Peacock Throne stood, supreme symbol of royalty. Whereas the Hindu rulers had built their palaces of wood, reserving the use of stone for religious edifices, the Mughals achieved some of their most splendid and durable architectural monuments in their palaces and royal apartments.

Akbar established an imperial civil service, the *Mansabdari* or 'ranking' service, based upon theoretical command of a number of horsemen. This was an aristocracy of talent. An escalator was

provided for the brave and the gifted. Almost three-quarters of
Akbar's chief officers were of Central Asian origin: Turks, Afghans,
Persians. But of the 416 supreme *mansabdars* of the empire, 47 were
Rajputs. Above them all, Raja Man Singh of Ambar, brother-in-law
to the emperor, had the supreme dignity of 5,000 horse. He was given
the posts of greatest trust and danger, such as that of Governor of
Kabul and of Bengal. The revenue department was run almost
entirely by Hindus. Under Akbar, a comprehensive survey of landed
rights throughout northern India was compiled by Raja Todar Mal, a
Kayastha. The Treasury was linked to every village in the land by an
intermediary network of revenue officials. The pattern thus laid down
remains essentially the pattern of the district revenue administration
in India and Pakistan today: one grade of official introduced by Todar
Mal, the *qanungo* or circle inspector, is still so called to this day.

Under the later Mughals, there was discrimination against Hindus
in the public service. Even in the Treasury department, Hindus were
displaced by Muslims. As the boundaries of the Mughal Empire were
pushed farther, until only the southernmost tip of India was beyond
the empire, so the policy of Islamic orthodoxy was increased.
Eventually, a revolt against Alamgir, the most bigoted of the
Mughals, was led by the Maratha prince, Sivaji. He deliberately set
out to recreate the apparatus of the classical Hindu state. His capital,
Raigad, was a hill fortress. Such a capital had obvious practical
advantages to a leader organising a resistance movement, but it also
imitated the symbolism laid down in the *Mahabharata* and other
classics. His palaces, council halls, and other offices were aligned to
the points of the compass as required in the *Arthashastra*. Sivaji
underwent the *abhisheka* coronation ritual, and chose a council or
Mantri Parisad of eight ministers, according to custom.[1] In later
years, Indian nationalists were to look at Sivaji as the link between
ancient Hindu India and modern Hindu nationalism.

After Alamgir's long reign (1658–1707) the Mughal Empire crumbled into pieces. At the height of their power, the Mughals had not
permitted any of their officials to gain independent position. On the
death of a high official, all his wealth became once again the property
of the emperor. But now, in the twilight of the Mughals, the
governors of the provinces set themselves up as independent rulers.
Even so, the framework of Mughal administration survived, even

---

[1] The Muslim Bahmani kingdom of the Deccan had assimilated certain Hindu
practices, including the Council of Eight. Sivaji may have adopted Hindu customs
through a Muslim intermediary.

though the effective control of the emperors was reduced to a few miles of territory around the capital. When the British came to establish their system of land revenue they were able to reconstruct a pattern of landed rights and authority from the debris of Akbar's empire.

François Bernier, a seventeenth-century traveller, called the Mughal capital 'a military encampment', and the Mughals shifted their capital city according to military necessity or to personal whim. Akbar made his capital at Allahabad, Lahore, Agra, and Fathpur Sikri, the 'city of victory' which he constructed in the wasteland, and which was abandoned at his death. His successors also shifted the capital from place to place, but finally in the wreck of the Mughal Empire the Emperor Shah Alam ('ruler of the world') returned to Delhi under the guarantee of the English East India Company in 1772. Thereafter, the Mughals kept up a shadowy puppet-show of sovereignty at Delhi until 1858, when their authority finally departed to the upstart British commercial city of Calcutta.

Both in Burma and in Ceylon, although powerful rulers succeeded in unifying the country under one rule, none was able to press on with the establishment of a system of government, capable of carrying on when the firm hand of a master was not holding affairs in his grip. We have seen how power in India followed the shifting of the capital (Map 6). The decline of the Sinhalese monarchy in the thirteenth century was symbolised by a succession of capitals. The great days of the monarchy saw the capital at Anuradhapura. The Chinese traveller, Fa Hsien, described the Brazen Palace, nine stories high, with its 1,600 pillars and its bronze roofs. As pressure from invaders increased, Anuradhapura was abandoned in AD 846. Then followed a drift southwards, away from the threatening pressures from south India. Polonnaruwa, Kurunegala, Gampola, Rayigama, and Kotte were in turn the capital. The Sinhalese kings had created an aristocratic civil service to supervise their great systems of irrigation. But dynasties from south India replaced the native monarchy, and they summoned to their aid mercenary, military supporters, as did the Sultans of Delhi. As power ebbed and flowed, Sinhalese princes regained the crown, but Ceylon was divided into three main kingdoms, with their capitals at Kotte in the south-west, Jaffna in the north, and Kandy in the central highlands. Kandy was never known to the Sinhalese by that name: to them it was always Maha Uvara, 'the Great City'. Amid the struggles of the kings, effective local authority passed to local leaders, members of a quasi-feudal aris-

58

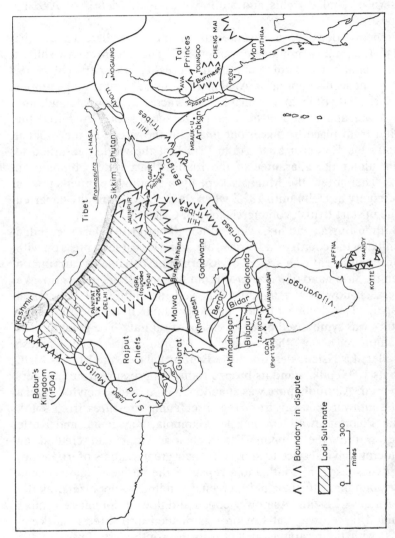

Map 6. Power in the balance, *c.* 1500.

tocracy. In the south the territorial leader was called Mudaliyar, in the Kandyan lands, Rate Mahatmaya, and in the Tamil north, Adigar and Maniagar. The last Sinhalese dynasty came to an end in 1739. Thereafter, the kings of Kandy belonged to a south Indian dynasty from Madura, and the court was modelled on the Malabar pattern. Surrounded by Tamil ministers and Malay warriors, the kings were increasingly alienated from the Kandyan Sinhalese chiefs.

At the last, the Burmese monarchy – though having no trace of foreign blood – became alienated from contact with the mass of the people. A united Burma was achieved three times between AD 1000 and 1800: under Anawratha, Bayinnaung, and Alaungpaya. After Alaungpaya the inevitable, internal disruption of the Burmese state began. Alaungpaya's dynasty, the Konbaung Dynasty, gave ten kings to Burma. Of the ten, only four completed their reigns and died natural deaths: of the others, one died of battle wounds, one was murdered, two became insane, and two were deposed.

The last dynasties did expand their area of control, exercising authority over Tai principalities east of the Salween river, even over Chiengmai, a feudatory of Ayuthia until 1776. They also forced ways through the hills to the west and north, annexing Arakan, Manipur, the Hukawng valley, and even for a brief while Assam, displacing the Ahom kings. These conquests stretched Burmese resources to the limit, and brought friction with other systems their equal, or superior in power. There were endless wars and the Irrawaddy heartland had to supply men and treasure. Burma might have survived if all the rulers had been as wise as Mindon Min, last but one. Under his son, Thibaw Min, the outer possessions were lost and the king ignored the advice of his wiser counsellors. So Burma, the last independent state of South Asia, could not survive: like her neighbour, Thailand.

Contradictions in the traditional system of government were not resolved. First, there was the Hinduised conception of divine kingship. This served to isolate the king from his people, creating an unworkable relationship with his ministers, whereby the king was dependent on the ministers for contact with the world outside, yet so high above them that he was under no constraint to behave like a constitutional monarch. The identification of king and capital produced political claustrophobia. The kingdom depended upon the auspiciousness, *mingala*, of the capital; and so, when luck began to run out for Burma, the site of the capital was changed six times under the Konbaung kings. An attempt to overthrow the last king but one, Mindon, in 1865, nearly succeeded: the conspirators killed the heir-apparent, the *Yuva Raja*. Thereafter, Mindon never left his capital city: the last king, Thibaw, never even left the royal palace. This self-isolation prevented any reform or renewal of the Burmese monarchy. Then, the Burmese kings never overcame the second great contradiction in the Buddhist attitude to the ruler. While Buddhism sees the king as specially meritorious, Buddhism also teaches that all temporal power is *maya*, illusion. The monk, who has renounced the world, is nearer to Nirvana than the king, who is still worldly. The confusion of being semi-divine, yet less than any monk, seems to have contributed towards that paranoia which royal inbreeding certainly engendered among the Burmese kings: the first queen of each was always his own sister. Believing in their own unquenchable majesty, the Konbaung kings defied the clearest omens of disaster: and time and again brought on their own destruction. Finally, the Burmese monarchy preserved, to the last, vestiges of its origins in tribal chieftainship. In a tribal society, he who aspires to possess great power must operate within the tribal context. Any super-organisation must be built out of tribal inter-relationships: military power must rest upon a confederacy of tribes, and must recognise the separate claims of the allied clans. The great leaders of Burma – and in this respect Bayinnaung was outstanding – recognised the need to gain the confidence of the different races and to respect their rights. Tabinshwehti (1531–50), though a Burmese, cut off that top-knot of hair which is the mark of the Burmese man, and wore a headdress in the Mon style. Bayinnaung appointed a Mon, Binnya Dala, as his commander in chief, and became a blood-brother of his lieutenants, including Mon officers, by the ceremonial of *thwe-thauk* in which each gave of his blood into a silver bowl and drank therefrom, signifying loyalty till death. Even Alaungpaya, the enemy of the Mons, realised the necessity for creating a confederacy wider than that of his Upper Burma followers, and he brought into his armies the Shan princes and their levies, Kachin tribal levies, and the wiry cavalry of Manipur. The failure of the later Konbaung kings to cherish the friendship of the non-Burmese tributary hill peoples on their borders contributed to the break-up of their kingdom. The last king, Thibaw, entirely alienated the hill peoples, and on the eve of the British annexation he was faced with two major rebellions. In Kachin-land a pretender arose, claiming to be a reincarnation of Hawsaing, a legendary Shan prince: he was joined by the Kachins and Shans and he terrorised the northern trade-routes. In the eastern Shan States a conspiracy of discontented *saophas* decided to topple over Thibaw, choosing a half-brother of the king, the Limbin prince, to head what was called the 'Limbin Confederacy'.

Whether as cause or effect, the Burmese kings never instituted anything like a centralised structure of administration. Mindon took steps to create a corps of administrators, paid by the state, not dependent on 'eating' their territories. But his efforts came too late.

The Burmese example demonstrates the centrifugal tendencies of the old south Asian political systems in the most dramatic way. Yet despite the instability at the upper levels, Burmese rural society, though less tightly knit together than Indian society, was able to maintain its own recognised structure of authority, based upon local custom and a web of local family loyalties.

In Burma, the kings were unable to evolve an outlook and a system which would effectively bring the parts together in a whole. The irrigation system of ancient Ceylon did provide a functional basis on which a national system of control and communication could develop. But the deterioration of the monarchy into a form of high-level faction, and the collapse of the national irrigation system which this aggravated, meant that the administrative pyramid crumbled. Finally, and most important, was the failure of Akbar's concept of an Indian synthesis between the Muslim conquerors and the Hindu conquered. Only in northern India did a settled system of centralised administration evolve. The assimilation of quasi-independent principalities into the empire was an operation requiring tact and patience. Alamgir, the world-shaker, believed that the Will of Allah required him to reverse the process of integration begun by his great-grandfather, and to assert the unilateral supremacy of Islam. In carrying out this policy he aroused a feeling of anti-Muslim nationalism – at any rate among the Marathas, if not also among other Hindus – and severed the links between the Muslim non-Indian elite and the mass of the people. The Mughal pattern of law and administration remained as the model for India (and Pakistan). But the centralised empire was doomed to disintegrate.

This survey of systems of government in South Asia appears to lead to the conclusion that the permanent institutions are those rooted among the people. Social structure, village associations, the spell of popular religion: while empires and kingdoms came and departed these were immutable.

4 Religion and Belief

Nowhere is that 'peculiar quality' of India – 'absorption, synthesis' – postulated by Jawaharlal Nehru, more evident than in the evolution of religion. Nehru has also observed that 'Hinduism as a faith is vague, amorphous, many-sided, all things to all men.... In its present form, as well as in the past, it embraces many beliefs and practices, from the highest to the lowest, often opposed to or contradicting each other.' Hinduism is a noble philosophy and a crude jungle cult; it is the creed of the mighty and of the meek; it has shaped the whole range of civilisation of India. As other religions have arisen – Buddhism, Islam, Sikhism, Christianity – Hinduism has both accepted and resisted. Although the dominating influence throughout South Asia, Hinduism has made no appeal to lands beyond; except for its one 'colony', tiny Bali, in Indonesia. The explanation must surely be that, in South Asia, Hinduism is part of the custom and belief of all parts of society, whereas in South East Asia it was imported as a part of the ceremonial of the royal court. Our examination of the relation of government to the people, and of the city to the countryside has demonstrated a certain division; one that is often described as the difference between the elite and the mass. Some writers have drawn a distinction between popular religion in South Asia, a superstitious propitiation of godlings and demons, and an esoteric philosophy, practised by the few, the intellectual elite. This distinction is often applied to Buddhism, as between the selfless teaching of Gautama and the heterodox practices associated with Animism and astrology. Islam also is differentiated, as between the austere faith of the Quran and the degenerate practices of some Indian Muslim sects. But the unique quality of religion in South Asia is the ability to span the distance between the vulgar and the divine, between earth and Heaven, which is not always apparent in other religions of other lands.

The lines of the familiar Protestant infants' hymn:

> There's a home for little children
> Above the bright blue sky

would have little meaning for South Asia. God, or Heaven, is not conceived as being (however loving) distant and other-worldly; God is in us, and all around us in the familiar setting of daily life. Popular

62

religion in South Asia, whether it goes by the name of Animism, Hinduism, Buddhism, or even Muhammadanism, is absorbed in the immediate, local power of the Spirits. The most primeval layer of religious experience, that of the original inhabitants, the Negrito, or of the autochthonous hillpeoples, is made up of demons and omens; a dark, malevolent world in which human beings are pawns or puppets, who may evade disaster only by strictly observing all the ritual precautions which custom prescribes. It is not difficult to imagine why these primitive people, living so precariously at the mercy of the hazards of nature were (and are) obsessed with the dangers behind every thought or move. The Spirits which ruled their lives were emanations of animals, trees, stones, streams, ancestors, rival tribes – a mirror of all the hazards surrounding their uncertain lives. Although powerless before their fury, one might avoid disaster by interpreting the omens correctly, through the medium of a seer who could glimpse the intentions of the Spirits through an animal sacrifice, made to please and propitiate them. Something must be paid to the Spirits to achieve success in any enterprise, such as a wedding, or to avert danger in any trial, such as illness. Life was sustained by the harvest: if the harvest failed, the tribe starved: and so the harvest must be secured by the fullest sacrifice that could be offered: the sacrifice of human blood. The fields must be fertilised by a blood offering: and to the present day, those Nagas of the India–Burma border who are not Christian believe that only human sacrifice will ensure the abundance of the harvest.

The dark Spirit world of the aboriginals was enlarged by the beliefs of the Australoid and the 'Mediterranean' immigrants into South Asia. They introduced a strong element of optimism or faith into the primitive world of local spirits. They developed the belief that life flowed ever onward through rocks, trees, beasts, birds, and humans. This early concept of transmigration or rebirth does not seem to have been connected to any idea of reward or punishment for good or bad actions, but to have arisen out of a love of living, the life-force. Some creatures were identified as specially potent: the serpent or *naga* was regarded as mysteriously wise, the eagle or *garuda* of the Hindus and *galon* of the Burmese was believed to be the monarch of the skies, and the egg from which these creatures came was seen as the emblem of creation. The identification between animals and men was symbolised in totemism: in gods half-human, half-animal in form, of which one is Ganesh, the elephant-headed god-child, the symbol of good fortune, and another is Hanuman with his monkey-head, personifying inquisitiveness, boldness, which may lead to mischief, but may broaden into an enterprising adventurousness. Because nature, gods, and men are so closely inter-connected, there is a strong belief that man can be possessed by the Spirits. Sometimes this possession is deliberately cultivated, as a means of discovering the intentions of the Spirits; sometimes ritual will be employed to cast out an evil Spirit from a possessed body. Beliefs such as these are not peculiar to South Asia, but they attain a remarkable intensity among all the religions of the area at the popular level.

Pantheistic Spirits, both high and low, play a prominent part in the lives of the village folk of South Asia. All the peoples of Burma believe in a shadow world, a mirror on a magnified scale of the human world, inhabited by the *Nats*. The Nats, or *Dewa Loka*, spirit people, are all around, and must be propitiated by offerings, and their special abodes in stream or tree or cave must be respected. The highest, the Thirty Seven Noble Nats, are seated upon that sacred mountain which features in all Asian cosmological systems as the axis of the universe. The king of the Nats is Tagya Min; his lieutenant, the Mahagiri Spirit. Several kings (notably Tabinshwehti) have been elevated to the Nat pantheon, and some queens; for example, one of Anawratha's queens, who offered herself as victim in the customary blood sacrifice to sanctify a new irrigation system, and who is worshipped as The Lady of the Weir. The Nats lived upon six planes; there are Nats of the Sky, Nats of the Earth, Ancestor Nats, evil spirits emanating from women dying in childbirth, and others ill-omened in their death. According to their rank, so long will the Nats live: those of highest rank live for 576 million years.

Ceylon has a Spirit world remarkably similar. All around are the *Yakkas*, troublesome sprites who torment the village folk. But at a higher level are the *Rakusu* – the *Raksasas* of Hindu mythology – for the most powerful, the ten-headed Ravana, king of Sri Lanka, was the opponent of Rama in the mythological war of the *Ramayana*. Hinduism also has its classes of Spirits, headed by the *Raksasas*, with middling Spirits, the *Pisacas* and *Vetalas* (or vampires) having a more restricted jurisdiction, while ghosts – *preta*, *bhuta* – exercise a purely local malevolence.

In parts of India, especially Bengal, there is an annual festival, Dasera, when the demons are first worshipped and propitiated and are then consigned to little boats to float away down the river. Popular Muhammadanism has incorporated this practice into the ritual of Khwaja Khizr, 'the green one', a water spirit identified with the prophet Elisha, who is ceremonially despatched upon a river voyage.

Possession by the Spirits may be deliberately cultivated, but the most elaborate ritual surrounds the exorcism of Spirits from those possessed by evil. The folk ritual of South Asia is replete with examples of so-called 'devil dancing' or *shamamism*, especially among the people of Kerala and Ceylon, and the Burmese. Buddhism, Hinduism, and even Islam have assimilated these dances in which, often by means of self-mutilation, the dancer attains a trance-like state of ecstasy in which he can command the supernatural. Protection against evil Spirits, and against all the dangers of life, might be secured by magic signs. The Burmese and other Mongoloid peoples tattooed their bodies from knee to navel, thus securing immunity. Amulets, containing magic formulae of words or of magic substances, were carried by most village folk from earliest days, in Ceylon and India.

Yet the main development in religion was the emphasis upon communion between man and nature, rather than the terror of the unknown. The cult of astrology linked together all classes and creeds. The village astrologer is indispensable in the social life of South Asia. He casts the child's horoscope soon after birth: it has been described as his passport through life. A marriage-union depends entirely and absolutely for its success upon the horoscopes of the prospective pair being harmonious; if the astrologer's report is adverse, the wedding cannot proceed. François Bernier, the seventeenth-century traveller observed: 'No circumstance can happen below, which is not written above. In every enterprise they consult their astrologers. When two armies have completed every preparation for battle, no consideration can induce the generals to commence the engagement until the *Sahet* [discovery of auspicious hour] be performed. In like manner, no commanding officer is nominated, no marriage takes place, and no journey is undertaken without consulting Monsieur the Astrologer.'

All this, we may say, was the legacy of the early peoples of South Asia; together, most probably, with many other features of Hinduism, which were assimilated into Buddhism and partly into Indian Islam. Even the caste system with its rules for eating, marriage, and all forms of social intercourse, may have been partially evolved before the Aryan invasions.

At one time it was believed that the Aryans brought a superior religion with them and imposed their ideas upon the subject Dravidians. Yet the beliefs of the Aryans in their original form have almost entirely disappeared from India. They brought with them a pantheon of gods which bears distinct resemblances to the Teutonic Valhalla: a band of physically powerful, coarse, brutal beings, quarrelling and fighting among each other. The principal Aryan ritual was the great horse sacrifice or *asvamedha*. A consecrated horse was set free to roam for a year, followed by a band of warriors. Wherever the horse strayed, the people were required to do homage, or to fight. If the horse had not been slayed by the end of one year, he was brought back for ritual slaughter. Another ritual, designed to glorify fighting, was the Maiden's Choice or *swayamvara*. Girls were offered in marriage to the victor in gladiatorial contests. Regular ritual revolved around the drinking of *soma*, a powerful drink or drug which appears to have produced a state of ultra-awareness, like mescalin. In this condition, the worshippers became aware of a higher power, to which the name *brahman* was attached. Those who attained *brahman*, 'the mysterious word', were *brahmachari*, or adepts. The objects of worship were the gods, among whom Agni, personifying fire, and Indra, the war-god, were especially honoured. The all-powerful Indra was especially admired by the conquering Aryans, who put into his mouth the hymn:

> In my glory I have passed beyond the sky
> and the great earth. Have I been drinking soma?

> I will pick up the earth
> and put it here or put it there. Have I been drinking soma?

When an Aryan died, he entered into the fire, on his funeral pyre, taking with him his wives and horses and cattle in one great immolation. This warlike religion was gradually softened by contact with India and the pre-existing Dravidian cults. The 'Hinduism' which emerged from this synthesis was even more like a palimpsest of beliefs, one overlaying the other, but with the old permeating the new.

The most important innovation was the introduction into the social system of a fundamental division between upper and lower castes no less complete than the modern doctrine of apartheid. *Varna*, colour, the earliest term in the vocabulary of caste, signifies the racial division which was formulated. The three 'twice-born' categories, Brahmin or priest, Kshattriya or warrior, Vaisya or cultivator, were formed from the Aryans. The fourth category, Sudra, were serfs, condemned to serve the twice-born. The religious justification for this division was found in the concept of rebirth, which was linked with an upper-caste version of the law of causality or *karma*. Because of sins in previous births, the Sudra had been born into the lowest human category. Because the chain of causality was so firmly shackled to him, he might not hope to rise into the class of the twice-born until hundreds, or perhaps thousands of existences on earth.

How did the Sudras meet this condemnation? It seems to be an almost universal human characteristic that if you are despised and rejected you look around for someone *you* can despise. The Sudras found in the remnants of the aboriginals, and among the slaves and condemned persons carrying out the most loathsome tasks, groups, who could be classed as sub-human, outside of caste altogether – Untouchables. But the Sudras may also have seen an escape from their dilemma by utter renunciation of life. By austerity, and by abstention from the habits of the conquerors – fighting and the use of force – by abstention even from perpetuating their own kind, by sexual continence, they might attain release from the burden of their condition. All this is conjectural: it may be that among the Aryans men began to turn away from the obsessive ritual, the cult of aggressiveness, and the growing power of the priests as the only group able to attain *brahman*, knowledge of the ultimate. Whichever is the reason, India saw attempts to find philosophies that would release men from the wheel of causality, while others turned away from the aggressive, assertive, masculine qualities of the Aryan gods back to the pantheism of the old gods, with their female, maternal overtones; fertility, nourishment, reconciliation.

Post-Vedic times saw the popular acceptance of gods who have evolved away from the Aryan warlords. Shiva, the god of fertility and procreation may have swallowed up the Aryan Rudra; while his consort is called Parvati in her fair, Aryan guise, Durga in her brown 'mediterranean' character and Kali in her dark, primordial form. Krishna appears as the avatar or reborn incarnation of Vishnu, source of the universe. Krishna, the dark god par excellence, triumphs over Indra in legends which seem to symbolise the conquest of the conqueror. Krishna is the antithesis of the brawling Aryan gods, playing his flute and flirting with the milkmaids. It is true that the pastoral, erotic Krishna is merged into an entirely different Krishna, contestant for power in northern India; but his last days, and his melancholy death in the forest, represent yet another literary tradition. Along with these later gods of Hinduism in human form there is a galaxy of zoomorphic deities, with the serpent always in attendance. While literary, epic Hinduism appealed to the higher, literary castes, the rural folk continued with their own versions of the great myths. Thus, while there is Ananta, the world serpent, there are local serpent shrines in remote villages, frequented especially by women; for it is believed that snakes can have union with women and give them children.

In the religious outlook of South Asia we have seen two vital themes emerge. There is the sense of a communion between the world of men, the world of nature, and the world of the Spirits, producing a holistic view of the universe. Then, secondly, there is the concept of race: a conquering, triumphant assertion that the Aryans (and later the higher castes of the Hindus) are superior to all other men. Both these views are emanations of a folk attitude. The third important factor in the religion of South Asia is the emergence of what one might call the spirit of man: the idea that man, the individual, not man in the mass, must find his own spiritual path. Christians call this salvation; and if this word is not altogether appropriate, it does signify the emphasis upon personal decision, and the search of the individual for a right relationship with God.

The period between the seventh century and fifth century BC was a time of spiritual searching throughout the ancient world: it saw the beginnings of Greek philosophy, the rise of the prophets of Israel, Confucius in China, and (according to Parsi tradition) the time of Zoroaster, the Persian. This period saw the birth of the Jain and Ajivika teaching, with the greatest of them all, 'the Light of Asia', Gautama the Buddha. Orthodox Hindu belief, *Sanatana Dharma*, 'the Eternal Truth', was recorded in a series of texts, the *Upanishads*, evolved over several centuries from about 1000 BC. They preach the doctrine of monism, belief in one Supreme Being. They deny any duality between Mind and Matter: *Brahman*, the universal soul is also in the individual *atman*. This unity represents the ultimate way whereby individuals can obtain release from the round of birth and death, *samsara* and achieve ultimate bliss. This release, *moksha* (which may be equated with salvation) is the solution to rebirth, or the transmigration of souls; it is all in men's *karma*, which is ineluctable.

This doctrine of causality, of an endless chain of rebirth was sufficiently overpowering to impel reformers to seek ways of liberation from the burden of causality. The first important heresy or sect was that of the Ajivikas; their leader, Makkhali Gosala, taught that *karma* could not be changed by deeds or works; all that men could do was to cultivate a rigorous asceticism. Jain belief was similar in imposing a regimen of total asceticism upon the monks (even forbidding the use of clothing) and demanding a considerable degree of austerity from the laity, to whom salvation could not yet come, because of their insufficient dedication. The life of the Jain leader, Mahavira, compares with that of Gautama: he was a prince who renounced his kingdom to roam northern India in search of salvation. His solution was to see the soul as imprisoned within matter. The individual might free his spirit by rigid self-discipline and control. The Jains believed that everything, animate and inanimate, contained a soul; it was considered imperative to avoid any possibility of damaging life or the soul in any form: hence Jains took the most elaborate precautions to ensure that they did not inhale or swallow or tread upon any tiny insect, for this would mean the taking of a life.

Alongside these cults of austerity, showing that salvation could be found only by subduing the body, Gautama preached a gentler doctrine, the Middle Way, the Noble Eightfold Path. In his search for enlightenment, the Buddha practised all the rigours of extreme asceticism. Finally, while seated under a pipal tree at Gaya in Bihar he received *bodhi* or illumination. Popular belief tells that he went through a torment in which he was assailed by Mara, Prince of Darkness, but he was sustained and sheltered by the great serpent. Arising from his vision, the Buddha travelled to the deer park at Sarnath near Banaras, where he delivered his message: man may liberate himself by observing the Eightfold Path: Right Understanding, Right Resolve, Right Speech, Right Action, Right Living, Right Effort, Right Mindfulness, and Right Meditation. Those who attain perfection in this path will obtain release from the endless wheel of existence: the soul will dissolve in *Nirvana* or *Nibbana*, 'the final blowing out' of the flame. A doctrine of annihilation, in which an omnipotent God has no place, might seem one of profound pessimism: yet Buddhism was saved from being negative by the emphasis placed upon free-will and humanity. The importance of tolerance, of compassion, of charity and almsgiving, all combined to generate a religion of warmth and love. Together with Jainism, Buddhism helped to create a revolutionary concept, that of *ahimsa* or harmlessness: the idea of a respect for others which evolves from self-respect. Jainism had made a popular appeal: its message was conveyed not in Sanskrit, the ritual language of the priests, but in the Prakrits, the colloquial dialects. But Jainism had insisted that only the monk could reach the goal. Buddhism also appealed through the vulgar tongue;

Pali, 'the text', was in the speech of the Bihar country. In addition, Buddhism saw the worlds of monks and men as complementary. It became the practice for every youth to enter a monastery as a novice. He would receive training in the scriptures, and he was then free to choose to take the vows of monkhood or return to the world. At any time of life – especially when the pressures became intolerable – a man might retreat to the monastery and put on the saffron robe. No kind of judgement was pronounced by monks or laymen if he then returned to the world again.

Buddhism has been compared, not inaptly, to Protestantism in its emphasis upon the human condition; like Protestantism it was to divide into a number of sects. Soon after the death of the Lord Buddha, his followers met together in a cave at Magadha to gather together his teachings; this meeting became known as the first great council. A second council met at Vesali about 376 BC (traditional date 443 BC) and here a schism developed between the orthodox *theravadi*, 'believers in the teaching of the elders', and the *mahasanghika*, 'members of the great community'. The third council was held under the patronage of Asoka at Pataliputta about 240 BC (traditional date 308 BC) and led to the establishment of the *theravada* doctrine as orthodox: it also heralded the development of Buddhism as an international religion.

The message of the Buddha was probably taken overseas before Asoka's day. Both Ceylon and Burma have their legends of visitations by the Buddha himself, and of the holy footprints which he left as his mark. Without taking this literally, it does appear probable that early converts included traders (because of their lowly caste-status, they welcomed a religion in revolt against caste) who took the message on their voyages. Yet when Asoka's brother, Mahinda, took the emperor's appeal to the king of Ceylon, this was accepted on behalf of all the people and Buddhism became the state religion. The fourth *theravada* council was held in Ceylon about 29–13 BC, when the texts were committed to writing. A rival fourth council was held by the *mahayana* school at Jalandhara, Kashmir, under the patronage of Kanishka about AD 100. This branch called themselves *mahayana*, 'greater vehicle' and referred to the older *theravada* doctrines as *hinayana*, 'lesser vehicle'. *Mahayana* raised Buddha to the role of God. The theory of avatars was assimilated from Hindu and Zoroastrian belief. Besides the Lord Buddha (who himself was seen as one of a long line of incarnations of the Adi Buddha or Original Spirit) there were *boddhisattvas*, or coming Buddhas: these were great souls who declined to pass into the final state of Nirvana in order to devote themselves to saving mankind. The most advanced of these *boddhisattvas* dwell in heavens, high above, but at an earlier stage of their journey they share in all the tribulations of mortals. Because many *mahayana* teachings assert the need for suffering and sacrifice, it has been suggested that, in the Greek kingdoms of the first and second centuries AD in north India, there was a mingling of Christian and Buddhist thought. It was from this milieu that missionaries departed to take the message to Central Asia and China, and it was to north India that celebrated Buddhist pilgrims such as Fa Hsien came to imbibe the true doctrine.

Great centres of learning grew up in India. There were the ancient cities of Kashi (Banaras) and Madura, where seekers sat at the feet of Hindu seers and ascetics. Taxila in the northwest was a meeting place for Greek and Indian scholarship. Nalanda in Bihar was the great university of Buddhism, where students gathered from as far away as China and Java. The curriculum included grammar, mechanics, medicine, logic, and metaphysics. As in medieval Oxford or Padua, disputation was a recognised mode of scholarly intercourse. Ujjain was one of the venerable seven sacred cities. Its scholarly reputation was specially associated with astronomy. From their ancient predilection for astrology, the Indians had developed the study of mathematics and astronomy to a high power. The Arabs (often regarded as the mainspring of modern science) looked to India. They called mathematics 'the Indian art' (*Hindisat*) and took their meridian in geography from Ujjain (*Azin*). It was believed that exactly 180° of the earth's surface was inhabitable, and that Ujjain's site marked the central line of this habitable zone. The chief method of dating the years used in India, the Vikrama Era (begins 58 BC), receives its name from a king, Vikramaditya, who took Ujjain as his capital.

Buddhist ascendancy began to wane after the downfall of the Maurya dynasty to which Asoka belonged; but for something like 800 years there was a struggle between Buddhism and an ineluctable Brahmanised Hinduism. The Maurya dynasty, according to some writers, sprang from Vaisya origins, and although the Buddha (himself a Kshattriya) preached against caste, rather than against the superior castes, there is reason to suppose that Buddhism was an aspect of lower caste resentment against priestly dominance. When Asoka imposed a ban upon animal sacrifice, he directly hit the power of the priests who derived much of their prestige from their unique ability to mediate between the people and the gods by performing sacrifices. Buddhism had acquired its supremacy when an emperor became its chief missionary. Brahmanical Hinduism regained its old supremacy by elevating kingship to the level of the divine, and assured its own indispensability by elaborating the priestly ritual which upheld the throne.

The revival of Hinduism was accompanied by the composition of major epic poems, the *Ramayana* and the *Mahabharata*. The former in its popular form tells how the wife of the deity Rama was kidnapped by Ravanna, the demon king of Lanka. She was rescued with the help of Hanuman, the monkey god, who organised a monkey chain whereby Rama could cross the narrow strait to the island. The *Mahabharata* tells of a mighty war, ending on the field of Kurukshetra. A later version incorporates the *Bhagavad Gita*, the 'Song of the Blessed One', celebrating Krishna, the most human manifestation of the Godhead. He was the foremost of the *avatars*, the reincarnations of God (the last in Hindu belief being the Buddha). Krishna expounds the 'discipline of action', *karma yoga*, as the path to salvation. The *Gita* was to have a profound influence on Gandhi.

To some extent Buddhism assisted its own downfall in India by moving away from the individual, personal outlook of the *theravada* doctrine, first to the majestic, infinite theology of *mahayana*, and then to the debased practices of Tantric Buddhism, sometimes called *vajrayana* or 'the vehicle of the thunderbolt'. Tantric Buddhism is the manipulation of occult power in order to achieve Nirvana. It was believed that the magic arts of the tantras could inculcate such power and wisdom that the goal of the *boddhisattva*, attainable by other means, only after three periods of *asankhya* (or uncountable aeons), might be reached in three rebirths – or even after only one rebirth. Tantra was a more extended form of *shamamism*. Many tantric rituals depended upon auto-suggestive employment of magic formulae, such as the famous *om mani padme hum*, 'the jewel is in the lotus'. The adept demonstrated his supernatural power over natural objects (the Indian rope trick is the most familiar example of a tantric exercise). Tantric magic flowed from the ability to manipulate and control sexual powers: among the priesthood there were female priests and archpriests, taking part in erotic feats. Tantric Buddhism lingered on in eastern India, in Bihar and Bengal, under the Pala dynasty. Tantric missionaries spread their doctrine to Nepal and Burma in the seventh and eighth centuries. Gradually, under Brahmanical pressure, the Tantric cults faded and fled, lingering on in 'the Lands of the Thunderbolt', Bhutan and Sikkim, to this day, and lasting for some centuries in the remote, riverine, jungle fastness of eastern Bengal and Assam.

Meanwhile, in Ceylon the original *theravada* Buddhism persisted, only partially infiltrated by south Indian Hinduism. An important contribution towards consolidating *theravada* Buddhism was the writing of Buddhaghosa. He was a monk, born in Andhra, who settled in the middle of the fifth century at Anuradhapura. Among his voluminous writings, his major work was *Visuddhimagga*, a compendium of the *theravada* canon. His works were venerated throughout South Asian Buddhist lands: the Burmese have adopted him, claiming that he was a Mon or Talaing who emigrated from south India. There was controversies between the various Sinhalese orders, and some inclined towards *mahayana* tenets, but royal support was given to the *maha vihara* (great monastery) which upheld orthodoxy. The main innovations were the worship of Buddha images and relics, especially the great tooth relic, supposed to have been brought from India about AD 311.

As we have seen, Burmese Buddhism included a powerful Tantric element. This mingled with Hinduism (adopted by the Mons) and with *theravada* Buddhism, first drawn from the Coromandel centre, Conjeveram. With the rise of Pagan, the Tantric Ari priesthood flourished. In the eleventh century, the king of Ceylon asked King Anawratha of Pagan for monks and copies of the scriptures. This established a link which has constantly been renewed. During the twelfth century, a Mon monk ordained in Ceylon became primate and adviser to the king. A new order of monks was set up in 1192, its first members all coming from Ceylon. Temples were built on the Sinhalese pattern, and the former practices began to be condemned. Another important mission to Ceylon was despatched by the king of Burma in 1495. Twenty-two monks were reordained at the *maha vihara*. On their return to Burma, they proceeded to reordain almost the entire *sangha* or monastic order according to the Kalyani rite (so named from the Kalyani stream in Ceylon). Burma repaid the debt over three hundred years later. After ordination in Ceylon had been restricted to the dominant Goyigama caste, some lower-caste novices came to Burma in 1802. They were ordained by the primate, and returned home, taking some Burmese monks with them. This Amarapura sect, which refuses to recognise caste distinctions, remains an important school of thought in modern Ceylon.

And so Buddhism was perpetuated on the extremities of South

Asia; in Ceylon, Burma, Nepal, Bhutan, and other little Himalayan valley-states. But in India, the homeland of the Buddha, his message was absorbed and submerged within the general outlook of Hinduism. Can one concur with Sardar Panikkar, the influential historian and publicist, in saying that 'India turned her back upon *ahimsa* when she rejected Gautama the Buddha'? To some extent this must be true: but *ahimsa* was perpetuated among the tiny Jain community in western India for two thousand years until, out of his childhood experience of Jainism, Gandhi was to absorb ideas which later experiences in the West were to transform into a moral and political synthesis.

As Buddhism, the religion of compassion, was fading from the Indian scene, Islam, the religion of brotherhood was knocking on the door. The first contacts came from Arab merchants and seamen, calling at all ports around the coasts of South Asia from Sind to Chittagong. This maritime introduction to Islam was voluntary, on a basis of equality between donor and recipient; the main force of Islam came through the north-western passes in the tracks of invading armies, and was involuntary and compelling. From the invasion of Mahmud of Ghazni onward, the impact was experienced: first and most in Punjab, then in the Gangetic plains, finally in Bengal and the Deccan. The lure of India and its reputed riches drew a steady flow of immigrants into the country from Western Asia. These foreigners made India their home. Yet the spirit of brotherhood which the Holy Prophet had preached seemingly excluded the people of Hindustan: *their* brothers were the Muslims of Central Asia and the Middle East. When they thought of marriage, they sent for a bride from their ancestral land. The indigenous Muslims of India were conscious of a different spectrum of identification. They embraced Islam for many different reasons. First, there were those whose conversion was voluntary: they heard the preaching of Muslim Sufis and Faqirs, and sought in Islam liberation from the bonds of their condition. These might be rare idealists, or more often (as later in response to Christianity) the oppressed, those outside of caste, who saw in a religion of equality release from their thraldom. A second category – probably the most numerous – were those who became Muslims in the hope of office, whether great or small: over the centuries the pressure was much towards embracing Islam, for the adventurer or the adventurous. The last category of conversion were those forcibly brought into the faith for fear of death or disability. Under Shahjahan and Alamgir, a systematic attack upon Hinduism was launched. At one time, worship at the great temple of Jagannath was impeded. Sati, and other Hindu customs were prohibited. Penal taxes were levied on the Hindus. Under this treatment, thousands embraced Islam: though many slipped back into Hinduism when the pressure was taken off. Almost all the Hindustani Muslims, or Nau (New) Muslims as they were called, remembered many of their ancestral ways. Rajput or Jat Muslims still retained their caste designations. Some kept up Hindu customs (a few practised female infanticide), while Hindu marriage ceremonial, especially the simulated capture of the bride, remained general. Indian Islam was permeated by the caste system. Muslims of high degree were known as *ashraf*, 'noble'; they would never intermarry with their inferiors, *ajlat*. The common folk shared each other's festivals: Muslims celebrated Holi (the Hindu spring festival), Diwali (festival of lamps) and Dasera, while Hindus joined in Muharrum, mourning for the death of Husain and Hassan. At this rite, enormous representations of the tombs of the martyrs called *taziyas* are carried in procession: bearing a resemblance to the processional cars (the so-called Juggernauts) of the Hindus.

Some Muslim sects adopted practices associated with the wandering Hindu ascetics, *sannyassis*. The rival Jalaliyan and Madariya sects both imitated Hindu practices. They went about virtually naked, using the narcotic *bhang*, and were said to swallow snakes and scorpions. Hinduism was challenged by the Islamic spirit of brotherhood; while the Sufi speculative philosophers generated within the lower levels of Hindu society a longing for a faith that would dissolve caste. Three Sufi orders settled in India, the Chishti and Firdausi in the Gangetic plain, and the Suhrawardi in Sind. They emphasised the virtues of quietism and contemplation. At its highest, Sufism led men into union with the Mind of God, renunciation of the world of action, and a quest for ultimate knowledge. At a lower level, Sufism encouraged speculation for its own sake, and a quest for sensation and sensualism through poetry, music, wine and boys. Sufism created a climate of opinion in which unorthodoxy could be heard without instant persecution.

The first great medieval Indian religious reformer was a Brahmin from the south, Ramanuja, who lived about AD 1150. He proclaimed the unity of God under the name of Vishnu, the Cause and Creator of all. Ramanuja accepted converts from every class; but his insistence upon castelessness did not survive him. Later votaries of Vishnu were known as Vairagis (Sanskrit, *vairagya*, 'devoid of passion'). They held that *Bismallah* ('In the name of God'), the Muslim (and Jewish) invocation, was addressed to Vishnu. While continuing to live in the world, they sought *mukti*, salvation. Among the Vairagis was one Kabir (1440–1518), a poor Muslim weaver of Banaras. He became the disciple of Ramananda, a follower of Ramanuja, who propounded *bhakti* or devotional religion. Ramananda made his appeal to the common, unlettered folk. He gathered together twelve disciples; besides Kabir, they included a barber, a leather-worker, and a high-caste Rajput. Kabir then organised his own religious order, not unlike the Friars of medieval Europe. He composed a corpus of rhymes and aphorisms which appealed to the everyday folk of northern India. He taught that God was in everything. He denied that any religion had a monopoly of divine wisdom. He condemned all formal ritual, all symbols, all claims to sanctity for places or persons or gods. Equally he condemned the path of withdrawal, the turning inward into self of the *sannyassi* or the yogi. To him who seeks, God is ever near.

> The man who is kind, who practises righteousness,
> who remains passive amidst the affairs of the world,
> who considers all creatures on earth as his own self:
> He attains the Immortal Being,
> the True God is ever with him.

When Kabir died, he was claimed both by Hindus and Mussulmans. His followers, the Kabirpanthis, still sing his songs and follow the religion of *bhakti*: but caste and Brahmanism have once again triumphed over a religion of egalitarianism and individualism. The Kabirpanthis are now merely sub-castes of the different castes to which their members originally belong; distinguished, if at all, from other sub-castes by being vegetarians and abstaining from alcohol.

Kabir's contemporary, Nanak (1469–1538), was to endure an even more extreme conclusion to his quest for universal truth. Nanak was born near Lahore, the son of a corn-merchant, a Khatri by caste. In early middle life he left his government post and his family and, accompanied by a Muslim musician, wandered across India and overseas, to Ceylon and Arabia. He spent the last years of his life, reunited with his family, preaching the *bhakti* doctrine of universalism. He retained belief in *karma* and rebirth, but rejected the Vedas, caste, idol worship, and the authority of the Brahmins. Punjabi Mussulmans were among his disciples. Nanak laid great emphasis upon the need for men to find a guide or master, a *guru*. Believing that God had laid the authority of the *guru* upon him, when Nanak approached death he appointed a disciple, Angad, as his successor. Angad put Nanak's teachings into the commercial script of Punjab, Gurmukhi, and instituted a common *langar* or free kitchen as a symbol of the open community of the Sikhs, the 'disciples'. There were ten *gurus* in succession; the community became organised in *misls* or clans, and was drawn into the disputes between the claimants to the Mughal throne. From being a religion of reconciliation, Sikhism became a warrior's creed, with its symbols (the uncut hair, the discus-bangle, the short sword, the brief nether garment) demonstrating readiness at all times to do battle. The Khalsa, the Pure, the Elect, as they often called themselves, took as part of their name *Singh* or lion as a sign of their ferocity, and one group, the *Akali* or *Nihang* ('naked ones') constituted themselves the commandos of the community, dedicated to seek death in combat. And so the Sikhs, from being mediators between Islam and Hinduism, became a fierce, proselytising religion apart. Sikhism has felt the grip of the caste system, for among the Khalsa there are groups which do not intermarry or eat together: Khatri (merchant), Jat (cultivator), Labana (carrier), and Mazbi (refuse disposer), to name the most important. The Jats emerged as leaders of the Sikh community, and their clans or *misls*, led by recognised chieftains, built up a military confederacy which finally became the Sikh kingdom of the Punjab.

Kabir, Nanak, and other reformers such as Tulsidas (1532–1623) were men of the people, and their message was given in the common tongue. But one further attempt at religious synthesis was to be made from above, by the Emperor Akbar, in his *Din-i-Ilahi* or *Tauhid-i-Ilahi*, the Divine Monotheism. The Emperor made reconciliation between Muslims and Hindus the cornerstone of his policy. His favourite wife was a Hindu, and he loved music and painting and wine (all forbidden by the Holy Prophet). Akbar had his Chamber of Worship (*Ibadat Khana*) in which he indulged in discussions and disputations with Jesuit missionaries, Zoroastrians, Jains and Hindus. Akbar collaborated with his associates Abul Fazl and Faizi in a comparative study of religion, from which emerged the Emperor's own religion in 1556. There were Hindu elements: cows were regarded as sacred, and worship was paid to the sun. Devotees were enrolled as *chelas* or disciples. The religion did extend beyond the circle of the court, but not to any important extent. The main effect seems to have been to excite derision among Hindus and to stir up the orthodox of Islam. Akbar's son and successor, Jahangir, continued his father's practices and enrolled *chelas*; thereafter the Divine Monotheism seems to have faded into the shadows.

If the middle ages in India were in some sense a renaissance or reformation in religion, the seventeenth and eighteenth centuries saw the counter-reformation. We have already noticed the particular case of Sikhism, in which synthesis was succeeded by separatism and militancy. Much the same happened in Islam and Hinduism. With the accession of Shahjahan, orthodoxy replaced eclectic liberalism in the court. Alamgir, his successor, was an even more dedicated Muslim who was initiated into the mystery of *suluk* or Islamic devotion. He spent his long life in attempting to convert India into a Muslim land. He believed that by smashing the power of the priests and temples he would break Brahmanical Hinduism: but persecution only served to arouse resistance. Whereas the Hindus had been content in the past to bow before the storm, to acquiesce and compromise, preserving the core of their religion, in the face of Alamgir's challenge they were compelled either to surrender (which many did) or they were aroused into forming something like an underground resistance movement. The policy of the court was in line with contemporary Indian Muslim feeling. There arose leaders to whom the title of *Mujahid* ('one who fights in a holy war') was accorded. They set up schools of Islamic orthodoxy at Deoband and Patna and tried to win over the mass of lax Muhammadans to strict observance of the Law and Tradition.

Revolts broke out among the Hindu feudatories of the empire – Rajputs, Jats, and Marathas. The latter threw up a brilliant guerrilla fighter, Sivaji, who defeated all the might of the empire. Sivaji was a warrior chief, of the Bhonsle clan by origin. When Alamgir died, his successor sent Shahu (grandson of Sivaji, and a state prisoner since childhood) to reign as a Mughal feudatory. Shahu appointed as his prime minister one of the less important members of the royal council: this was the Peshwa, who was a Chitpavan Brahmin. Rapidly the Peshwas made themselves the actual rulers of Maharashtriya, and the Brahmins ensured their superiority. Thus we find in 1790 an order issued to the Prabhu (writer) caste, ordering them to stop practising the priestly offices of the Brahmins, to cease from reciting the Vedas, to visit only temples open to Sudras, and to salute the Brahmins. All over India, Brahmin control over the temples and holy places was tightened, their privileges were reasserted and their caste exclusiveness re-enforced. All this was possible as the central Mughal power tottered and fell, and all over India semi-independent princelings and chieftains arose, who were delighted to lean upon the wisdom and prestige of the Brahmins. And so, as the eighteenth century lengthened, and as government counted ever for less, so Hindus and Muslims throughout India drew apart into their separate traditions to await the outcome of the 'time of troubles'.

The problem of synthesis or separation did not confront religion in Ceylon or Burma. The Burmese, over the centuries, associated the ruling families among the Shans – and to a much lesser extent the other hill peoples – with *theravada* Buddhism. To cultivate Buddhist rites, and to accept Buddhist missionaries into your territory was often a means for tribal leaders to demonstrate their social and political superiority. In Ceylon, the Hinduism of the Tamils and the Buddhism of the Sinhalese seem to have co-existed down to the end. The confrontation which came in Ceylon was to be between the old, indigenous faiths and the religion of the adventurers from the West: the Portuguese, followed by the Dutch. This was to be the next dilemma: was a synthesis possible between the East and the West?

5 The Entry of the West

The encounters between East and West may be said to have started when the Aryans entered India. The invasion of Alexander (325 BC) saw the birth of the most fruitful period of contacts. It seems possible that Alexander actually met Candragupta (in Greek, Sandrocottus). Megasthenes, the Greek historian, was sent as ambassador to Pataliputta, and compiled the first Western account of India. There is even a possibility that Asoka may have had a Greek mother: there are suggestions that his father married a daughter of Seleucus. The Hellenic kingdoms on the northwestern border of India lasted for several centuries, and provided a meeting place for Buddhist, Greek, and later Christian ideas. The Buddha was even assimilated into the hagiology of medieval European Christendom: as an Indian prince, Josaphat (a corruption of *boddhisattva*), he underwent all the experiences of Gautama. Josaphat, and his disciple Balaam, were accepted as saints by the Greek Orthodox Church, and later by Rome (November 27 is their saints' day).[1]

Contacts between East and West were plentiful during the age of the Antonines, while Thomas the disciple took the message of Jesus Christ to south India soon after His life upon earth. Hundreds of years later, Alfred, King of Wessex, is supposed to have sent envoys to find the Thomasite Christians – the Malabar Church, as it became known. But with the rise of militant Islam in the Arab world, almost all connection between Europe and Asia ceased, while the later dominance of the Mongol hordes over the trans-Continental plains and steppes from Hungary to the Amur and the Yellow Sea further restricted communication. There were occasional voyagers like Friar Odoric, and of course the observant Marco Polo, but their narratives were dismissed as romances by their sceptical fellow countrymen.

Trade continued: but through a network of intermediaries. The Venetians and Genoese traded to Constantinople and the Levant: Aleppo, Damascus, Cairo. The caravan routes wound their way to the Gulf and the Red Sea. From thence, sea-captains – Arab, Indian, Malay – plied with India and South East Asia. This elaborate

---

[1] Tolstoy reveals in his *Confession* that it was the story of Josaphat which made him resolve to renounce his wife. Gandhi was influenced by Tolstoy's example to give up the marriage bed. So have East and West reacted upon each other.

and costly international trade was at last circumvented by the Portuguese, in their epic exploration of the route to the East round the coast of Southern Africa, through the legendary Sea of Darkness, dreaded by all ocean-going mariners. By 1460, they had reached only Sierra Leone. Then, in a splendid surge forward, Bartholomew Dias rounded the Cape of Good Hope in 1486 and in 1498 Vasco da Gama sailed into the south Indian port of Calicut. He was guided across the Indian Ocean from Zanzibar by a pilot said to be a 'Moor': perhaps an Arab, perhaps an Indian.

The Portuguese were quick to assess the potentialities of the situation. They appreciated that their ships were faster, and their guns better than any in the Indian Seas. They may or may not have realised that a crumbling political situation gave them special opportunities. Vijayanagar, the dominant Hindu power in south India was about to topple over; the Muslim States were jostling for predominance. The main challenge to the Portuguese on the seas came from Egypt and Turkey. The Sultan of Egypt, prodded by Venice (alive to the threat to the Mediterranean spice trade), despatched a fleet which was joined by ships sent by Sulaiman the Magnificent to wipe out the Portuguese. An encounter took place off Diu (1509), and the Portuguese were victorious. This sea-battle settled the future of the Indian Ocean area for more than four centuries. Next year the Portuguese seized Goa, and the year following they captured Malacca (1511). With Ormuz in the Persian Gulf, and Socotra off the entrance to the Red Sea in their hands, they now commanded the key positions around the Indian Ocean. No ship could sail between the Levantine trading area to the west, and the trading area of South East Asia and the Far East, without encountering the Portuguese. Proudly, Manuel, King of Portugal, styled himself 'Lord of the Conquest, Navigation and Commerce of Ethiopia, Arabia, Persia and India', Francis I of France might refer slightingly to this ruler of a tiny kingdom as 'the Grocer King'; yet he and all Europe had to acknowledge that the spices, gold and other riches of Asia were now subject to Portugal's control. The Portuguese understood both their power and their weakness. At sea, no one could withstand them; on land their limited numbers and exiguous resources would have shown up their weakness in relation to monarchs able to call upon hordes of warriors. The Portuguese confined their activities to the seas.

Manpower was the main Portuguese problem. Their young heroes might achieve the impossible by their heroism: but their numbers were few, and could not be replenished. Portuguese military power

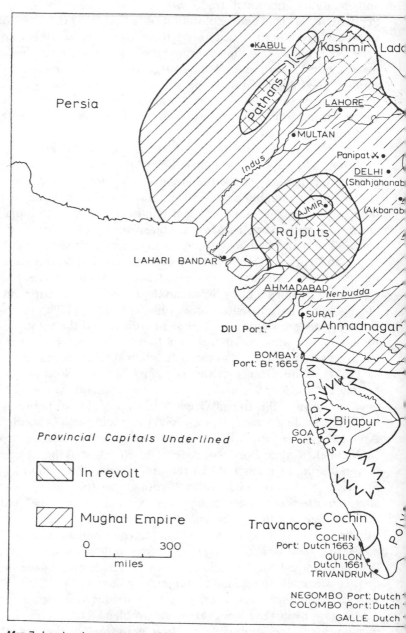

Map 7. Land and sea power, c. 1650.

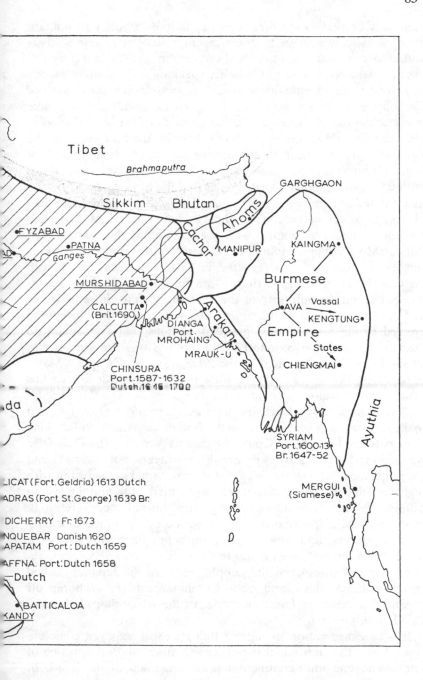

Tibet

Brahmaputra

Sikkim   Bhutan

GARGHGAON

Cachar   Ahoms

•FYZABAD

•PATNA
Ganges

MANIPUR

KAINGMA•

Burmese

•AVA   Vassal

KENGTUNG•

MURSHIDABAD

CALCUTTA
(Brit 1690)

DIANGA
Port.
MROHAING

Arakan

Empire

States

CHIENGMAI•

MRAUK-U

CHINSURA
Port.1587-1632
Dutch.1616 1700

da

SYRIAM
Port.1600-13
Br. 1647-52

Ayuthia

LICAT (Fort. Geldria) 1613 Dutch

ADRAS (Fort St.George) 1639 Br.

DICHERRY Fr.1673

NQUEBAR Danish 1620
APATAM   Port : Dutch 1659

MERGUI
(Siamese)

AFFNA. Port:Dutch 1658

—Dutch

•BATTICALOA

KANDY

and Catholic zeal found themselves in accord: a policy of militant evangelism, combined with encouragement to Portuguese soldiers and sailors to marry into the local population, produced a mixed or *mestiço* Asian community: Catholic, speaking a Portuguese patois, and loyal to the Lusitanian cause. The outstanding missionary of Catholicism in Asia was St Francis Xavier (1506–52), a Jesuit, like many of the pioneer evangelists. He arrived at Goa in 1542, and in ten years visited Ceylon, upper India, Malaya, the Moluccas and the Far East. His sojourn in these outposts of Christendom created for Asian Catholics the same sense of local identification with a universal faith which the legendary visits of the Buddha to Ceylon and Burma had inspired so many centuries before. The Viceroy of the Indies had his headquarters at Goa; Goa the Golden. Portuguese forts and settlements under his control were scattered along the coast of East Africa (Mozambique, Mombasa, Malindi), with Ormuz in the Persian Gulf, Colombo Fort (erected in 1518), Malacca, and Macao (settled, 1557). In addition there were colonies of renegade Portuguese, beyond the authority of the Viceroy, such as those in Timor and Arakan. At each of their ports and settlements the Portuguese erected strong fortifications, guarded by guns, but they made no attempt at territorial conquest. Their empire was the sea: as was symbolised by the titles held by the *fidalgos*, such as 'Captain-Major of the Japan Voyage'. For their trading the Portuguese designed ships which were enormous by contemporary standards. The 'Great Ship' or *Nao*, known to the English sailors as a 'carrack' was designed to make one voyage a year: such was the *Nao de carreira da India* which plied between Lisbon and Goa. One famous *Nao*, the *Madre de Dios* was captured off the Azores by English privateers, homeward bound from India in 1592: she was a 1,600 ton ship, broad in the beam, with high poop and forecastle, but only lightly armed. Slow and sluggish to sail, the *Nao* was often the victim of pirates, and still more often sunk in storms. The ship's chances were lessened by the practice of all – captain, officers, and crew – taking on board their own goods for trade, to an amount often equal to the official cargo. These 'mountains of wood' astonished the peoples of Asia; the Japanese called them the Black Ships, and when Commodore Perry anchored off Japan three centuries later, memories of the Black Ships helped to gain him respect.

It is an exaggeration to suggest that Portugal acquired complete control over the maritime trade of Asia: a much larger proportion of inter-island and inter-continental trade remained in the hands of

Arabs, Malays, Indians and Chinese. But the Portuguese did establish a trading network wider than any previously in operation. It was their achievement to link the trade of India and China, and to export the produce of Asia direct to Europe. A debased Portuguese became the lingua franca of the ports of South and South East Asia, taking over a role hitherto mainly filled by coastal Malay.[1] When the Dutch and the English later arrived upon the scene, they adopted this commercial Portuguese for their own use in trade. Robert Clive, on his first voyage out to India was driven by storms across the Atlantic to Brazil. There he acquired a good knowledge of Portuguese, and during his thirty years in India he never learned an Indian language; making do in Madras and Bengal with his Portuguese. Among the more common words of Portuguese origin assimilated into Eurasian and Indian speech are *caste*, *cobra*, *mosquito*, *aya* (nurse), *cameez* (shirt), *towlia* (towel, Portuguese, *toalha*), *gram* (pulse), *plantain* (banana), *peon* (messenger), *maistry* (craftsman), *almyra* (cupboard), *pomfret* (fish), *compradore* (commercial agent). By constant usage on Portuguese lips other loan words from the languages of Asia have passed into international use. Such are *monsoon*, *typhoon*, *palanquin*, *mandarin*, *mango*, *curry*, *catamaran*, *batta* (extra pay), *chop* (seal), *nabob* (*nawab*, prince), *betel* (aid to digestion), *copra* (dried coconut).

Portuguese predominance in South and East Asia lasted nearly a century. The famous Papal Bull of 1494, which divided the newly discovered lands of the world between Spain and Portugal, confined Spain's activities to the Philippines. The newly emerging maritime Protestant powers of Europe, the English and the Dutch, were far behind the Portuguese in their knowledge of the sea and ships, and were absorbed in fighting Spain in the narrow waters around their own shores. Conditions in South Asia favoured the Portuguese. Not until late in the sixteenth century did the Mughals become the masters of northern India, while the peninsula was disputed between rival princes. The island of Ceylon was torn into three by the rivalries of royal contenders. On the borders of Burma, the independent kings of Arakan were glad to call upon Portuguese sea-power to confront the rulers of Bengal to the west, and the renascent Toungoo dynasty of Burma. At no time did the Portuguese dominate the politics of

---

[1] Malay has produced many nautical terms used throughout Asia, e.g., *sampan*, *prau*, *junk*. Many of these 'Malay' words were, in turn, borrowed from south Indian traders speaking Tamil. The vocabularies of South Asia illustrate Nehru's thesis of 'absorption' and 'synthesis' completely.

South Asia, but by applying the leverage of their sea-power and fire-power at points of weakness or division they succeeded in exercising an influence out of all proportion to their actual strength.

On the west coast of India, the central point of their Afro-Asian empire, the Portuguese were confined to their headquarters at Goa, together with other tiny territories: the island of Diu, Daman, Cochin, and Quilon. From 1510 to 1595, Goa was constantly under siege, by sea and land, from rival powers in the peninsula. Consequently, the Portuguese did not penetrate inland: indeed it was not until the beginning of the nineteenth century that, as an ally of the British, Portugal was able to occupy the *Nuevas Conquistas*, the hinterland of Goa. The City of Goa was dominated by its churches, monasteries, convents, and seminaries, with the cathedral of St Paul crowning all; a centre of pilgrimage and festival, with its sacred relic, the body of St Francis Xavier, which lay in a golden casket, defying decay and corruption. This ecclesiastical magnificence served to demonstrate that the Church was as powerful in Portuguese India as the Crown. Like the Viceroy, the Archbishop of Goa exercised authority throughout the Portuguese possessions in Asia, and indeed beyond. From time to time, the Archbishop was invested with the office of Viceroy. The Church was supported by a power which could reach out to the highest lay official, and terrorise the populace at large: the Inquisition. The Inquisition was established at Goa in 1560, to maintain spiritual discipline among all Christians and non-Christians. Its most terrible instrument was the *auto-da-fé*, death by burning. Between 1600 and 1773 (when the Inquisition was abolished) over seventy *auto-da-fé* were held at Goa, and over eight hundred victims perished at the stake. Long before the Inquisition departed, the Old Goa – weakened by pestilence – had sunk into a ruin, the greatness had departed. But something lasting had been created; a fusion between the Catholic enterprise of the crusading *fidalgos*, and the tenacity and shrewdness of the people of the west coast whom they had conquered. Goa might subside into the twilight which follows an imperial sunset, but the Goanese spirit remained: Christian and distinct.

Ceylon provided the Portuguese with wider opportunities. The island had become divided between three dynasties, each claiming to be the legitimate overlord: their capitals were Jaffna, Kandy, and Kotte near Colombo. This last controlled the valuable cinnamon plantations of the west and south-west coastal plain. The king of Kotte hoped that Portuguese protection would preserve his realm against the rival kingdoms, and (even more pressing) against the plotting of his brothers. The king agreed to pay 400 *bahars* of cinnamon annually, and in 1540 he sent an embassy to Lisbon to seek a guarantee that his grandson, Dharma Pal Astane, would succeed to the throne. Joao III of Portugal solemnly crowned a golden statue of the young prince (1543) and promised to safeguard the succession. The Portuguese fort at Colombo was strengthened, and the education of the prince was entrusted to the Franciscans. In 1557, the boy became a Catholic, being baptised Don Juan Dharmapala; eight years later the capital at Kotte was abandoned (under attack from the rival claimants to the throne) and Dharmapala made Colombo his residence. In 1580, he ceded his throne to the king of Portugal, Don Henrique; though he did not die until 1597. Exercising the claim of the Kotte kings to rule the whole island, the Portuguese advanced into the mountains and captured Kandy. But under the pressure of guerrilla raids, they were compelled to withdraw. In the north, Catholic missionaries made many converts among the fisher people of the offshore isle of Mannar. The king of Jaffna led a force to kill the Christians; in retaliation, the Portuguese invaded the Jaffna peninsula. Unable to consolidate their hold on Jaffna, they withdrew to Mannar where they erected a fort (1561). Only after fifty years were the Portuguese able to even the score with Jaffna: then, the king was captured, deported to Goa, and Jaffna annexed in 1619.

Under Portuguese rule, the old administrative hierarchy, from village to province, was largely preserved. Almost all the hereditary officials at the lower levels continued in the Portuguese service, as did some of the high-ranking *mudalyiars*. The Sinhalese system of *rajakariya* was taken over; the Portuguese military forces, called *lascarins*, were hereditary conscripts, commanded by hereditary officers. The tributary obligations of many of the people were commuted into payment of taxes to revenue farmers or landlords, who were required to pay fixed sums to the government (the Captain-General). Some *fidalgos* settled down as landlord-tax collectors, but mostly the office was taken up by hereditary officials. In order to determine the state of their revenues, the Portuguese compiled the *tombo*, a land register of agricultural holdings.

All the Sinhalese who were awarded positions of rank and responsibility were required to embrace Christianity, and most adopted Portuguese surnames, such as Fernando, Pieris, Mendis, da Costa, da Silva. There was widespread intermarriage between Portuguese and Sinhalese: so much so, that some authorities have stated that all the

Low Country population of Ceylon are now ethnically (though not culturally) Eurasians – all have some trace of a Portuguese ancestor among their forebears. Many of the townspeople became Catholics, as also did most of the fisher communities. Christianity attracted the highest born – partly because of its intellectual appeal and also as the religion of the establishment – and Christianity attracted the lowest born – as a means of attaining social parity for the low caste fisherman with the high caste cultivator.

Between Ceylon and Malacca there were several Portuguese colonies; but these had no official status under the *Estado da India*: they were the haunt of freebooters and renegades. Hooghly (on the river of that name) lay on the fringe of Mughal India. Akbar gave permission to the Portuguese to occupy the town in return for an assured supply of luxury goods from China. Augustinian monks arrived in 1599 and founded a monastery and a church: but most of the arrivals were soldiers of fortune. Dianga, near Chittagong, was even worse: a scorpion's nest of pirates and slave traders. They were tolerated because they provided auxiliaries to the king of Arakan in his encounters with his enemies. Outstanding among these renegade Portuguese was Felipe de Brito, a cabin boy turned buccaneer; a man of courage and some vision. Despatched by the king of Arakan to attack Pegu, and its outport, Syriam, he conceived the plan of taking Syriam for Portugal. De Brito went to Goa and obtained Viceregal support: the Viceroy even awarded him the hand of his niece (whose mother was Javanese) in marriage. He returned to Syriam with Portuguese ships and established his command – a few score Portuguese, some Eurasians, Negroes, and Malabaris. De Brito preyed upon shipping in the Bay of Bengal, and compelled all foreign traders to berth at Syriam. Then he took to raiding into Lower Burma, and finally in 1612 sacked Toungoo. This provoked the king of Ava, and he mustered his forces to conquer Syriam. De Brito was betrayed and his stronghold captured. The Burmese king impaled him upon a stake, facing his fortifications, and left him to linger for days between life and death, gazing in agony on his little kingdom. The Portuguese captives were marched away into Upper Burma, and settled in villages near Ava to provide gunners for the Burmese army. Centuries later, their descendants still looked on themselves as Catholics, and the women still wore the *mañtilla*, the veil of Iberia.

The great adventure of the conquest of the Eastern seas, and of Brazil, exhausted the Portuguese nation and exterminated its bravest sons. The population of Portugal was replenished from Africa, South

America and the East, but the *bravura* achievement could not be sustained. The eclipse came when the Portuguese royal line ran out of sons, and the crown of Portugal passed to the rulers of Spain in 1580. The animosity which England and the Netherlands directed towards Spain, the Catholic protagonist in overcoming Protestantism, was now directed against Portugal. If the Portuguese mission in Asia had been in some sense the last Catholic Crusade against the infidel, the English and Dutch entry into Asia was an extension of the Protestant cause: economic warfare against Madrid and Rome.

During the old Burgundian time, commercial contacts had grown up between Antwerp, Bruges, and other ports of the Netherlands with Lisbon. The scientific spirit was alive among sixteenth-century Duchmen, and they produced the best map-makers and geographers of the day. The maps and charts of pioneers like Jan Linschoten, revealed the way to the East. Dutch and English determined to make use of that way. The first moves were made by England. The capture of the *Madre de Dios* created a sensation in England. When the cargo was unloaded at Dartmouth for transhipment to London, ten coasters had to be chartered. Spices, silks, calicoes, quilts, carpets, ivories, pearls, *chinoiserie*, were among the haul. The London merchants began to discuss how they might enter into this trade: especially those banded together in the Levant Company, importing oriental goods through the Middle East. However, the financial resources of England were puny compared with Dutch enterprise. The Dutch had earned for themselves the nickname of 'waggoners of the seas'. No more than the English did they have the ships to embark upon the protracted voyages to the East, but more adaptable than the English they launched into the spice trade with vigour. Their need was more urgent: they had to divert the profits of Asia from Portugal to Holland if they were to survive. With these profits they could hire the mercenary armies and subsidise the diplomatic arrangements whereby they could defeat Spain.

The main Dutch effort was directed towards the Moluccas, the Great East, the islands of Indonesia where the most profitable spices could be procured. Yet as early as 1612, Hendrik Brouwer observed that the Coromandel coast was 'the left arm of the Moluccas and neighbouring islands, since without the cottons from thence trade is dead in the Moluccas'. The main trading problem of the Europeans was that Asia did not need their commodities! To buy Asian products, they were compelled to pay silver or gold. Because of the flood of precious metals from South America, it was profitable to export bullion (especially Spanish *rials*) to the East, where they had a premium value. But this could not solve the trading problem. If the merchants of Indonesia did not want European goods, such as woollen broadcloth, it was necessary to discover what they did want. One answer was to market the fine cottons woven in India: and so the Dutch became heavily engaged in a purely inter-Asian trading network. Like the Portuguese, the Dutch insisted upon enforcing a monopoly over the commodities most in demand; mainly in order to maintain a high selling price. Like the Portuguese, the Dutch began to strengthen their hand by building fortified settlements under their own control. They established what they called a *Gouvernement* on the Coromandel coast, with headquarters at Pulicat in 1617. At once they embarked upon the task of extinguishing the Portuguese *Estado da India*. Ceylon felt the first impact of their drive and ruthlessness. Notwithstanding their previous experiences with Portugal, the rulers of Ceylon still fondly believed that they could employ the Europeans for their own purposes. Certainly they were successful in expelling the Portuguese, but as they were to wryly observe later: 'We gave pepper, and in exchange got ginger.'

When Rajasinha inherited the throne of Kandy in 1628 he started negotiations with the Dutch at Pulicat: at length, after ten years, a definite alliance was concluded between Rajasinha II and the Dutch East India Company in which the king assigned a monopoly of the spice trade to the Company in return for aid against Portugal. The Dutch first seized the east-coast ports of Batticaloa and Trincomalee (1639) and then launched their attack upon the main cinnamon country on the west coast. Galle and Negombo, with their fortifications, were captured in 1640. Meanwhile, in Europe, eighty years of Hapsburg rule in Portugal were over and the native Portuguese dynasty restored at Lisbon. Hostilities between the Netherlands and Portugal were terminated; but the Dutch Company refused to accept that the armistice applied to the eastern seas, until 1645. The Portuguese were allowed a last breathing-space, but in 1652 hostilities were resumed. After a long siege, the Portuguese remnant in Colombo Fort ('Seventy-three very emaciated soldiers, all that remained there, including some with broken arms and minus a leg') capitulated in May, 1656. The last Portuguese stronghold was reduced in 1658: Jaffna.

As they eliminated the common enemy, the Dutch were supposed to hand over the captured places to Rajasinha: but they put him off by demanding that he first pay the bill they presented for the cost of the war. The king attempted to stir up rebellion against the new occupants of the cinnamon lands. This did not unseat them: but equally, Dutch attempts to penetrate to the stronghold of Kandy were foiled. Both sides had to recognise an impasse. On the coast, the Dutch operated a community organised on commercial lines; in the interior, the Sinhalese preserved their almost anti-commercial society based upon *rajakariya*. Like the Portuguese, the Dutch left the infrastructure of administration much as they found it, only introducing Dutchmen at the provincial level. They organised a special department to regulate the supply of cinnamon, and extended their monopoly to other spices and luxury products. The greatest innovation was in the sphere of law. Dutch legal experts combined with Tamil scholars to compile a code of Tamil laws, the *Thesavalamai*, which was systematically applied to the Tamils of the north. After the disorders of two centuries, law and custom in the Low Country areas of Sinhalese occupation were in a state of confusion. Dutch Roman law was therefore introduced and a system of *Land Raads*, or County Courts, was established.

Because the Dutch national struggle was founded in the Protestant resistance to the Catholic Counter-Reformation, the Catholic Church was persecuted in Ceylon. An attempt was made to convert the native Catholics to Calvinism; and some among those who had embraced Christianity in order to retain high office were duly ready to accept the change. But others defied the new rulers. The Catholic churches were turned over to Protestant ministers, and Catholic priests forbidden to carry on in the Dutch possessions. But devoted missionaries from Portuguese India continued to sustain their flocks in secret. Calvinism made a definite advance among the urban Tamils of the north, who turned to the Western education provided by the Protestants as a means for developing their talents. Among the common people, the Dutch tolerated the continuance of Buddhism and Hinduism as the Portuguese had never done.

In South India, the Dutch were able to establish themselves on the Malabar coast as the dominant trading power, capturing Cochin and Quilon from Portugal in the 1660s. On the Coromandel coast they made their headquarters at Negapatam (1689), building another castle, while they also founded a settlement at Chinsura, near Hooghly in Bengal. Dutch adventures in prospecting for trade in Burma were largely unsuccessful. They followed their usual technique of treading upon the heels of the Portuguese, and from about 1627 to 1677 were active at Syriam, Pegu and Ava, as well as in

Arakan. Finding no profits and many losses, they withdrew.

As we noted, the English interest in the East came as early as that of the Dutch: the English East India Company was founded in 1600, two years before the United Dutch Company. But English financial resources were insufficient to mount the kind of sustained assault upon the commerce of Asia which the Dutch so rapidly built into an empire. The Dutch strongly resented English competition, and claimed that they were taking advantage of the openings created by the Netherlanders to pick up the leavings of their enterprise. Certainly, in their early voyages the English deserved much of the contempt expressed by their Dutch rivals. Some of the English ventures were little more than raids, in which the captains obtained their cargoes by looting other ships. However, the profits from these ventures were so enormous that the merchants of the City of London began to invest seriously in the Company's trade. Because in the spice islands of Indonesia the English were at the mercy of the Dutch, they looked more and more to India for their trade.

When English ships began to drop anchor in Swally Roadstead, off Surat, the Portuguese mercantile community there took alarm, and tried to persuade the Mughal governor to exclude them. When Captain Best arrived in 1612 with *Red Dragon* and *Hosiander*, he was attacked by four Portuguese galleons and six frigates. Taking advantage of the difficulty of fighting an action so near the shore, Best succeeded, by navigational skill, in defeating the Portuguese admiral. This defeat, in full view of the Mughal governor, elevated the prestige of the English. Two years later, the governor ordered four English ships to join in attacking Portuguese Daman. The English refused, and when the governor sailed out to attack them, he was repulsed in a second battle off Swally. Recognising that the English could threaten the pilgrim route from Surat to the Red Sea (the only maritime connection which interested the continentally-minded Mughals), the governor, and later the emperor, gave permission for an English 'Factory' or warehouse to be situated at Surat. Here the English made their headquarters in the East. The Chief and the Factors led a corporate life not unlike that of a Cambridge college, trying to make up by pomp and pageantry what they lacked of actual power to impress their Indian hosts.

The English tried to imitate the Portuguese by building tall ships for their Indian trade. Because English shipbuilders had no experience of constructing such vessels, the East India Company established its own yards at Deptford on the Thames. Among the first ships built was *Trade's Increase*, a monster of 1,100 tons. Perhaps not surprisingly, she was heavy and slow, and on her first voyage (1610–11), while being overhauled at Bantam, she was set on fire and became a loss. The Company abandoned the policy of constructing such huge craft, but still the size of their vessels (many over 500 tons) was larger than the ships then voyaging to the New World. The English were not able to gain much of a share in the trade of the more costly spices – clove, nutmeg, mace, and cinnamon – but mainly imported pepper. Between six and seven million pounds of pepper were imported into Europe annually, and the English Company re-exported a large part of their supplies to the continent of Europe. The price varied considerably, according to the scarcity or abundance of supplies, between 26 pence and 15 pence per pound. The English were unable to develop an inter-continental or inter-island trade in Asia to anything like the extent achieved by the Portuguese and the Dutch. But they quickly realised the potential market for Indian textiles in the West. They imported fine white cottons, and *pintadoes*, the painted calicoes of Gujarat. Searching for other sources of piece-goods, the Company looked to the extreme south of India, beyond the reach of the Muslim rulers. In 1640 they moved to Madraspatam, where a petty ruler gave them a strip of shore on lease. The place was not specially well-situated, being an open roadstead, where ships could not venture inshore. But there was a village of hardy fishermen, prepared to take out their little craft in all weathers, who would act as a link between sea and shore. And so Madras, the first pocket of British territory in India, came into being.

On the west coast, the English obtained a semi-independent position when Charles II received as part of the dowry of his bride, Catherine of Braganza, the Portuguese island of Bombay (Bom Bahia='good harbour'). At first, Bombay was a doubtful asset, not having access to trading commodities, and being much afflicted by pirates. Gradually it took over from Surat as the main English stronghold on the west coast and in 1687 became the headquarters of the Company in India. Meanwhile, the English were trying to gain a foothold in Bengal. Ejected from Hooghly, they finally settled at a village called Sutanutti in 1690, mainly because it was far away from the provincial capital, Murshidabad, and the authority of the Mughals, while marshy ground behind the river gave some protection against attack. The little settlement expanded to take in the neighbouring villages of Calcutta and Govindpur: in 1698, the Company became *zamindar* or revenue farmer for the three villages, and a fort

(Fort William, in honour of King William III) was thrown up. Whereas in the Portuguese and Dutch possessions there was strict control from home, the English Company determined to give its settlements a measure of local self-government. Madras was provided with a municipal corporation, like an English borough, in 1687, with Mayor, Town Clerk, and Recorder as judiciary. In 1726, Calcutta and Bombay were endowed with Mayor and Aldermen, alongside Madras. It would be straining truth to pretend that these local government institutions made much difference to the outlook of the English servants of the Company, or to the Indian, Armenian and Portuguese traders and artisans who were helping to bring prosperity to the growing English settlements.

The later decades of the seventeenth century, and the early years of the eighteenth century were the high noon of the English East India Company; dividends were monotonously high, and the senior servants of the Company flourished. These were the years of Elihu Yale, founder of a university, and Thomas Pitt, 'Diamond' Pitt, grandfather of one prime minister and great-grandfather of another; these men 'shook the Pagoda Tree' with advantage at Madras. Also, during these years the Company discovered its greatest asset: the China tea trade. It was in 1677 that 100 lb. of tea was sent back to London: during the year 1765, 5,000,000 lb. were imported, and by 1800 the total was 24,000,000 lb. So was the British nation comforted and the United States of America lost.

Before this time, the English Company had been compelled to divert its attention from trade to politics and war. Just as the Dutch effort in the East during the seventeenth century was an extension of a struggle for existence in Europe, so the emergence of a British Empire in Asia during the eighteenth century stemmed from a European conflict.

Besides the English and Dutch companies, other West European maritime powers made their bid for the wealth of Asia. The Danes established settlements at Tranquebar in the south, and Serampore (Sri Rampur) in Bengal, while a Prussian Company and the Ostend Company (sponsored by the Austrian Empire) made somewhat unsuccessful efforts to break into the Eastern trade. The most important of these later comers was the French *Compagnie des Indes*. Established in 1664 by Colbert, the Company set up its headquarters in India at Pondicherry. The French appeared to be on the threshold of great gains in Siam in the 1680s, when Constant Phaulkon made his bid for power. Four companies of French infantry garrisoned the port of Mergui, then under Siamese suzerainty during 1688: but in the same year Phaulkon was murdered and the French precipitately retired. The French Company languished until rejuvenated by the financier Law, but although new posts were established at Chandernagore near Hooghly and on the Malabar coast of Mahé, the real centre of French activity in the East was in the faraway islands of Mauritius and Réunion. In 1744, the War of the Austrian Succession involved almost all the nations of Western Europe, including France and Britain. French naval power in the Indian Ocean was strengthened, and in 1746 Madras was captured from the sea. This was the beginning of seventy years of naval warfare in the Eastern Seas which led the British and the French to cast their eyes upon every harbour and anchorage from Cape Town to Manilla. Eventually the struggle for dominance was won by the Royal Navy, and in the process Britain acquired such naval stations as Penang (1786) and Trincomalee (1795). Of greater significance in the internal history of South Asia was the discovery by the Governor of Pondicherry, Joseph Dupleix, that he could manipulate the political leaders of south India by a comparatively limited deployment of disciplined military power, in support of shrewd diplomatic juggling. The first demonstration came in 1746 when the Nawab of Arcot sent troops to take over Madras from the French. With cannon and musket the French dispersed the Nawab's forces. Three years later, the web of plot and counter-plot in south India led to the elevation of a French accomplice to the office of Subahdar of the Deccan: still nominally the Viceroy of the Mughal emperor at Delhi, but actually the independent ruler of Hyderabad, the premier state of the peninsula.

This challenge led the British to take up the same game of military and political manoeuvre. The British command was held by Major Stringer Lawrence, an old regular soldier. The English Company had no military officers of rank, but in one of its Writers or clerks, Robert Clive (1725–1774), they had a general of genius. Clive raised local military forces, outfought the French and halted their plans for dominating Hyderabad and the Deccan. Clive returned to London, and was sent back to Madras with a formidable body of regular British troops, as well as a squadron of the Royal Navy, to finish off the campaign against the French. At this moment, the semi-independent Subahdar of Bengal, Siraj-ud-daula ('Lamp of the State'), decided that the British menaced the legitimate rulers of India, and sent an expedition to wipe out the settlement of Calcutta. The internment of the British in the stifling guard room called the

Black Hole was followed by the arrival of Clive's forces, abortive negotiations with Siraj-ud-daula, and the almost farcical victory at Plassey (1757). Perhaps what was most significant about this episode was the active support given to the British cause by the bankers of Calcutta, the Seths. The Indians who were to dominate the future already saw that their advantage was served by the British, not the declining Mughal authority.

The sequence of events which followed must have appeared quite unreal to the cautious British Merchants and Factors of the Company. After Plassey, Clive negotiated the establishment of a new regime in Bengal. When the rising Muslim prince of the north, the Nawab Wazir of Oudh (the titular first minister to the emperor), decided to overthrow the British settlement, he was decisively defeated at the battle of Baxar (1765) by Major Hector Munro. Unlike Plassey, this was a hard-fought action, in which the drill and fire-power of the battalions raised by the British overcame the thrust and manoeuvre of the Nawab's greatly superior forces. After the battle, Clive, newly-returned to Bengal, dictated terms to the Mughal emperor at Allahabad. The emperor, Shah Alam ('Ruler of the World'), was also compelled to deal with the Marathas and the Afghans before he was finally blinded and killed, the emperor of an empire of ghosts and shadows. At the Allahabad encounter in 1765, the emperor was established in the districts of Kora and Allahabad with an annual income of twenty-six lakhs of rupees (£260,000) guaranteed by the Company. In return, the British were assigned the *diwani* (the government and revenues) of Bengal, which then included Bihar and Orissa.

Still the British hesitated to 'stand forth as diwan'; they appointed Indian *naibs* or deputies to carry out the collection of the revenues and the administration of justice. Only slowly did the British assume the responsibilities which the weakness of the old order thrust upon them. As late as the 1830s, the British were still issuing rupees inscribed with the name and titles of the emperor (long since dead) Shah Alam.

During the half-century 1750–1800 in which the supreme power of India was in suspense, while the Muslims, the Marathas, the Sikhs, and the British contested under the pretence that the Mughal Empire still remained, the British were – in a sense – an Indian rather than an exterior factor. It is true that the British could rely upon sea-power which gave them a range and mobility denied to the other contestants. But in the internecine struggles of the sub-continent they relied very largely upon Indian resources and Indian troops and entered into the game of bargain and counter-bargain in which the Indian rulers plotted and manoeuvred. Some writers have suggested that during this period the British were upon the brink of that 'absorption, synthesis' which the spirit of India has exercised over so many would-be conquerors. It is true that, superficially, the British traders, diplomats – and later administrators – were assimilated into the Indian environment. The Presidency towns – Calcutta, Madras, Bombay – were, in terms of law and social habits, an extension overseas of England. But 'up-country', in the *mofussil*, the English made little attempt to recreate the image of their native land. How could they? A few hundred foreigners, isolated, serving for perhaps twenty or thirty years continuously in India, they were no longer British but (in the idiom of the times) Anglo-Indians, Nabobs. Except upon formal occasions, they abandoned their stifling, constricting European clothes for loose cotton garments, patterned after the Indian style. Their food was largely Indian (supplemented by wines and spirits from Europe) and they enjoyed the *hookah* or hubble-bubble-pipe, they chewed *betel*, and some turned to *afim*, opium. They enthusiastically took up Indian sports; they hunted tiger from the back of the elephant, they speared the boar, and they played polo. Almost all Englishmen had Indian concubines or wives. It is often assumed that access to what was commonly known as a 'sleeping dictionary' gave the English in the eighteenth century a fluent knowledge of Indian languages. This is debatable. Certainly the Anglo-Indian vocabulary was saturated with Indian words and phrases (something of its flavour can be found in Thackeray's characters: Colonel Newcombe, and Jos Sedley in *Vanity Fair*). But most British officials were content to pick up a competent knowledge of Persian, the language of administration and of justice; their understanding of the vernaculars went little further than *bazaar bat*, the language of the market place. It is true that the rediscovery of the Indian classics was originally the work of Englishmen: Sir William Jones, 'Asiatic Jones', revealed the scope of the *Vedas*, and his pioneer studies were supplemented by the research of Colebrooke, Prinsep, and H. H. Wilson. But a class of officials, recruited in their teens, by patronage (and only incidentally by merit) could not be expected to produce an intellectual elite. Most of the English in India were like the medieval Franks in Outremer, the Christian kingdoms of the Holy Land: they adopted such customs as seemed convenient and agreeable, but they remained Westerners in the East. A few

British officials married high-born ladies, Rajput or Mughal princesses. Even these men – among whom Charles Metcalfe, acting Governor General, and Ochterlony, the Resident at Delhi were outstanding – though they might move more gracefully into an Indian style of living, did not attempt to discover an intellectual or social synthesis. A few figures of mixed blood emerged, such as Skinner and Gardiner, both leaders of irregular cavalry. They received a modicum of respect. But most of the Eurasians were despised and rejected by Europeans and Indians alike, and they were compelled to create their own narrow cultural milieu from which a few outstanding thinkers emerge, such as Henry Derozio of Calcutta and Ananda Coomaraswamy of Ceylon. By the early nineteenth century, the British in India were striving to create the separate world of 'the Station' – the cantonments and the civil lines, with the main road invariably called The Mall, and invariably leading to the Club, the Sahib's haven. This was more like apartheid than synthesis.[1].

For half a century, it seemed that beyond the fringes of British power in India European adventurers might create their own sphere of influence and action. The eagerness of Indian chiefs and princes to master the military techniques which (it seemed) gave such advantages to the British and the French meant that any European with pretensions to military expertise could find a ready market for his services. Some of these adventurers rose to command thousands of men; like Count Benoît de Boigne, the aristocratic Savoyard, who gave the Marathas a disciplined army. Some aspired to carve out their own kingdoms: like George Thomas, the sailor from Tipperary, who nearly achieved his ambition of making the Punjab British – under his control. Few of these adventurers left any permanent mark upon India. One who did was Claude Martin (1732–1800) a French soldier of fortune who took service under the British East India Company, and then found employment at the court of the Nawab Wazir of Oudh, where he began by casting guns and other military pieces, and ended by providing a kind of Sears-Roebuck mail-order service for

---

[1] In one of those moments of bitterness to which he was prone, Jawaharlal Nehru observed that the only Indian word which had been taken into the English language was *loot*. This was an exaggeration, but the number of Indian words fully assimilated is small: loot, thug, dinghy, bazaar, verandah, bungalow, pyjama, towel, puttee. Some sporting terms are partially absorbed: shikar, gymkhana, chukker (in polo); and some culinary terms: curry, chutney, kedgeree. Many more hover on the edge of the English language, where generations of British soldiers have left them: bakshish, pukka, chota peg, char (*chae*, tea), and hundreds more.

the most extravagant princes of the day. General Martin amassed a fortune, and built himself a baroque palace at Lucknow which he called Constantia. Knowing that the Nawab would assuredly seize his palace after his death, Martin directed that he should be buried in the vaults below: this converted the palace into a tomb, and the Nawab's Islamic respect for the tomb was stronger than his covetousness. The palace became a school for European and Eurasian boys: La Martinière. The inquirer may still see the general, if he descends deep down, past bats and lizards, to the dungeon where a huge sarcophagus stands in pitch blackness, guarded by the towering figures of four French soldiers of the Guard.

The role of the British as a factor from within the Indian scene, rather than from without, was emphasised by their religious policy. The English East India Company had no desire to imitate the Portuguese in their Catholicism or the Dutch in their Protestantism. During most of the eighteenth century, the Company's ships trading to India were of a fixed tonnage: 499 tons: it is alleged because English law required ships of over 500 tons burthen to carry a chaplain. The British actually prohibited Christian missionaries to settle within their jurisdiction, and cheerfully complied with whatever custom or usage might require in recognition of Muslim or Hindu rights.

The Portuguese policy of militant evangelism had yielded little. One attempt was made in the direction of synthesis by Robert de Nobili, an Italian noble, who went to Goa as a member of the Society of Jesus in 1605. He settled in Madura, the principal centre of Hindu learning in south India. De Nobili dressed like a Brahmin, and conformed strictly to Brahmin rules of diet, living accordingly to a code of austerity. He acquired a good knowledge of Tamil, and then of Sanskrit, and he was able to become familiar with the *Vedanta* doctrine. He evolved a syncretic vision of Hindu-Christian mysticism, and a number of conversions of Brahmins followed. The converts continued to observe all the ritual of their caste, and prayer and festival were adapted from Brahmin forms of worship. In 1623, Pope Gregory XV gave his sanction to certain of these practices. But de Nobili's dream of acceptance by the Madura Brahmins of a revealed religion within a familiar framework did not transpire. Only scattered congregations remained as evidence of his mission, where low and high caste Hindus pursued their separate devotions in a manner not very different from those of their Hindu caste-fellows.

The next Christian initiative came at the beginning of the eighteenth century, when German Protestant missionaries arrived in Danish Tranquebar (1705). The English Society for the Propagation of Christian Knowledge, excluded from English territory, supported their work, especially that of C. F. Schwartz, who acquired a unique influence throughout south India, with men as diverse as the Raja of Tanjore, Sultan Hyder Ali, and Robert Clive. Schwartz adopted a gradualist, quietist approach, relying upon the fostering of good relations, and the promotion of education to disseminate Christian principles indirectly.

The Danish settlement in Bengal, Serampore, provided the first centre for Protestant missionaries in north India. William Carey (1761–1834), a Baptist shoemaker, was unable to pursue his mission in the *mofussil*, up-country in Bengal, because he had no licence from the East India Company. With his friends, Ward, a printer, and Marshman, a schoolmaster, he set up the Baptist mission in Danish territory. Perhaps because these men came not from the upper-middle class sector of Anglican (Episcopalian) religion, but from the lower-middle class sector of Radical Dissent, they saw problems in terms of self-help and practical self-education. They saw the need to translate the Bible into the vernacular languages of India, if they were to reach the ordinary people. Besides translations of the scriptures, the Serampore missionaries produced grammars, and popular stories and instructional works in the vernaculars. Ward, the printer, was able to design and cast type for most of the vernacular scripts: the Baptist Mission Press embarked upon the first major printing and publishing enterprise in India. Books and pamphlets were followed by newspapers: in 1818, from Serampore came the first newspaper in an Indian tongue, *Samachar Darpan* (The Mirror of Knowledge) in Bengali. At the same time, *The Friend of India* was launched, first as a monthly, and then as a weekly journal, providing serious comment and information. These journals investigated social evils, such as *sati*, the burning of widows. Also in 1818, Serampore College was opened, with courses in arts, science, and jurisprudence, as well as theology. The greater part of the teaching was carried on in Bengali, with English reserved for 'the specially diligent and able'. A charter granted by the king of Denmark in 1827 endowed the college with academic status equivalent to that of the universities of Copenhagen and Kiel (then Danish) with power to grant degrees. And so in Serampore, on the banks of the Hooghly, soon after 1800, the principal elements in the modern South Asia – popular linguistic identification ('linguism'), the press, the university, social consciousness – all came to light. The West and South Asia were about to come to grips with each other in terms not merely of power and profit, but also of ideas and principles.

6 Economic and Social Change in Modern Times

Throughout the world, the period since 1800 has witnessed greater change, flowing from scientific, technological and commercial advancement, than any comparable century and a half since history began. In South Asia, economic change has not come surging in like a flood, but has crept forward an inch here, and yet jumped ahead a mile there. In his *India at the Death of Akbar* (1920) W. H. Moreland wrote: 'What was the surface of India like at the time of Akbar's death? I should answer that on the whole it was very like the India which we know today.' Even in 1920, India was among the first eight industrial nations in the new world: yet Moreland's assessment was true of nine-tenths of the country.

The greatest changes have emerged since about 1860. India's economic advances have been stimulated by great wars in other continents: first by the American Civil War and then by the First and Second World Wars. Economic progress is often measured by industrial development, but 90 per cent of the people of India continued to live in the countryside and to be dependent upon agriculture: which is dependent upon the vagaries of the monsoon. The rural annals have been marked not so much by progress as by catastrophe: by famine and even by plague. The government intervened to counteract nature – by famine measures, by vast irrigation schemes, and by attempts to improve agriculture. But almost all improvements were eaten up by rising population figures. India's peoples and problems are so vast that they defy simple solutions. Ceylon and Burma, so much smaller in scale, were able to achieve a modest break-through towards prosperity by producing raw materials in demand in world markets. To them, the spectacular advance in communications of the later nineteenth century held out a means to establish a flourishing export trade. Lacking an adequate labour force of their own, they looked to the bottomless reservoir of Indian manpower to meet the new need. And yet the mobility which this migration brought had only the most limited consequences. The vast majority of peoples in South Asia lived and died in the same district – often in the same village.

The growth of the population remained slow and unsteady until the end of the nineteenth century. The latest estimates (as reproduced in the *Cambridge Economic History of India*) suggest that about the year 1600 AD the total population numbered perhaps 140 million. Thereafter there was a slow increase, and in areas devastated by invasion probably a decrease. There were terrible periods of famine, as in Bihar, 1670–71, when 100,000 people died in the vicinity of Patna alone, but the worst affliction followed the introduction of British rule in Bengal where in 1770–71 about one-third of the population perished. However, it is now believed that by 1800 the total throughout India had risen to 180 million. All these figures are rough estimates, made many years later. The first census, carried out between 1867 and 1872 showed a figure between 236–249 million. Thereafter, there was a steady rise and the first regular census in 1881 showed a population of 254 million. Two decades later, despite a series of famines in northern India, the total was over 294 million. By 1921 there were 312 million, and thereafter the 'population explosion' so much discussed in our time took over. The 1941 census showed a total of 389 million.

The increase in the rest of South Asia was equally rapid. The first attempt to calculate Ceylon's population was made in 1824: the total was placed at 851,940. Ten years later, the population was given as 1,167,700, and by 1911 had risen to 4,106,350. Some of this increase came from Indian Coolie immigration: for example, between 1843 and 1859, 903,557 Indians entered Ceylon, and only a small proportion ever returned to India. By 1931 the population had risen to 5,312,000; the 1953 census recorded a total of 8,098,637.

Ceylon's increase – the highest in the region – was followed by a considerably greater rise in Burma than in India. On the eve of the British invasion (1824), Burma's population is estimated to have totalled 4 million. In 1901, the census covered almost the entire country and showed a total of 10.5 million. At the 1921 census the population was 13.2 million, and in 1941, 16.8 million.

Burma, as well as Ceylon, received a large Indian influx. Beginning about 1870, and coming mainly from the poor and crowded districts of Madras, Indians entered in hundreds of thousands. Cheap sea passages encouraged seasonal migration, but many Indians settled in the country, and by 1931 there were more than a million resident in

Burma. Overall, there was less movement among the population of India than in almost any other country. But as industrialisation and plantations created a demand for labour, so migration developed into Bengal and Assam in the east, and into Bombay and other west coast areas. Internal migration was accompanied by labour migration over long distances overseas in addition to the short-range migration to Ceylon, Burma and Malaya (Map 12). When slavery was abolished throughout the British Empire the sugar planters urgently needed replacements. These were obtained by the recruitment of indentured labourers under contracts which bound them to estates for five years without option. The recruits largely came from the overcrowded districts of Bihar and those beyond, around Banaras. Some were drawn from the Tamil districts, also overpopulated. The recruits went under government supervision in specially chartered ships. Their first destination was Mauritius (from 1834), then British Guiana (from 1838), followed by Trinidad, Natal, and even Fiji (1879). The population structure of these sugar colonies was radically altered. Over a million Indian labourers went overseas in the forty years before 1870: the figure may have been much higher. These numbers had no great effect on the steady increase in the overall population of India.

A significant development, not easy to quantify, was the shift in the balance among different religions. In Burma, the Indian influx led to an enormous increase in the Hindu element, while among the indigenous peoples (particularly the Karens) conversion to Christianity led to the emergence of a new group: the Christians numbered 300,000 by 1941. Similarly in Ceylon, Indian immigration added to the existing Tamil community, and increased the proportion of Hindus; while a small but significant process of conversion by Protestant missionaries added to the older Catholic community to make the Christians a powerful force. Both in Burma and Ceylon, these changes in the religious balance were to have political consequences; but this shift was of greatest significance in India. There was a large increase in the Christian community, and also a substantial rise in the number of Sikhs through conversion. But of greatest importance was the process of conversion to Islam which was most obvious in Punjab, and to a lesser extent in Bengal. The Muslims formed about one-fifth of the population early in the nineteenth century; a hundred years later they constituted a quarter of the total. When the losses to Sikhism and Christianity are added, it is not difficult to understand why Hinduism became increasingly militant, to check this 'drain' from the community.[1]

Great numerical changes occurred in the cities. The armies of people which had gathered around a princely court, or a seat of Mughal government, found their occupations gone under the British, and numbers declined heavily. Murshidabad, Poona, even Delhi faded in importance. Delhi had been the greatest city between Constantinople and Peking: from a population of a million, the city had fallen to about 125,000 by the early nineteenth century. By contrast, other places rose in importance. When we first hear of Cawnpore in 1775, it was a village. The British established a frontier military cantonment there; then in 1863 the railway arrived, and Cawnpore became a junction for five main lines. Government ordnance factories and cotton mills followed, and by 1931 the population had reached 219,000. The most spectacular increases occurred in the great port cities. Throughout the nineteenth century the volume of trade rose steeply: Bombay had over 40 per cent of foreign trade, and Calcutta almost 40 per cent. From petty settlements, these ports expanded into conurbations numbering a million each by the First World War.

Indian conditions seem to produce large cities and small market towns – with nothing in between. The small towns remained small: their function to supply a rural neighbourhood, and to provide a centre for administration and amenity. In the Gangetic plains, and other areas of unchanging rural settlement, the village pattern also remained largely static. Parent villages might produce new colonies, on the borders of cultivation: but the characteristic Indian village was an ancient settlement, rising several feet above the surrounding fields because its site was the deposit of hundreds of years of accumulated waste-products. Only in certain regions did a new rural pattern develop: where jungle or waste was reclaimed to cultivation. In western Punjab vast tracts were opened up by irrigation. In Burma, the delta area, long devastated by war and invasion, was brought under

---

[1] For example, the population of Punjab in 1881 included 43.8 per cent Hindus, 40.6 per cent Muslims, and 8.2 per cent Sikhs. By 1931, the proportion of Hindus had declined to 30.2 per cent, while Muslims had increased to 42.4 per cent and Sikhs had increased to 14.3 per cent. These changes were hardly affected by relative fecundity or emigration/immigration. They were almost entirely due to religious conversion. The all-India proportion of Hindus to total population fell from 74 per cent in 1881 to 69 per cent in 1911.

cultivation by Burmese pioneers coming down from Upper Burma. Where these new rural settlements came into being, a frontier society developed: more individualistic than the old, more ready to adapt, to utilise change as an ally – and also more rugged, crude, and prepared to shape or break the law according to individual will.

The population increase throughout South Asia became the crucial factor in economic development during the second half of the nineteenth century. At the beginning of the century, the area was under-populated. This meant that there was more land than cultivators: those who owned agricultural land were looking for tenants, while the farmer discontented with his landlord could always move elsewhere. In *Rambles and Recollections of an Indian Official* (first published in 1844) Colonel W. H. Sleeman observes: 'Nine-tenths of the immediate cultivators of the soil in India are little farmers, who hold a lease for one or more years, as the case may be, of their lands which they cultivate with their own stock. One of these cultivators, with a good plough and bullocks, and a good character, can always get good land on moderate terms from holders of villages.' From about 1880, the pressure of the people upon the land was such as to constitute over-population: despite the extension of the area of cultivation. Only Burma could be said to be still under-populated; although the area under paddy in Lower Burma increased from 993,000 acres in 1855 to 9,911,000 acres in 1931, there were still frontier areas where virgin land might be brought under the plough. In India and Ceylon the growing land shortage produced serious problems for the peasantry as the nineteenth century progressed.

The first great changes came in Bengal, Bihar and Orissa, the area of the Permanent Settlement. This measure granted virtually all rights in the soil to great landlords or zamindars who owned tracts of land supporting thousands of cultivators. The cultivators lost all their customary rights, and became tenants at will. Although the landlords' liability for land revenue was fixed for all time, the peasants enjoyed no security at all; the economic law of supply and demand was allowed to operate freely. Bengal was one of the first provinces to feel the effects of the population increase, and from the mid-nineteenth century, rack-renting was general. F. W. Maitland characterised the passage from a medieval to a modern society as from Status to Contract. The enforcement of English ideas of contract upon the Bengali peasantry meant that they were liable to be taken to the Courts and imprisoned for debt. An attempt was made to provide some protection for tenants under an Act of 1859, but a combination of ignorance and need for land led to the Act's being generally ineffective.

Even when the cultivators established their rights to the land, the new legal system helped to undo them. Formerly, land had been regarded as different from other commodities: a trust, rather than a property to be bought and sold. From ancient times, the peasants had been accustomed to tide over the period between seed-time and harvest by borrowing from the moneylender; while family events, such as marriages, were invariably financed by a loan. Now, the moneylender took as his security a bond on his debtor's land; and if the debtor failed, he foreclosed, and seized the land. The most dramatic example of this transfer of land to the moneylending class was seen in Lower Burma, where during the 1930s depression, 48 per cent of the farm land passed into the hands of absentee owners: two-thirds of this alienated land was owned by Chettiars, moneylenders from Madras.

Rural indebtedness and land alienation were eventually tackled by legislation, and by co-operative credit schemes promoted by the government. But where grievances were worst, there were outbursts of rural protest; such as the Pabna rent disturbances of 1872–3 in Bengal, and the much more widespread agitation among the Maratha peasants in the districts around Poona in 1875. Subsequently, the Deccan Agriculturalists' Relief Act was passed in 1879 to create conciliation machinery to relieve indebtedness.

Besides rising population and the changeover from status to contract, the other major influence on the rural community was the revolution in communications. During the early nineteenth century, apart from the great rivers and the ocean, there were no means whereby people or goods could travel long distances. There were an infinite variety of small 'neighbourhood' regions, more or less self-contained. In consequence, there were great variations in prices and wages: each neighbourhood fixed its own levels. There was no incentive to produce for the market, except for a certain, known local demand. In the case of crop failure, the local population might starve when in another part of India there was no shortage. This local, limited economy was reinforced by a complex tariff system which erected trade barriers every few miles. Gradually, as South Asia came under British rule, these barriers were reduced; still there remained the customs line which stretched across the whole of India from the Indus to the Mahanadi in Madras, a distance of 2,300 miles. This barrier consisted of an impenetrable thorn hedge, patrolled by a force of 12,000 men. At length, its purpose was limited to securing the salt duties, and when the method of collection was changed the barrier was abolished in 1879. But in dissolving the differences between local economies, the three main agents of change were the telegraph, the steamship, and the railroad. The telegraph system began with a line from Calcutta to Agra: the first message was sent in March, 1854. The system covered all India by 1857: the sepoy mutineers called the telegraph 'the string that strangled us'. In June 1870, the British Indian Telegraph Company's direct cable from Bombay to England was completed, while shortly after India was connected with China, Singapore and Australia. International trade, which hitherto had been a speculation in the unknown, now became amenable to statistical forecasting.

The first line of railway, from Bombay to Thana, was opened by the Great Indian Peninsular Railway in 1853, and the first section of line from Calcutta to Raniganj in 1855. The Mutiny demonstrated the need for good communications, and the main trunk lines were pushed ahead in the 1860s. Railroad mileage totalled 288 in 1857; in 1861 it was 1,599 miles, and by 1871, 5,077 miles. Ceylon's main lines were built in the same period: the formidable task of driving the railway up from Colombo over mountain ridges to Kandy was completed between 1858 and 1867. Both in India and Ceylon, the problem of finding capital to finance railroad construction led to government participation in this sphere. The British authorities were fully imbued with the *laissez faire* theory of the importance of restricting the government's role to the minimum: but the inability of business enterprise to meet the need for expansion necessitated state action. The first Indian lines were constructed by private enterprise, on a basis of agreed interest rates, guaranteed by the government of India. This method proved unexpectedly burdensome to the state (costs exceeding anticipation) and from 1870, the government undertook direct construction and management of new rail networks. In Ceylon, railways were owned and operated by the government from the beginning. As the first 'guaranteed' lines came to the end of the contracts, their government purchased these companies and began direct operation.[1] Communications in Burma were first developed by

---

[1] When the government acquired the East India Railway in 1879, it took over collieries operated by the company, and began to sell coal to the general public in competition with British business. This example of state trading anticipated nationalisation in Britain by seventy years. Later, railway workshops undertook contracts for engineering work of various sorts.

water: the Irrawaddy Flotilla and the Arracan Flotilla provided fleets of paddle-steamers, carrying passenger and cargo traffic. A railroad (a government line) was built as far as Prome by 1877, and was carried north to Mandalay and Myitkyina by 1898. The river Irrawaddy was not spanned until the great Ava bridge was built in 1934. By 1914, there were over 31,000 miles of track in the Indian Empire, including a network of feeder branch lines. Indian nationalists protested strongly at the huge investment of public money in this enterprise, but from 1900 the railways began to make an annual profit. The First Five Year Plan (1952) noted: 'The Indian railway system is the largest nationalised undertaking in the country. It is one of the few railway systems in the world with a net earning power adequate to meet all fixed charges and provide substantial sums for development and reserves.'

The various railroad systems operated largely on a regional basis. In the plains, the lines used the broad gauge; the metre gauge was employed in the Deccan and other hilly areas, while narrow gauge lines served some mountain stations, such as Darjeeling. Transhipment was limited between different gauges. Between Burma and India there was no rail communication, while the railroads stopped short at the frontiers of Afghanistan and Persia. The railroad imperialism practised by Germany and Russia in the Near and Far East was absent.

The opening of the Suez Canal in 1869 shortened the voyage between England and India by 4,000 miles. Shortly afterwards, the development of the iron ship, powered by the compound tandem engine, diverted the freight trade from sail to steam. While the clippers could still offer cheaper rates, the speed and certainty of the steamship led to its dominance of the Eastern trade routes. Over the half-century 1860–1910, transport costs, by rail and sea, came tumbling down. Between the 1890s and the early twentieth century, freight rates between Bombay and England fell by 27 per cent, while internal rail charges fell between 30 and 40 per cent. These changes led increasingly to the agricultural products of South Asia finding their way into Western markets.

At the beginning of the nineteenth century, agricultural exports still followed the traditional pattern of the spice trade. Ceylon had a monopoly of the world's supply of cinnamon. The British took over the Dutch practice of operating this trade as a profitable government monopoly. The Ceylon government monopoly was abolished in 1833, and the plantations handed over to private companies. The East

India Company, under its charter, enjoyed a monopoly of trade between Asia and Europe and this monopoly gave the Company powerful weapons in determining the pattern of trade, industry, and agricultural production in India. However, it seems that the Company's interests became secondary to the operations of its own officials as well as European and Asian merchants. Between 1793 and 1833 the Company's monopoly was breached, and finally abolished. From the end of the eighteenth century, the Company began to export indigo to Europe. Production was first concentrated around Calcutta, but gradually Bihar came to be the main producing area. The plant was cultivated by individual peasants and the blue dye processed in crude factories under European management. Cultivation entailed much ploughing and weeding, and was unpopular with the peasants, but they were induced to do the work by being offered advances of payment, whereby they bound themselves to put a proportion of their land into indigo. Once enmeshed into a financial relationship with a planter, the peasant found himself obliged to grow indigo for ever. Demand grew, and despite competition from the West Indies and elsewhere, India emerged as the main supplier.

As India's closer connection with world markets led to a demand for other crops which commanded higher prices, the peasants increasingly resented their obligation to the indigo planters. During 1860 and 1861, this resentment was expressed in a mass movement of protest. There was some rioting, but in general the people combined in passive resistance to the planters. A Commission of Inquiry gave little relief to the peasants. Production was increased – often by the planters using coercive methods – and reached its peak in 1895. Then came the German invention of aniline dyes, first marketed in 1897. By 1901, indigo exports were only half the total of five years before. The Bihar planters struggled on, but gradually they disappeared; though indigo still survives as a small-scale cottage industry.

The next agricultural product to attain importance as an export was jute. Requiring much water, jute was also mainly grown in Bengal. It was an ancient cottage industry: *chatis*, or lengths of coarse jute fibre, being woven to make bags. Demand was given a fillip by war – the Crimean War, with its trench operations, requiring thousands of sandbags. As an industrial process, jute manufacture was first developed at Dundee in Scotland, about 1833. A former sea captain, George Ackland, went into partnership with a Bengali merchant, Byamsunder Sen, to import machinery from Dundee which was set up in a mill at Rishra, a few miles up the Hooghly from Calcutta. The

Rishra mill went into production in 1855. By 1885 there were 24 mills, near Calcutta, employing 52,000 operatives: by 1914 there were 70 mills and 200,000 workers. While manufacture was concentrated around Calcutta, production spread to wide areas of Bihar, Bengal and Assam, with East Bengal as the main source of supply.

Jute, like indigo, was grown by peasant farmers, but perhaps the most spectacular example of 'industrial agriculture' on a peasant basis was the paddy crop of Burma. This developed mainly as an export crop, and owed its spectacular expansion to the revolution in communications of the 1860s and after, which opened up the markets of India and Europe to Burma. The value of Burma's exports increased more than thirty-fold between 1868 and 1926 (from Rs. 32 million to Rs. 654 million) and Burma became the fourth largest producer of paddy (after China, India and Japan) and the largest exporter in the world. Although the marketing and processing of the rice was entirely in the hands of foreigners – Indians and Europeans – the Burmese peasant farmer benefited from the increased prosperity. Comparison with India demonstrated that the peasant in Burma enjoyed a demonstrably higher standard of living, with plentiful food, a sufficiency of attractive clothes, and a modicum of household appliances. Because of this prosperity, prices and wages were higher in Burma than in India. In 1914, a clerk in a public office in India received an average salary of Rs. 38 a month: in Burma, the monthly average was Rs. 62. The Burmese peasant acquired the notion that wealth was a function of nature: when the world slump closed down over Burma, and the market price of paddy fell in 1930 from Rs. 200 per hundred baskets to Rs. 50 per hundred, the cultivators were ruined: nothing had been put by in case of misfortune. In some districts, money disappeared, and the community reverted to the economy of barter.

Certain other products were grown in South Asia mainly for export, notably cotton. In addition, plantation crops produced by industrial methods became features of the economy. The East India Company had propped up its shaky Indian finances by the profits earned on the export of tea from China to Europe. This remained the last commodity in which the Company retained a monopoly: down to 1834. When Assam was annexed to British India from Burmese rule (in 1826) the tea bush was found growing wild. The Governor-General, Bentinck, set up a committee to promote tea-growing in India. Plants were brought from China, and the Assam Tea Company was formed in 1839, receiving a grant of hill country for its culture.

Because the tea gardens were projected in an uninhabited wilderness, it was necessary to recruit labour from a long distance away: many were aboriginals from the Bengal hill districts. Indian tea, with its full-bodied flavour, appealed to the mass of British consumers more than the delicate Chinese varieties: the demand seemed unlimited. In 1850, there was one tea estate, with an annual output of 216,000 lb. By 1870 there were 295 different estates, and total output had reached 6,251,143 lb. The great majority were British owned and operated.

Now came the turn of Ceylon. European planters had opened up much of the Kandyan hill country to the culture of coffee. The first plantation was started in 1823, and by 1848 there were 367 estates with about 60,000 acres being cultivated. The Kandyans showed no inclination to work on the estates, so thousands of coolies were brought in from southern India. Many came under a system of engagement which virtually tied them to the estates and kept them in bondage. Despite some wild speculation, coffee-growing steadily expanded and in the 1870s over 200,000 acres were under cultivation. Then appeared *hemileia vastatrix*, the coffee bug. Gradually its devastation spread all over the island, and the planters began to abandon their estates. Meanwhile, Brazil was coming forward as a rival coffee exporter. The Ceylon industry wilted and died: by 1905, only 3,500 acres remained under coffee . But disaster had been averted, largely by the efforts of Sir William Gregory, Governor in the 1870s, and Dr Thwaites, the chief government botanist. They used all their influence to persuade the planters to change over to tea production. During the 1880s and 1890s, tea gardens multiplied, and Ceylon emerged with the third largest tea industry in the world. By 1910 there were 390,000 acres under tea culture and the amount exported totalled 182,070,094 lb. After independence, India produced half of the world's tea exports (1952: 614,513,000 lb.), Ceylon well over one-quarter (1952: 316,842,000 lb.), and Pakistan about one-fifteenth (1952: 51,538,000 lb.).

Plantation production figured high as an export commodity; but because most of the plantations were foreign-owned, and their profits returned to Europe, this development only indirectly benefited the people of South Asia. The development of jute, paddy, cotton, etc., by peasant cultivation did give greater returns, but the changeover to commercial crops helped to bring about a general increase in prices, and also brought about a decline in food production. The process of adjustment from a local price structure to participation in a world price structure was worked out only over many decades, and in the process some sections of the population were adversely affected. The changeover to commercial crops, combined with rising prices, and set against the sudden and not expected rise in population, produced a combination of circumstances in which any additional calamity could lead to disaster. The second half of the nineteenth century in India was a period when famines became the recurrent feature of life for millions of people.

After the terrible Bengal famine of 1769–70, came the great hunger of the Carnatic from 1780 to 1783, caused by the ravages of Hyder Ali's armies. In 1790–2, famine came again to Madras; and for the first time an attempt was made to relieve the starving by employing them on public works. Every few years, calamity struck again in the south, and less often in the north. But these famines are more accurately described as dearth than disaster. Famine in its most terrible form reappeared in Orissa only in 1866.

At this time India was only just beginning to be associated with the world economy: but the rulers were imbued with the belief that the *laissez faire* doctrines of Nassau Senior and the Manchester school were universally applicable. In case of shortage, no attempt should be made to interfere with the law of supply and demand: let prices rise, as local supplies proved insufficient to meet the demand, and the appropriate quantities of foodgrains would be brought into the market from elsewhere until equilibrium had again been established. Unfortunately, this doctrine was first put to the test in Orissa, which in the 1860s was dependent upon local food-growing, its communications with the outside world being limited to open shores where ships could not ride at anchor during monsoon storms. The crisis came suddenly: in April it appeared that all might be well – then, in May, the population was starving. Sealed from the outside world by the monsoon, relief could not be supplied until November: by which time a quarter of the population had died. The great mistake was the initial decision to leave the law of supply and demand to solve the situation. The Lieutenant-Governor of Bengal visited Orissa and declared that if he were to interfere with prices he would be 'no better than a dacoit or thief'. The famine emphasised the importance of developing an adequate network of communications: but the main lesson was the need to anticipate disaster. Slowly, a Famine Code was evolved, designed to be put into operation as soon as a failure of the monsoon, or other warning-signal, indicated a probable shortage.

When, in 1873, the rains failed in Bihar, the government put a comprehensive relief scheme into effect: a million tons of rice were imported, and no lives were lost. But the cost, £6.5 million, appeared monstrous to the careful Victorian guardians of public finance. The main remedy was to provide work for all those threatened with starvation (over three million were employed during the Bombay famine of 1876–8) and to provide food supplies from government stocks while scarcity prices prevailed. The great famine of 1876–8 covered the whole of peninsular India, affecting a population of more than 58 million. Its total cost to the government exceeded £11 million.

The nineteenth century closed with the worst disasters of all: the famines of 1896–7, and 1899–1900. The 1896 famine began with a total failure of the rains over most of India. The crop yield for the year was between 45 and 75 per cent of the normal, in different provinces. Despite food riots in the towns, the government refused to supplement the normal sales of food grains. Prices rose – even in areas not directly affected by drought. To food shortage was added the miseries of epidemic disease, such as cholera and smallpox. The Famine Code operations provided employment and relief for millions, and the numbers of deaths were small. On the heels of this crisis came the famine of 1899, affecting about 30 million people. Those affected crowded into the relief camps: when Lord Curzon, then Viceroy, inspected the relief works he was reminded of 'the children of Israel toiling at the pyramids'. Disease was restricted by a much wider use of inoculation: still, the Famine Commission which inquired into the calamity estimated that 1.5 million deaths above the average had been caused by famine.

After 1900, this cycle of disasters came to a halt. When dearth struck the United Provinces in 1907–8, the preventative measures entirely eliminated the characteristic features of a famine – emaciated faces and bodies, wandering bands of victims seeking succour, acts of violence and desperation. Analysing the Bengal famine of 1896–7, an official, L. P. Shirres wrote: 'The famine of 1896–97 marks the close of the era of famines in Bengal, in the sense in which the word famine has hitherto been understood, and the commencement of an era of poor relief. . . . It may be confidently asserted that never again will Bengal be devastated by one of those awful calamities which a century ago were called famines.'

For over forty years it seemed that this prediction was well-founded. Despite a leap in population figures, the rise of industry and the extension of irrigation, together with improved methods of agriculture, kept famine at bay. Then in 1943 came the unthinkable: a famine in Bengal which killed 1.5 million people. The cause was the Japanese invasion of Burma, and the stoppage of the export of the 1942 rice harvest. Even within Burma there were severe shortages. While bags of rice lay rotting in railway sidings and beside the river banks in Lower Burma, a few hundred miles away in Upper Burma the people were on the verge of starvation. The old 'neighbourhood' economy had returned, with plenty only a few miles away from dearth. Bengal, though producing its own rice, relied upon Burma rice to make up deficiencies. In 1943, Bengal's paddy harvest was poor: though estimates prepared afterwards by a Famine Commission established that there was food enough in the province for 49 of the 52 weeks in the year. But the wartime situation aggravated the difficulties. Demand was heavy from the industrial areas around Calcutta and other booming wartime installations. Supplies were sucked out of the countryside, and prices soared. The Bengal ministers, led by Fazl-ul-Haq, did nothing. When at last the central government intervened, and imposed controls and food rationing, there was chaos in the distribution system. Thousands had to die before normal conditions were restored.

After independence, regional shortages have created conditions in India akin to famine, with abnormal prices and acute shortages in different regions. Each time, however, the emergency provision of supplies from the United States, Canada and Australia has averted catastrophe. Before independence, the doctrine of financial self-sufficiency was still current in the world, and India's capacity to call a halt – even if only temporarily – to population outstripping food resources, owed much to the huge programme of irrigation.

Certain canals had been built for irrigation purposes under the Mughals, but these had long fallen into decay. The first British enterprise in canal construction was the Ganges canal system, begun in 1842 and completed in 1854. The British military engineers who designed the Ganges canals had no models from which to borrow: the science of canal engineering had to be evolved out of experience. The Ganges canals were linked with a system drawing upon the river Jumna. Together they added some 1.5 million acres of fertile farmland, growing sugar-cane, wheat and other heavy crops, to the tillage of what were later the United Provinces (Uttar Pradesh). The next great development came in Punjab. 'The Land of the Five Rivers' is so called because the rivers which branch out like the fingers of a hand (with Indus as the arm) form the life-lines of cultivation. Apart from the fertile country which lies under the rain-shadow of the Himalayan foothills, and the lands adjoining the rivers, the old Punjab was a waste of sandy semi-desert, where only stunted trees and thorn bushes grew. The people of these barren wastes were mainly nomads, camel drovers and cattle thieves. When the British defeated the Sikh armies, Lawrence, the new rulers of the British Punjab, set about canal building, in order to provide land for occupancy by the disbanded Sikh soldiery. The first project, the Bari Doab canal, was started in 1851; but mistakes and difficulties delayed the completion of the work until 1861. The canal opened up 800,000 acres of new land in the *Manjha*, the middle-land of Punjab. The next main work was the Sutlej or Sirhind canal which irrigated the eastern Punjab. Opened in 1882, this scheme carried the water of the upper Sutlej across the natural drainage of the country to bring 1,116,000 acres under the plough. Finally, the western Punjab, the country of the Chenab, Jhelum and Indus rivers, was canalised. Here the canals entered the back-lands, which were entirely uninhabited: yet these were to prove the most fertile of the great irrigation schemes. Here it was necessary to create a new society out of nothing. Roads, villages, schools, all had to be planned and built. Most important, the pioneers who were to create fertility in the wilderness had to be picked and planted in their holdings with systematic care. In all this, the planners of the canal colonies (as they were called) went far beyond the *laissez faire* notion of the function of government as the maintenance of law and order, and in many ways anticipated the concept of a planned economy which only became accepted in Britain after the Second World War.

Although Punjab saw the most dramatic feats in making the desert blossom as the rose, irrigation went forward throughout India. We may instance the Son canals in Bihar (1875) irrigating 655,000 acres; the Cauvery Delta system in Madras (1889) feeding 1,070,000 acres, followed in the same province by the Godavari Delta system (1890) and the Krishna Delta system (1898), both over 1 million acres. Canal construction went on steadily until independence; two of the more important later works being the Sarda canal in UP (1930) irrigating 1,297,000 acres, and the Sukkur Barrage on the Indus, on which work began in 1923, which was planned to bring 5 million acres into cultivation. The total gross area irrigated by tanks, wells, and all artificial means in 1939 was 60 million acres: of these over 34 million acres were supplied by government irrigation works: this represented nearly 13 per cent of the total cultivated area in India.

Ceylon, like South India, has always relied largely upon 'tanks' or reservoirs to sustain agriculture. Ceylon's 'dry zone' included vast tracts which had once been under cultivation but which had become scrub jungle. During the second half of the nineteenth century, the colonial government began to rebuild the *bunds*, the great banks which had held back the waters of the ancient irrigation tanks. There was nothing original in this restoration: the British engineers laid their lines down upon the lines traced by the ancient Sinhalese tank-builders. By bringing these reservoirs back into operation, thousands of acres of good land were added to cultivation.

Lower Burma's paddy lands required no artificial irrigation, but water is scarce in the dry zone of Upper Burma, where ancient sluices and dams still exist. In the Mandalay and Sagaing divisions, the British extended the area of artificial irrigation, fed by the Irrawaddy, until by 1939 an area of 1.5 million acres was being fed by canal works.

It seems generally accepted that these developments throughout South Asia helped to raise agricultural production to a level where, in the early twentieth century, the great mass of the rural population was enjoying a modest improvement in standards of living. This improvement was very marked in the expanding areas, like Punjab or Burma, and was minimal in the areas where population pressure had not been accompanied by agricultural improvement, such as the inland districts in the south of Madras. It appears that by the early twentieth century the tendency for prices to increase before wages rose to compensate had at last been overtaken. On one side, the farmers with substantial holdings had benefited; on the other side, the labourers were better off; but the small cultivators still lived near the margin of subsistence. Prices rose until the movement was reversed by the depression of the 1930s. If 1870 is taken as a starting point (1870=100) then by 1914 the price index had reached 144. After the First World War the highest point was reached in 1920 when it stood at 281; then prices fell abruptly (1921=236) followed by a slow decline (1928=201) and then with the great depression another heavy fall: by the mid 1930s the index had returned to the figures of 1900 (1935=119), but by the Second World War they had recovered slightly (1939=134).

The commercial outlook for India was unsettled during most of the nineteenth century. The boom of the 1860s did not provide a permanent basis for development. The early years of the twentieth century were a period of trade depression, but there was a general

movement of economic consolidation which was given a fillip by the
First World War. The 1920s brought a time of commercial prosperity:
while the 1930s were for India (as for the world) a period of difficulty.
The Second World War initiated another period of somewhat febrile
prosperity, which lasted into the first years of independence.

Trade at the beginning of the nineteenth century followed the
immemorial pattern. Its scale was limited, and was confined to goods,
small in bulk, of a luxury nature: much of it was specialised, like the
muslins of Dacca. The first great changes occurred in foreign trade.
The ending of monopolies, the revolution in communications,
together with the industrial revolution in Britain and other Western
countries, all combined to transform the character of the foreign
trade. India's traditional fine textiles – calicoes, silks, muslins – could
not compete against industrial Lancashire. The export of traditional
Asian vegetable products, such as indigo, cinnamon, and lac continued, until substitutes were invented. But the new development was
the growth of large-scale exports of bulk products, such as cotton,
rice, jute. Both in volume and in value, exports showed great
increases after about 1870. The growth of trade was much affected by
the kind of commercial organisation which handled traffic, and by the
effects of world conditions upon Asia. In this regard, India had
severe disadvantages as a trading nation: the Indian rupee gradually
lost its value, while the 'drain' of India's balances to Britain (even if
for services rendered) was crippling for a poor country.

The mechanism of trade in early nineteenth-century India remained simple and undifferentiated. Trading houses were usually
partnerships (whether the partners were English, Armenian, Parsi,
Marwari, or Gujarati). The various commercial functions, such as
banking, insurance, brokerage, were not divided on specialised lines
but were combined under the operations of a partnership. There was
already a considerable mixing of Indian and British capital and
business activity. The big business concerns had their head offices in
Bombay and Calcutta, which developed a cosmopolitan commercial
character, quite distinct from the old administrative cities. Colombo
and Rangoon acquired much the same character later in the
nineteenth century. The import-export merchants became known as
agency houses. Confidence in their capacity was badly shaken when
the collapse of Barretto and Company of Calcutta in 1828 led to a
series of catastrophic failures among the leading agency houses, in
which the investments of many, British and Indian, disappeared. The
East India Company strenuously opposed the establishment of banks

on a joint stock basis, and the exchange banks only began to spread after the termination of the Company's rule in 1858. The Oriental Bank was set up in 1851. The Chartered Bank followed in 1853, and the Mercantile Bank in 1858. These and other banks established a financial network which linked up the Indian Ocean area and the Far East with the City of London. But the modernisation of the South Asian commercial scene remained the function of merchant houses, and a type of organisation peculiar to South Asia known as the managing agency. When a new venture was being promoted (such as a manufacturing plant, a plantation, or a trading venture), the promoters would approach an established managing agency. The promoters might be Indian or British, and they might have technical and financial resources, or merely a concession. In any case, they would turn to the agency because of its reputation, which would encourage confidence in the venture, and stimulate investment. The agency would also have managers, accountants, and possibly technical staff, who could provide a ready-made nucleus for launching the new venture. It is usual to argue that this system enabled much more rapid economic expansion in a country deficient in an entrepreneurial structure: but it is also argued that the managing agency system inculcated a type of development in which investment and control in business and industry was promoted from a dangerously narrow base.

The first period of expansion was stimulated by the American Civil War cotton boom. Despite the Confederate efforts to ship cotton through the Federal blockade, by 1862 Lancashire was running desperately short. Indian exports rose from 835,000 bales to nearly twice this figure, and at largely inflated prices. Encouraged by the boom a large number of new banks were opened. Then in 1866, the bubble was pricked. At the beginning of the year there were 24 exchange banks in Bombay and 22 in Calcutta: at the year's end there were only 7 such banks left in India. However, the cotton trade recovered, and with the speeding up of communications, overseas trade expanded again.

In far-away Nevada, the discovery of the Comstock Lode in 1859 set off the flow of a river of silver which led eventually to a fall in the value of the metal. Many countries had currencies based upon a fixed ratio between silver and gold. These countries discovered that they were being adversely affected by finding their gold disappearing in exchange for devalued silver. Most of the European countries adopted a monometallic gold system, such as Britain had long followed. India's currency, being based entirely on the silver rupee, was at a special disadvantage. Because the value of silver fell between 1873 and 1893 from five shillings to three shillings an ounce (or $1.25 to $0.75 US) the value of the rupee diminished from two shillings to 1*s*. 3*d*. It is likely that devaluation stimulated Indian exports. But it is certain that this devaluation increased the burden of debt which India was acquiring for railway building and other public purposes, and scared away foreign capital from investing in Indian enterprises. British banks doing business in India were compelled to hold their capital in London and operate upon a margin unless they were prepared to see about one-third of their capital disappear through depreciation: the Oriental Bank which suffered a shrinkage of capital in this way was a casualty of the silver crisis.

Another peculiar feature of India's relations with world markets was the treatment of the difference between India's exports and imports. The five years 1874–9 saw India export products worth £24 million per annum more than the cost of imports: during the next five year period the favourable balance rose to over £30 million per annum. Rather more than one-third of this annual surplus was spent on gold, and was either (quite literally) buried or was placed upon the arms, ears, or noses of the women of India. Another third went in repayment of interest on loans raised in London and in dividends. The last third paid for the 'Home Charges', as they were called: the cost of the British Army in India, of government purchases in England, and of the pensions of British officials retired from India. The interest and dividends and the Home Charges became known as 'the drain' in the terminology of Indian nationalists: one of their main sources of resentment against British rule. A dispassionate inquiry suggests that India did indeed have a grievance. Mainly as a result of external wars, and also the cost of the Sepoy Revolt (over £40 million) all charged to India, the public debt rose to £70 million in 1858 and £220 million in 1900. The rate of increase continued to accelerate: £17 million in 1901, and £25 million in 1913. Only about half of this was on account of new economic development.

Another grievance was India's forcible exposure to the benefits of free trade. After the Sepoy Revolt of 1857, the government of India was sorely in need of revenue and, among other fiscal measures, it established moderate duties on all imports, as well as low duties on exports (mainly raw materials). The import duties gave some advantages to India's infant industries: also, they aroused the wrath of the English cotton industry, and Lancashire members of parliament put strong pressure on the government to introduce free trade. Lord

Lytton acceded to this pressure in 1879: the duties were abolished from 1882. It is worth recalling that his Council (composed almost entirely of British officials) opposed the abolition of the import duties on cotton manufactures and insisted on putting their protest before the British government. The Council continued to object, and in 1894, the duties on imported cotton manufactures were reimposed: but a corresponding excise duty was placed on Indian cotton goods. The Council again protested, and were over-ruled. A few concessions were granted, early in the twentieth century, but not until 1916 was a protective tariff policy begun. While British goods were no longer able to compete with Indian manufactures, Japanese mills were able to undersell Indian textiles, despite high tariffs.

The effects of currency fluctuations were again felt by India after the First World War: an attempt to revalue the rupee at 2*s*. failed, and the rupee was stabilised at 1*s*. 6*d*. by 1925. When Britain and other countries left the gold standard, in 1931, the new high value of gold led to quantities of hoarded Indian gold being put into the market by rich and poor: this made India's finances remarkably steady during the 1930s.

If India's trade and finances were moulded by the imperial yoke, Burma and Ceylon had the additional disadvantage of being financially subordinate both to Britain and India. The 'drain' from India to Britain had its equivalent in the 'drain' brought about by Indian emigrants to Burma and Ceylon who remitted substantial sums out of their earnings or profits to their places of origin. The expanding trading surpluses of Burma and Ceylon permitted them to absorb the remittance drain, but during the great depression this became a serious adverse item. The chief group of Indian capitalists in Ceylon and Burma (as also in Malaya) were the Chettiars. Although the term *Chetti* (Tamil, *Shetti*) is often applied to any Indian shopkeeper in South East Asia, the bankers and moneylenders belong to the Nattukottai Chettiar clan or subcaste. They operate on a partnership basis, within their own Association, which has offices in different countries and a head office in Madras. The Chettiars are financiers, not entrepreneurs: but they exercised an important role as middlemen between the land-owning, land-tilling indigenous community and the foreign banks and business houses. The Chettiars have their own financial network, determining rates of interest and creditworthiness. When the nineteenth century was about to end, the Chettiars decided that the world was about to end: in 1900, they called in all their money, suspended business, and closed their books, as if by one unified decision. During the depression, the hazardous balance between debit and credit maintained by so many Burmese and Sinhalese collapsed disastrously. The Chettiars' tight hold upon the rural community was blatantly demonstrated. Great resentment was felt by many Burmese and Sinhalese against the community – even the tolerant and charitable premier of Burma, U Nu talked about 'the Chettiar with the swollen abdomen' – and this resentment has been extended to the whole Indian domiciled community.

However, Burma and Ceylon were able to attain a wide measure of prosperity during the late nineteenth century and after, such as was denied to India, by the export of a small number of raw materials in general world demand. India, with its uncertain monsoon and enormous population could not develop by any simple process: the much more difficult task of industrialisation was needed to supplement agricultural improvement. We have noticed how agricultural production and trade led to manufacturing industrialisation in the jute business: this was the pattern in other industries.

Before we can consider industrial development we have to remember the previous de-industrialisation of India. The British were attracted to India first by its fine textiles. In 1798–9, the East India Company exported hand-woven piece-goods to the value of £3 million. By 1830, India was being flooded with the textiles of Lancashire. Indian domestic production had shrunk, and many weavers had become day-labourers.

The foundation for industrialisation in the nineteenth century was coal; and this India possessed in good supply and good quality. The main fields, at Raniganj, Jharia, Bokara and Karanpura are all within two hundred miles of Calcutta. The earliest mining companies were launched by Calcutta merchants. For example, Dwarkanath Tagore, a merchant prince-philosopher, controller of Carr, Tagore & Co., owned enterprises in such various fields as indigo, saltpetre, and sugar; and he promoted one of the earliest coal mines. Output of coal rose steeply. From 36,000 tons in 1839, it climbed to 91,000 tons in 1845; a million tons in 1880; six million in 1900; and 22 million tons in 1917. Demand levelled off after the war, and by 1940 the Bengal coal-fields were producing 30 million tons per annum, including two million tons for export.

Calcutta benefited enormously from its close proximity to this supply; but Bombay had other advantages, including an enterprising and adaptable business community, among whom the Parsis and the Gujaratis are outstanding. The Parsis had developed an important shipbuilding industry during the days of sail. From the mid-nineteenth century they pioneered the Indian textile industry. Bombay has the advantage of that damp climate which gave Manchester its lead in cotton manufacture. Bombay was also close to the cotton-growing districts of the Deccan. The first mill was opened in 1851 by Cowasji Nanabhoy Davar; twenty years later, there were a dozen mills in Bombay, mainly owned by Parsis. The most outstanding of these entrepreneurs was Jamshetji Nusserwanji Tata (1839–1904). He acquired his first wealth in the American Civil War cotton boom. Thereafter, he pioneered the newly-opened trade of Shanghai. He operated a mill in Bombay for a brief period, and then determined to develop a textile industry upon lines of his own. After thoroughly investigating the Lancashire industry, he chose to establish his factory (known as the Empress Mills) at Nagpur in the Central Provinces. There was no industry in the area; but the site lay in the centre of the cotton lands, rail communications were good, and the Warora coal mines lay within easy access. Tata's original capital amounted to Rs 15,000,000 (then equal to £150,000). The mills started production in 1877. On the technical side, Tata relied on English advisers, but his managers were Indian. From the beginning, the mills succeeded and dividends of 20 per cent were declared each year.

Tata was a model employer, providing incentives to his workers to stay with the firm, and watching over their working conditions. Other Indian industries were much more grim, and all the evils which accompanied the industrial revolution in Europe – such as sweated child labour – were prevalent in India to a worse degree. The only ameliorating feature of Indian industrialisation was its casual incidence. Workers were not sucked into an urban *lumpenproletariat* as in Europe. The rate of absenteeism was enormous; workers absented themselves for family reasons, or for the festivals of their religion or tribe, as they pleased. After a few months or years in industry they would drift back to their villages. Because the demand for labour outran the supply, these casual attitudes to discipline were accepted. At the mill conditions were uncertain. Workers were usually hired by middle-men, called *sardars*, who would levy commission on the worker's pay, rent accommodation, and lend money at high rates: the worker was reminded to pay up on pay day by the attention of the *sardar*'s strongarm men.

Following agitation in the press and the House of Commons, a commission of inquiry investigated conditions in 1875. They found that the Bombay mill-hands worked from sunrise to sunset; that there were no fixed weekly holidays; and that children started work at eight years of age, or less. There were no safety regulations to protect workers against industrial accidents. The only humane aspect of the system was the absence of discipline, and the casual behaviour of labour. The inquiry was followed by a Factory Act of 1881, which applied throughout British India to all factories employing a hundred persons or more. Children under seven were excluded from employment; children between eight and twelve must not work more than nine hours daily, and must have four free days a month. Accident prevention measures were laid down; employees must be given a midday break. Further industrial legislation followed in 1891: a year after the founding of the first Indian trade union, the Bombay Millhands Association (1890) which, however, lacked a constitution and received no subscriptions from members. In 1922, Indian legislation was amended to adopt the provisions of the Draft Convention of the 1921 International Labour Conference at Washington. Enforcement has never been easy when management and often labour attempt to evade the law. The textile workers have led the way in combining against the employers to protect their rights.

The Indian cotton industry received a great stimulus from the 1914–18 War, in which military contracts, together with a home demand starved of all imported goods, set the mills running at full capacity. There were 193 Indian cotton mills in 1900, employing 161,189 hands; in 1918 there were 262 mills and 282,227 employees. Expansion continued, stimulated by post-war tariffs, and the Second World War saw the Indian textile industry supplying the defence effort outside India. The number of mills in 1936 had grown to 379, employing 417,803 operatives, and in 1943 there were 401 mills and 502,650 workers. The workforce increased four times during the first four decades of the twentieth century, but productivity increased about eightfold during this period. The efficiency of Indian factory labour remains conditioned by an attitude to life and work relating to the rhythm of the countryside rather than the tempo of the town.

While cotton was providing the foundation for India's industrial development, J. N. Tata was planning further diversification of his interests. As a patriot, he decided that India must have a modern steel industry. Once again he went into the open countryside, and fixed upon a site where millions of tons of iron ore were lying loose upon the surface. This tract lay in the territory of a minor prince, the Maharaja of Mourbhanj, who granted Tata a lease of twenty square miles of land. Tata's agents attempted to raise the necessary capital in London, but they met with difficulties. It was decided to raise the money in India although, hitherto, Indian investors had hesitated to put their money into industry; preferring traditional, safe investments, especially property. However, the name of Tata was a sufficient guarantee to produce the required capital – £1,630,000 – within three weeks. The centre of operations was a village about 170 miles from Calcutta named Sakchi: later it was named Jamshedpur, in honour of the great industrial pioneer. Construction of the iron and steel plant began late in 1908; the first iron was made in December 1911. The first industrial steel to be made in India was cast in 1913. The onset of war stimulated development into full production: Tata's supplied rails for military lines in Iraq, Palestine, East Africa, and Salonika. A large scheme of extension began in 1917, and was completed in 1924. Tata's employed 40,000 men and produced more steel in a year than any steel plant outside the United States. Many of the labourers were aboriginals, Santhals and Khols. Jamshedpur grew into a vast company town, with every kind of social service supplied by Tata's.

Tata enterprises pioneered other developments, such as vast hydro-electric schemes, and the first airline in India. Other Indian industrial giants emerged in the twentieth century. Right up to 1911, the major portion of Indian industry was controlled by British business: a group of fifteen managing agents controlled 189 industrial units in 1911. With the exception of Tata's, no Indian managing house controlled more than five industrial units. From the 1930s onwards, the position was transformed. The Parsi dominance of the cotton industry was overturned. Marwaris and Gujaratis took over about four-fifths of the Ahmadabad sector of the industry and about half the Bombay city industry. Later, the Marwaris took over a sizeable sector of the jute industry. They came to dominate industrial sugar production. Finally, they took over much of the newspaper industry. By the time of independence, Marwari participation in industrial ownership and control was almost equal to that of all the other Indian business communities. The rise to power of this group has never been analysed in sociological terms. It would appear that the elite in Indian society shows a tendency to move away from business. As one generation acquires wealth in a trade or industry, the next generation moves into higher administration, landed interests, or intellectual pursuits. Certain communities have remained loyal to the family business – the Tata dynasty are an outstanding example. But the whole subject awaits systematic investigation.

At other levels of society, despite the rigidity of the Indian caste system, a certain ebb and flow is noticeable. In general, the Brahmins, the priestly caste, have lost their former unchallenged superiority. Even in south India, the Brahmin stronghold, they have been elbowed out of the higher professions. The middle castes, the Vaisyas, have consolidated their position during the last century, and now command economic and social esteem. Among the low castes, many remain fixed at the bottom of the social scale. Yet industrialisation has afforded an opportunity to some to attain a higher status. The lowly *khalasi* caste of tent-pitchers from Bombay found new occupations in the nineteenth century as sailors and riggers. In modern industry, the *khalasi* will be found as the skilled steel-erector, or oil driller; an aristocrat of the labour force.

Yet it cannot be too often recalled that right up to the middle of the twentieth century, three-quarters of the population were dependent upon agriculture. The 1951 Census of India (following partition) reported a total population of 353 million, of whom 295 million lived in the countryside, and 249 million were directly engaged in agriculture. Of this great majority of India's peoples, the First Five Year Plan observed 'the rural economy has been largely static'. The same must be said of rural sociology.

Much the same conclusion is true of Ceylon. The Goyigama caste, the yeomen, remain the dominant element in society, while the scions of leading families still manage the social and political machine. Only in Burma can one say that the traditional leadership deriving from rural authority or official status has now ceased to be of much importance in the scale of social or economic enterprise. Yet in Burma, as throughout South Asia, what might be called the opportunity for mobility is severely limited.

From this climate of limitation and inertia those who desired change had to look in the areas where social and economic change had already begun (to state the obvious). The districts of Gujarat north of Bombay and adjacent to Ahmadabad saw the spread of progressive agriculture, commercial enterprise, and small-scale industrialisation. Similar developments took place in Punjab where the spread of the canals stimulated other innovations. These were the exceptions. Over most of India the energies of the rising middle class were channelled into administration and politics. In so far as the British rulers were in charge of the direction the country was taking, their active encouragement of change and reform was shortlived: they fell back on a cautious policy designed to reinforce existing institutions rather than any effort to speed up the processes of change.

7 The Policy and Purpose of British Government

In the year 1800, the British Empire in South Asia was limited to the great province of Bengal (then including Bihar and Orissa), some districts in the south linked with Madras, the island of Bombay, and the low country of Ceylon. After half a century of conquest, South Asia had become a wholly British sphere of influence (Map 8). The boundaries of direct British rule had been pushed forward hundreds of miles as far as Peshawar in the northwest (1849) and Rangoon in the east (1852). There were a few additions yet to be made. British power extended in the northwest into the Afghan hills, and the independent kingdom of Ava or Upper Burma was extinguished in 1886. Yet even though the Union Jack flew from Aden to Singapore, unchallenged and unchallengeable, this empire remained a curious, patchwork affair. Vast territories, some as large as France or Germany, remained under the rule of their own princes; while thousands of miles of borderland, hillside and mountain, were never brought within the loosest form of British administration. Apart from a brief period from about 1849 to 1857, British policy, both in London and in India, was firmly set against any further accession of territory.

Britain remained a naval power and a trading nation; there were always voices ready in influential quarters to further the acquisition of a naval base, or a free port; and, as steam replaced sail, so the need arose for coaling stations all over the East. But whenever an adventurous military commander or Governor-General attempted to extend the empire on land, there was always a strong movement to halt, and sometimes to reverse the expansion. Expansion there was: in part to counter the rivalry of France (in the Indian Ocean up to 1810, and again in Burma in the 1880s), but much more to eliminate the local rivalry of restless Indian princes. When these princes were prepared to accept a kind of fossil independence, and where the British found themselves confronted by nothing more menacing than tribal chieftains, they left the local leaders to their own ways.

Indeed, when the British unexpectedly found themselves masters of Bengal, they first planned to perpetuate the existing system of government: though hoping to manipulate the governors to their own profit. Edmund Burke exclaimed: 'God forbid we should pass judgement on a people who framed their laws and institutions prior to our insect origin of yesterday.' Yet it was Burke who first stated the principle of 'trusteeship': of British rule for the good of India. Partly to protect Bengal from the unchecked exploitation of the East India Company's officials, partly to protect English party politics from the enormous pressure which the East India Company, gorged on Indian profits, might exert, William Pitt as Prime Minister passed legislation (1784) to bring India within the control of the British government. He despatched Lord Cornwallis (five years after his surrender at York-town) to be the first parliamentary Governor-General of India.

In order to put a check upon the adventurers who swarmed out to India to 'shake the pagoda tree', regulations introduced by Cornwallis restricted all senior appointments in the administration to members of the Civil Service, who were required to enter into a Covenant not to engage in trade or to accept presents. Because these 'Covenanted' civil servants received a monopoly of all posts, Indians were virtually excluded from all but the subordinate positions in the administration and the judiciary.

The structure of government as it evolved at the end of the eighteenth century may be said to have had an indigenous infrastructure and a foreign superstructure. The basic functions of government were the collection of revenue, mainly derived from agriculture and the land, and the dispensation of justice. As in Mughal times, the main unit of government was the district, the *zila*, and the factotum of government was the district officer or Collector. The districts constituted in the eighteenth century were enormous: the population of Mymensingh, in Bengal, is greater than that of Switzerland, while Vizagapatam in Madras is bigger than Denmark both in population and area. In the early days, the Collectors in Bengal dealt only with the great landlords, ensuring that they remitted the revenues due. The preservation of law and order was limited to ensuring that no actual revolt broke out in the district. As British rule extended beyond the area of Bengal and the permanent settlement, so its character began to change. After wars with Tipu Sultan in south India, the East India Company acquired new tracts of territory. One important area, the Baramahal, was placed under the administration of a soldier, Colonel Alexander Read, with another military officer, Thomas Munro, as his assistant. Unlike the Bengal Collectors, Munro lived among the people. For eight or nine months every year

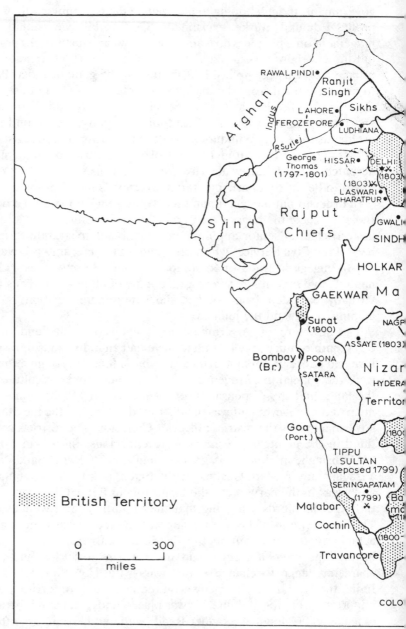

Map 8. The British gain control, *c*. 1800.

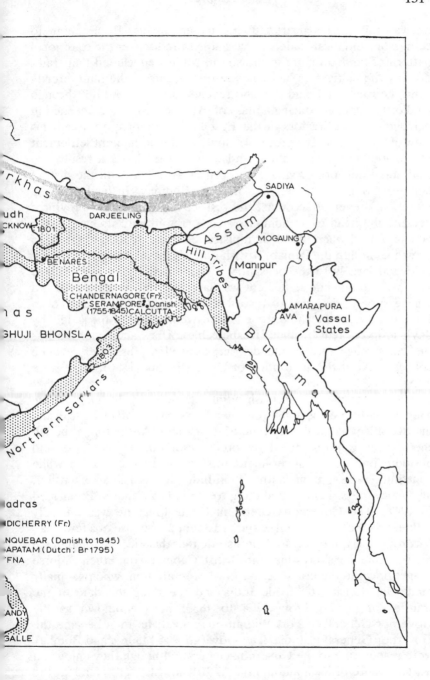

'rkhas

udh

CKNOW 1801

BENARES

Bengal

h a s

GHUJI BHONSLA

Northern Sarkars

DARJEELING

SADIYA

A s s a m

MOGAUNG

Hill Tribes

Manipur

CHANDERNAGORE(Fr)
SERAMPORE Danish
(1755-1845)CALCUTTA

1803

B u r m a

AMARAPURA
AVA

Vassal
States

adras

DICHERRY (Fr)

NQUEBAR (Danish to 1845)
APATAM (Dutch : Br 1795)
FNA

ANDY

GALLE

he was touring his district, living under canvas. By listening to cultivators and local leaders he was able to rediscover the traditional pattern of landed tenure in the south. Munro concluded that traditionally the cultivators had enjoyed their rights in the land directly from the ruler, and paid the land revenue directly, and not through landlords. After producing a mass of evidence, Munro succeeded in persuading the Directors of the East India Company to accept his view of the system. The process of applying the permanent settlement throughout India was halted, and even reversed. As a result, the traditional network of village authority was linked with the district administration in Madras, and later in Bombay. Instead of being merely a keeper of accounts, the district officer in these provinces became the head of an administrative pyramid with its base in the village. Later, when British administration was extended to the Agra provinces and to the Punjab, British officials found that landed rights belonged largely to the peasantry under the so-called joint village system. The revenue settlement was largely founded upon field and village surveys designed to record traditional landed rights. To an even greater extent, the district officer lived his life in the saddle by day and in the tent by night. Responsible for law and order, he was the chief magistrate in the district, as well as the chief revenue collector. After the annexation of Upper Burma (1886), there were altogether 240 districts.

In the districts, then, British administration largely followed the Mughal pattern of personal rule by a hierarchy of officials, with the district officer as the cornerstone of the system. At the top, although the British Raj resembled its predecessors in its aloofness and absolute power, the government took on a dual character: while constituting the supreme authority in India, it was also an extension, an agency, of parliament and the government in London. From 1774 to 1947, 'The Governor-General in Council', as he was officially called, was the government of India. Except in the case of a few weak Viceroys, it is quite easy to demonstrate that the Viceroy could make the supreme decisions which the British Cabinet would then endorse – right down to the last Viceroy, Lord Mountbatten, who personally made the decision to divide India and speed up the date of the transfer of power. From 1774 to 1833, he was known as the Governor-General of Fort William in Bengal; he then became the Governor-General of India. The Governors of Madras and Bombay were responsible to the Governor-General, although they enjoyed a wide measure of local autonomy. As British rule was extended, the new territories were formed into provinces whose heads were called Lieutenant-Governors or Chief Commissioners, and who were held much more tightly in rein by the Governor-General.

As a trading concern, the East India Company had set up Councils in its main centres which corresponded to the Boards of Directors of commercial companies. Originally, the Governor-General and the Governors of Madras and Bombay each had a Council of three members, but after 1833, the Councils of Madras and Bombay were limited to two members (together with the Governor) while the Governor-General's Council was slowly expanded until, in the 1920s, there were six members, as well as the Commander-in-Chief. By the Act of 1833, the Council was to include a Law Member, who was required to be a barrister. The first Law Member was Macaulay, from 1834–8. The Governor-General's Council functioned much more like the Cabinet of an American President than that of a British Prime Minister: its members were individually responsible for departments of government rather than exercising a corporate responsibility for policy-making. The Governor-General was the unchallenged ruler of India, and it was largely during the 'reign' of such expansionists as Wellesley (1798–1805) and Dalhousie (1848–56) that the outward frontiers of British power leaped forward.

The only member of the Council in a strong enough position to challenge the Governor-General was the Commander-in-Chief; there were several notable duels between the civil and military chiefs, only one (Kitchener versus Curzon) being won by the military. Nevertheless, the role of the Army in India was infinitely greater than that of the military in England. The forces of the East India Company in 1795 included 53 Indian infantry battalions, 7 European battalions, and 8 Indian cavalry regiments. By 1824, the Company's troops had increased to 144 Indian battalions, 7 European battalions, and 21 cavalry regiments. In addition, there was a large contingent of the British Army in India. Large numbers of British officers were needed for the Company's Army, and, as the British territories in India expanded (in 1856 their area was more than double that of 1800), these military officers offered almost the only available source of recruitment of administrators in the new provinces. After the annexation of the Punjab, half the rulers of the new province were drawn from the Covenanted Civil Service, and half from officers seconded from the Army. This dualism continued in the provincial administration of the Punjab, the Central Provinces, Assam, and Burma down into the twentieth century.

Ceylon escaped from the control of the East India Company in 1802, to become a Crown Colony, but the structure of its administration remained a miniature facsimile of the Indian model. The Governor of Ceylon, like the Governor-General of India, was appointed by the Crown, usually from English public life. But the backbone of the administration was provided by an elite Ceylon Civil Service, selected from British candidates. From 1833, the Governor of Ceylon had an Executive Council consisting of four senior civil servants and the Officer Commanding the troops. Also in 1833, the island was divided into five Provinces – later to be re-formed into nine Provinces. Each Province was divided into two or more districts, nineteen in all. The head of a Province was called the Government Agent, and the head of a district the Assistant Government Agent. To an even greater degree than in India, the infrastructure of local administration remained fixed in the hereditary pattern of leadership established under the Ceylonese kings, with local sub-district officials bearing traditional titles such as Mudaliyar and Rate Mahatmaya.

Already, at the end of the eighteenth century, some voices in England and in India were challenging the policy of *laissez aller* which the East India Company had taken up towards the responsibility of governing India. There were two main schools of reformers anxious to breach the cautious traditionalism of the Company: the Evangelicals, whose missionary fire had brought into existence a number of Protestant Missionary Societies in the late eighteenth century, and the Utilitarians or Philosophical Radicals, a pressure group which sought to dismantle medieval obstacles to the Industrial Revolution in England. The main achievement of the Evangelicals was the abolition of the slave trade and slavery itself in the British Empire; the Utilitarians' influence was more obliquely effected through political and legal reform measures. In South Asia, Utilitarianism operated most distinctly in the sphere of legal reform. The two movements crystallised in the great educational debate, but their influence permeated almost all the activities of officials and non-officials in the two decades before the great Sepoy Revolt.

The first breach was in 1813, when Wilberforce secured the admission of Christian missionaries into the Company's territories in India, but a long struggle lay ahead. The traditionalists or preservationists included some of the most respected names among high officials of the Company. Munro had seen the consequences of ill-judged change in the Permanent Settlement: 'We proceed in a country of which we know little or nothing as if we knew everything', he wrote. Mountstuart Elphinstone (1779–1859) who was responsible for introducing British administration into the country of the Marathas, noted: 'My first plan, and it certainly was the wisest . . . was to leave everything as I found it.' The Preservationists were not obscurantist. When Captain John Briggs, a district officer under Elphinstone visited his chief one day he asked him why a pile of Marathi books lay in the corner of his tent.

'To educate the natives.'

'But that is our highroad back to Europe', commented Briggs.

'We are bound under all circumstances to do our duty to them', was Elphinstone's reply.

But what was this duty? The division between the Preservationists and the Innovators was most direct over education.

The first support given to education by the British government in India was devoted to fostering studies in the classical languages of Oriental learning, Arabic and Sanskrit. In 1770, Warren Hastings had founded the *Madrassa* or Islamic College at Calcutta, and in 1791 Jonathan Duncan established the Banaras Sanskrit College. A despatch from the Directors in 1813 ordered that £10,000 per annum 'be set apart and applied to the revival and improvement of literature, and the encouragement of the learned natives of India, and for the introduction and promotion of a knowledge of the sciences among the inhabitants'. Clearly intended as a compromise, this directive aroused influential supporters of classical studies (often called the Orientalists) who ensured that the annual grant was applied to existing classical institutions. From 1823, the grant was administered by a Committee of Public Instruction for Bengal. The Committee included some non-officials, both European and Indian, but officials predominated. At first, the Orientalists had their way. They were not diverted by a despatch from the Directors in 1824 (said to be the work of James Mill, their secretary, a leading Utilitarian): 'The great end should not have been to teach Hindoo learning, but useful learning. . . . In professing to establish seminaries for the purpose of teaching mere Hindoo or mere Muhammadan literature, you bound yourselves to teach a good deal of what was frivolous, not a little of what was mischievous, and a small remainder indeed in which utility was in any way concerned.' The situation changed in the 1830s when the reformers gained the ascendancy. Macaulay became a member in 1834, along with Charles Trevelyan, who was to marry Macaulay's sister. Macaulay became the champion of English education. Trevelyan urged a middle course; he regarded the role of English as similar to that of Latin in the Europe of the Renaissance: a language of scholarship which would open the door to the entry of the vernacular languages as the vehicles of literature and education.

In the end, Trevelyan's policy was largely accepted. The explanation lay in the decision in the 1830s to replace Persian, hitherto the official language of the law courts and of administration, by English at the higher levels, and by Bengali and Urdu at the lower levels. However, Trevelyan's belief in cross-fertilisation between English and the vernaculars was largely stultified. He had urged the setting up of a network of district schools, but, in an effort to effect a compromise in the controversy between the preservationists and the innovators, Lord Auckland, the Governor-General in 1839, restored stipends to certain Arabic and Sanskrit copyists, shelved plans for vernacular schools, and substituted proposals for developing Central Colleges. The Committee of Public Instruction wanted to go further, and in 1840 pressed for a university in Bengal. Among these cross-currents of policy, the decisive changes were the substitution of English for Persian in higher administration and law, and the concentration of higher education in the central, English-language colleges. These changes served to displace the Muslims from their privileged place in the law, deriving from their knowledge of Persian and Arabic, and to give a stimulus to the rise of a new English-speaking Indian middle class elite, drawn almost exclusively from a small adaptable group among the Brahmin and Kayastha castes. More generally, these changes served to widen the gap between the higher administration (together with the elite Indian middle-men) and the mass of the people.

A similar movement took place in Ceylon. The most important stimulus to change was the inquiry conducted by W. M. G. Colebrooke and C. H. Cameron. They insisted that the language of the courts and the administration must be English, and they urged a greater concentration on English education, together with the establishment at Colombo of a government university college. A Central School Commission was established in 1841, and next year grants in aid were instituted. Colombo Academy became the Royal College, but Ceylon had to wait another ninety years for its own autonomous university.

Cameron also took up the question of law reform. Ceylon, however, continued the anachronistic application of Roman-Dutch law: superseded in the Netherlands by the Code Napoleon in 1809. It was left to Macaulay to carry through the codification of criminal law in India, to replace the tangle of Islamic law previously applied. Macaulay was instructed that his guiding principle should be 'the ascertaining of truth with the smallest possible cost of time and money whether to the State or to the individual and the suppression of crime with the smallest possible infliction of suffering whether to the innocent or the guilty'. The code was completed by 1837, though it was not brought into force until 1862. It was subsequently introduced into Burma, Ceylon, Malaya and British Borneo.

The reforms flowed most strongly during the period when Lord William Bentinck was Governor-General (1828–35). He it was who told Jeremy Bentham, greatest of the Utilitarians, that he went to India as his disciple. On his monument is inscribed Macaulay's tribute that 'He never forgot that the end of government is the happiness of the governed'. During his administration, in 1829, the custom of sati – the self-burning of a widow upon her husband's funeral pyre – was finally prohibited. The sati controversy also divided the preservationists from the innovators, as in the education debate. Soon after Bentinck departed, another important liberal measure was introduced. In 1823, a press censorship had been imposed: in 1835, Metcalf, Bentinck's temporary successor, abolished all restrictions, declaring: 'if India could only be preserved as a part of the British Empire by keeping its inhabitants in a state of ignorance, our domination would be a curse . . . and ought to cease'.

During Bentinck's administration, something was done to restore to Indians a share (though still a very minor share) in the government of their own country. Of the Cornwallis regulations which had excluded Indians from the higher levels of administration, Thomas Munro had observed: 'There is no instance in the world of so humiliating a sentence having ever been passed on a nation.' John Clark Marshman, editor of the Serampore newspaper *The Friend of India*, called this 'the ostracism of a whole people'. Under Bentinck, a new grade of civil judge, Principal Sadr Amin, was created, and the office of Deputy Collector was thrown open to Indians. The Act of 1833 which revised the Company's Charter provided (Clause 87) 'that no person, by reason of his birth, creed or colour, shall be disqualified from holding any office in our service'. The Directors followed this with a despatch of 1834 (again ascribed to James Mill) declaring 'there shall be no governing caste in India . . . no subject of the king, whether Indian or British or mixed descent shall be excluded'. The 1833 Act also provided that recruitment to the Covenanted Civil Service should be based upon a qualifying examination. However, this provision was not implemented. As entry into the Covenanted Service was open only to those who could secure a nomination from one of the Directors – a prize much sought after – no Indian could expect nomination. One Director conceived the plan of nominating the adopted son of Ram Mohan Ray to a vacancy, but it came to nothing. In 1838, the Committee of Public Instruction recommended for all posts beneath the Covenanted Civil Service that 'public examination, open to all candidates . . . should be annually held by officers appointed by the Government' and that the successful candidates should have first claim on appointments. This was accepted, and increasingly the highest grades filled by appointment in India went to young Indians with English-language education. Already, in 1853, *The Friend of India* declared that 'India is a despotism tempered by examinations'.

The prospect of the renewal of the Company's Charter in 1853 brought about the formation of the first political pressure groups in India and in England. The British Indian Association was formed in 1851; the Bombay Association and the Madras Native Association came into being in 1852. However, it appears that the terms of the 1853 Charter were substantially modelled upon the opinions of three men: C. E. Trevelyan, J. C. Marshman, and Alexander Duff, a Scots missionary. Three provisions were of special importance: the introduction of a competitive system of entry into the Covenanted Civil Service, a renewed declaration of educational responsibility and the first move towards setting up a legislature in India.

A committee was appointed, with Macaulay as chairman, to draft rules for the new examination system. They advised the adoption of an examination of an entirely academic character, with English, History, and Mathematics as the subjects scoring the highest marks (1,000 maximum each) while Sanskrit and Arabic were given a low rating (375 maximum) and the Indian vernacular languages were totally excluded as 'of no value except for the purpose of communication with natives of India'. The new type of civil servant was known in India as a 'Competition Wallah'. The first Indian to succeed in entering the Covenanted Service through competition was Satyendranath Tagore (elder brother of the poet, Rabindranath Tagore) who gained his place in 1864; in 1869, four young Indians succeeded in entering the service.

The new start in education was heralded by a despatch of 1854 which is usually linked with the name of Sir Charles Wood, the responsible minister, though it was drafted by Marshman and Duff.

This reaffirmed that: 'The education we desire to see extended in India must be effected by means of the English language in the higher branches of instruction, and by that of the vernacular languages of the great mass of the people'. Once again, the chief effect was to create a superstructure, but without an infrastructure of primary and secondary schools. Stimulated by the Wood despatch, the new Universities of Calcutta, Bombay and Madras came into being early in 1857 on the model of the University of London as it then existed: i.e. as an examining body, incorporating a number of separate university colleges.

The Charter of 1853 included the first move towards introducing a legislature into the government of India. The Governor-General's Council (the Commander-in-Chief, and four other members) was augmented for legislative purposes by six additional persons to form a Legislative Council of twelve members, with the Governor-General in the Chair. The six additional members were the Chief Justice of Bengal, another judge, and representatives of Bengal, Madras, Bombay, and the North-Western Provinces. The entire membership was British, and all were officials: yet the additional members showed themselves far from being yes-men. This independence was especially irksome to Canning after the 1857 Revolt, and also to Bartle Frere, who was mainly responsible for initiating legislation. Writing to Sir Charles Wood in London, Frere commented: 'You can have little idea how much India is altered. . . . The sympathy which Englishmen . . . felt for the natives has changed to a general feeling of repugnance . . . all this feeling is inevitably reciprocated by the natives.' He went on: 'Unless you have some barometer and safety-valve in the shape of a deliberative Council I believe you will always be liable to unlooked-for and dangerous explosions.' Frere insisted upon the necessity 'of learning what the natives think of our measures and how the native community will be affected by them': his idea was to have a Council rather like the darbar of an Indian prince. The Indian Councils Act of 1861 reconstituted the Legislative Council, with the Executive Council again forming the nucleus, supplemented by additional members, between six and twelve in number, of whom half were non-officials. These additional members were nominated by the Viceroy, and held office for two years. Whereas the previous arrangement had allowed the Legislative Council to conduct its affairs in a free imitation of Parliament, the Council of 1861 was stricly held down to what it could and could not do.

The Act also established augmented Councils for Bombay and

Madras empowered to legislate for their own territories. Bengal obtained its own Legislative Council in 1862, and a fourth provincial Council was set up for the North-Western Provinces in 1886. The provincial Councils were also strictly confined to law-making; they were allowed no criticism or even comment on wider issues at all. The first Indian members of the Councils were aristocrats, like the Maharaja of Patiala, or retired officials, like Sir Sayyid Ahmad Khan. As proceedings were all in English, the Indian members almost always preserved a dignified silence. Without opposition, the work was concluded with great celerity. Whatever value the legislatures might have possessed as sounding-boards of public opinion was more than offset by the practice (which became a fixed rule from 1864) of the Viceroy and his government to spend six months of every year at Simla in the Himalayan heights, far away from the dusty plains.

It is customary to regard the Sepoy Revolt of 1857 as the watershed between medieval and modern India, and so, in many ways, it is. Yet in terms of British initiative the 1850s saw the drying up of modernising, progressive policies and the beginning of a long period of preservationist conservatism. From 1857 to 1914 might be called a period of reconstruction, following the earlier period of reform.

Whereas the Utilitarians had pressed for the same reforms in India as in England, the attitude which became predominant from the 1850s saw the problems of India as quite different and distinct from those of England. There was a definite tone of racialism in the growing conviction that India could not expect to tread the same path as Britain because of differences – which some stated frankly to be an inferiority – between the Asiatic and the European. Calcutta, Bombay and Madras obtained their universities only twenty years after the foundation of the University of London; entry into the elite Civil Service of India for all comers, by open competition, came almost twenty years before the same reform was generally introduced for the elite Civil Service of Britain. But these were the last effects of the spirit of progressive innovation. India and Ceylon had to wait for ninety years before full parliamentary government and full self-government were conceded to the 'lesser breeds without the law'.

Here is one example of the change in attitude: J. C. Marshman was succeeded as editor of *The Friend of India* in 1852 by Meredith Townsend (later editor of the *Spectator*). Already in March 1857 (before the Mutiny) we find Townsend commenting editorially on a proposal to alter the legal status of Europeans in India: 'All the parliaments in the world cannot make a native and a European equal.' The change in the British attitude in India did not go unnoticed, even at that time. In 1863, G. O. Trevelyan (son of Charles Trevelyan) was going through the old files of *The Friend of India* for 1836. He comments: 'The tone of the articles indicated the existence in Anglo-Indian society of a spirit which has passed away and left but little trace. . . . Thirty years ago the education of the people of the country was the favourite subject of conversation.' He went on to describe the contempt for Indians, the racial arrogance of his own day.[1]

The Queen's Proclamation of 1858 which announced the end of the rule of the East India Company was an attempt to counteract this rising tide of intolerance (Map 9). The Queen instructed Lord Derby who drafted the Proclamation that it 'should breathe feelings of generosity, benevolence and religious feeling, pointing out the privileges which the Indians will receive in being placed on an equality with the subjects of the British Crown'. The leaders of Indian opinion treasured the Queen's promises, especially that which stated: 'It is our further will that, so far as may be, our subjects of whatever race or creed, be freely and impartially admitted to offices in our service.' But, as *The Friend of India* pointed out (1861): 'Our rulers preferred the inconsistency of proclaiming an impossible equality without practising it.' Far from welcoming the emergence of a new class of Indians, English-educated, and Western in outlook, the British rulers of India seemed to wish to smother this emergent elite. While John Lawrence was Viceroy (1864–9) he initiated a scheme for the annual award of nine Queen's Scholarships, tenable in England. Instituted in 1868, the scholarships were suspended in the following year and were never actually awarded again. Then, in 1876, the upper age limit for competing for the Indian Civil Service was lowered from 21 to 19, effectively excluding Indians educated in their own country from entry. Between 1868 and 1875, eleven Indians had entered the service; between 1876 and 1883, only one passed in. Discontent with these inequalities led progressive Indians to turn from questions of social reform to the organisation of a political movement.

The government of India repulsed the educated vanguard of Indians, although they had been supporters during the Sepoy Revolt, when so many of the tradition-minded groups joined the Mutineers. The 'Babus' – doctors, professors, government officials – had been a

---

[1] See G. O. Trevelyan, *The Competition Wallah*, London, 1866, for a vivid impression of race relations in India after the Sepoy Revolt.

special target, along with the Europeans, and many had suffered death or mutilation. But now the British looked with favour to the landlords (many of whom had joined in the Revolt) and to the martial classes – Sikhs, Rajputs, and Punjabi Muslims. British policy was devoted largely to maintaining the existing balance of forces within society. *The Friend of India*, always a reliable barometer, summed up this policy in an editorial: 'Avoid change; by removing obstructions rather than by supplying new stimulants, slowly develop, but do not violently upheave; leave rich and poor to themselves and their natural relations within the limits that prevent oppression' (December, 1873). The main innovation of the post-Mutiny years was the development of a network of municipalities. This was designed, in part, to draw upon the traditional feeling of local loyalty, as a Resolution issued by Lord Lawrence's administration made clear:

> The people of this country are perfectly capable of administering their own local affairs. The municipal feeling is deeply rooted in them. The village communities . . . are the most abiding of Indian institutions. They maintained the framework of society while successive swarms of invaders swept over the country. In the cities also, the people cluster in their wards, trade guilds and panchayats and show much capacity for corporate action. . . . Holding the position we do in India, every view of duty and policy should induce us to leave as much as possible of the business of the country to be done by the people . . . and to confine ourselves to . . . influencing and directing in a general way all the movements of the social machine.

Following this Resolution, legislation was enacted for most of the provinces, and the major towns obtained municipal councils (e.g. Delhi, Agra, Allahabad, 1863; Dacca, Patna, Jubbalpore, 1864; Burdwan, Gaya, 1865; Trichinopoly, 1866; Lahore, Rawalpindi, 1867). Although the new municipalities might introduce certain much-needed public utilities, they gave no scope for self-government. Lord Hobart, Governor of Madras observed quite bluntly (1874): 'The population of a municipality does not govern itself.' Local government remained firmly under the control of the Indian Civil Service, and this service remained predominantly British. Here is the view of a representative British member of that service, John Beames, in the 1880s: 'In the course of my long experience I have constantly found natives deficient in courage, shirking responsibility, careless and indolent. From what I have seen of the large number of natives who have served under me during the last twenty-nine years, I do not think they possess the qualifications which fit them to be admitted to the Covenanted Civil Service.'

Such an attitude was not confined to British officials in India. Lord Salisbury as Prime Minister observed when Dadabhai Naoroji attempted to enter the House of Commons: 'I doubt if we have yet got to that point where a British constituency would elect a black man.' When reproached for his intolerance, Salisbury made things worse by explaining that 'the colour is not exactly black, but at all events he is a man of another race'. The middle class Indian demand for fuller participation in the Civil Service was sidetracked. In 1889 the Indian Civil Service numbered 896, of whom 12 were Indians. By 1915, the total strength of the ICS had risen to 1,371, of whom 63 were Indians.

Increasingly as they came to believe that the government of India – the Viceroy and his Council – would never listen to their requests, Indians began to co-operate with the Radical wing of the Liberal Party in England, and with the Irish Nationalists, also beginning their long agitation for self-rule. Largely because of the efforts of Henry Fawcett, MP (sometimes called 'the Member for India') an Act was passed in 1870 to provide 'additional facilities for the employment of Natives of India of proved merit and ability in the Civil Service of Her Majesty in India'. But British officialdom in India was able to negative this measure. At last, under the Viceroyalty of Lord Lytton, a romantic conservative with a strong feeling for aristocracy, an alternative elite Civil Service, the Statutory Service, was established. The test for entry was not to be ability in the examination room, but family and status. Lytton's intention to appoint aristocratic Indians largely failed because the scions of princely families were aware that this service was not regarded as equal to the Covenanted Service, and also because the fossil dignity which was the consequence of British rule had left them unfitted for the responsibility and initiative of high administration. The intention was to build up the Statutory Service to one-fifth the size of the Covenanted Service – about 200 altogether – but in the end 69 such appointments were filled.

Only the leaders of the Muslim community were favourable to the 'Statutory' scheme. Experience had shown that Muslims, with their late entry into Westernised education, were no match for the scholarly Hindu castes: the first successful Muslim candidate did not enter the Covenanted Service until 1885: twenty-one years after the first Hindu. Where entry into the middle grades of the Civil Service was by open competition (as in Bengal), the Muslims had suffered gravely. By the 1880s in the Bengal Presidency (which included Bihar and Assam) Muslims formed 31 per cent of the population, but held 8.5 per cent of 'gazetted' (i.e. middle and upper) posts. Only where entry was by nomination did the Muslims hold their ground. Thus, in the North-Western Provinces and Oudh (later United Provinces) Muslims formed only 13 per cent of the population, but through entry by nomination retained 45 per cent of gazetted posts. The policy of the forward-looking leaders of the Muslim community was to call upon the British government to maintain Muslim privileges, while pushing ahead with plans for educational reform which would make the Muslims able to compete with their more enterprising Hindu rivals. Consequently, Sir Sayyid and his supporters urged that Muslims confine their political activity to professions of loyalty to the British government. The more advanced elements among profession-al, middle class leaders – and these included the small Parsi and Christian communities, as well as the scholarly Hindus – began to promote associations for social and political reform, culminating in the foundation of the Indian National Congress in 1885.

At first, these aspirations received some encouragement from forward-looking Viceroys, whatever discouragement British officials might offer. Lord Ripon (1880–4) was a reformer with genuine sympathy for India. His predecessor had again muzzled the press by the Vernacular Press Act of 1878: Ripon repealed the Act, and also went on to introduce proposals calculated to make municipalities more free of official control, and to extend local self-government to the Districts. But the measure which aroused most feeling was the Ilbert Bill (called after Sir Courtenay Ilbert, the Law Member) designed to put British or 'domiciled European' residents in India on the same legal footing with the rest of the population. This measure aroused the racialism now rampant and led to furious feeling in the clubs and in the press. A writer to the newspaper *The Englishman* who called himself 'Britannicus' summed things up: 'The only people who have any right in India are the British; the so-called Indians have no right whatever.'

Happily, there was another note in the speech of Englishmen. John Bright warned his countrymen that India could not be accepted only as 'a field for English ambition and for English greed'. Lord Dufferin, Viceroy from 1884 to 1888, had sufficient political imagination to see that the newly emergent progressive leadership could be made into political allies. Emphasising the need to associate the professional, middle class with the government, he urged London to 'give quickly and with good grace whatever it may be possible or desirable to accord'. He saw the autocratic nature of the government of India as a weakness: it was 'an isolated rock in the middle of tempestuous seas'. His plans received the same cautious, captious reception from the British government in London as did all the reforming proposals for India. Draft legislation was postponed from session to session. Despite pressure from individuals, 'the system' had taken over. This is well expressed by Sir Charles Dilke, that brilliant Radical voluptuary, in his book *Problems of Greater Britain*, which appeared in 1890, and went into four editions within a few months. Dilke wrote: 'Persons do not count for much in India. The Indian governmental system is too regular, the codes are too complete, traditions too strong, to give much room to human personality. No one man can really change the policy, and the greatest alterations of recent times have taken place gradually by the help of scores of distinguished men.' At last, in 1892, Dufferin's proposals to associate non-official Indians more closely with the government were in part implemented in the Indian Councils Act. The Conservative government, led by Lord Salisbury with his racial prejudices, had opposed any introduction of representation by election. The Bill was introduced into the House of Commons by Curzon, as Under Secretary for India, in a speech which reflected the attitude of the English ruling class, then and for years to come. 'Who are the people of India?' he asked, and went on:

> The people of India are the voiceless millions who can neither read nor write. . . . The people of India are the ryots and the peasants whose life is not one of political aspiration but of mute penury and toil. The plans and policy of the Congress Party in India would leave this vast amorphous residuum absolutely untouched. . . . That party contains a number of intelligent, liberal-minded and public-spirited men . . . but as to their relationship with the people of India, the constituency which the Congress Party represents cannot be described as otherwise than a microscopic minority of the total population.

During debates upon the Bill, Gladstone offered the hope that the Indians with experience of municipal government might provide leadership on the Councils; but he added: 'All the parts of the British Empire present to us a simple problem in comparison with the problems which India presents.' A Liberal member, C. E. Schwann, introduced an amendment to make the Councils partly elected. He withdrew his proposal after an assurance that the principle would be accepted, though not formally included in the Act.

The Act of 1892 increased the number of additional (that is non-official Indian) members of the Governor-General's Legislative Council from six to ten, and the maximum number from twelve to sixteen. The Madras and Bombay Legislative Councils were expanded more widely: the maximum number of additional members could now be fixed at twenty, of whom not less than half must be non-officials. Bengal's maximum was also raised to twenty, while that of the North-Western Provinces became fifteen: the non-official proportion was smaller in both cases than for Madras and Bombay.

The principle upon which the new members were to be appointed was that of providing representation of 'different races, classes, and localities'. The draft rules adopted for schemes of representation for the central and provincial legislatures laid down: (1) the determination of the number of interests to be represented, (2) the selection of members on the recommendation of bodies speaking for those interests, and (3) appointment to the remaining seats by nomination. For the central legislature, five out of the ten non-official members were chosen by the non-official members of the provincial legislatures. The latter were chosen to represent such 'interests' as the landlords, the mercantile community and the universities; but the largest 'constituency' was that of local self-government. Between three and four seats in each province were allotted to the municipalities and district boards, whose members formed electoral colleges. These local bodies, in turn, were partly elected and partly nominated. Systems of election varied. The municipal electorate was minute. In most provinces it comprised less than two per cent of the urban population, though in Bengal it was somewhat higher (perhaps 5 per cent). Even in large towns there were seldom more than four or five hundred voters, and many voters avoided going to the polls, because there was no secret ballot, and to record a vote might be to earn the enmity of a powerful citizen. Some municipalities were elected on a ward basis, but some allocated the seats on the basis of 'interests'. In many towns, the basic division was between Hindus and Muslims. In general, the Hindus owned more property, and thus controlled more votes. In Lahore, in the 1880s, the Muslim population numbered 60,000, and the Hindus 35,000: yet only seven members were Muslims, while nine were Hindus. To rectify such inequalities, several municipalities (especially in the Punjab) were reconstituted, giving so many seats to the Hindu community, so many to the Muslims. For example, Amritsar adopted this system in 1895, and Multan in 1899. Rangoon Municipality, which became a two-thirds elected body in 1882, had five Burmese members, five Europeans and Armenians, two Chinese, two Hindus, two Muslims, and one Karen: besides a member elected by the Chamber of Commerce.

The system of 'communal' electorates, established in some local bodies, began to be favoured by the minorities for the legislatures. Of the forty-three members elected by municipalities to the provincial legislatures between 1892 and 1909, forty were lawyers, and only a tiny minority were Muslim. Of fifty-four elected by the district boards, ten were landlords and thirty-six were lawyers, with Hindus again dominant. Discontent arose from two directions; the progressive, middle class leaders of the Congress chafed at the limited opportunity in the legislatures and the Civil Service which they were given, while the Muslim leaders began to feel that even these limited openings were showing how, given open competition or election by majority vote, the Muslim minority must always be outpaced by the Hindu majority.

Although administered as a frontier province of India, Burma retained its own national character. The invasion of Upper Burma and occupation of Mandalay required only a minor military expedition, but subsequently guerilla bands under traditional leaders began a jungle war which lasted five years and spread to Lower Burma, occupied thirty years earlier. To suppress the revolt over 32,000 troops, mainly Indian, had to be brought in. Gradually, they were replaced by military police battalions, mainly recruited in Punjab, and this was only part of the 'Indianisation' of Burma which now took place. The central areas of Rangoon formed an Indian city, though Mandalay retained its traditional character.

After the first two heads of the administration, who had spent their working lives in Burma, the Lieutenant-Governors were all men whose previous administrative experience was in an Indian province. In the district administration, Indian Army officers, who were no longer employed in civil posts elsewhere in India, still played an important role as Deputy Commissioners and Commissioners. Burma was regarded as a backwater, avoided by all ambitious officials.

Time stood still in the government of India. Even the most modest change was resented. Lord Curzon (Viceroy, 1899–1905) declared in 1900: 'Every year an increasing number of the 900 and odd higher posts that were meant and ought to have been exclusively reserved for Europeans are being filched away by the superior wits of the natives'; at that moment there were 33 Indians, as against 988 British members of the Indian Civil Service. Also, in 1900, Curzon wrote: 'My own belief is that the Congress is tottering to its fall, and one of my greatest ambitions while in India is to assist it to a peaceful demise.' This oft-quoted miscalculation was not so far from the mark: the progressive, reforming Congress leaders who loved to repeat Queen Victoria's declaration of 1858 had almost reached the end of the road of peaceful, purposeless constitutional agitation. It may be argued that unwittingly Curzon provided a lifeline to the Congress by his plan for the partition of Bengal. We need not embrace the theory that the creation of a new province of Eastern Bengal and Assam, designed to afford greater opportunity to the Muslim community, was an instalment of a master-plan to 'Divide and Rule' the peoples of India. At this time, a missionary working in Madras observed: 'The impression exists that administration is for the government rather than the people . . . revenue matters rule rather than the needs of the people.' The division of Bengal derived from an administrative rather than a political motive. However, the belief that this was a machiavellian plot to set the Hindus and the Muslims of Bengal against each other triggered off an agitation against partition which gave a fillip to the 'Extremist' wing of Indian nationalism. The return of the Liberal Party to power in England after twenty years in the wilderness also encouraged the Moderates to believe that there would now be a genuine partnership between men of goodwill on both sides.

Yet the racial hostility between Englishmen and Indians (which even Curzon's critics admit he tried to break by punishing any case of race oppression which he could uncover) had now become so intense that even British Liberals could not understand the challenge of the hour. The new Liberal Secretary of State was John Morley (1906–10), the disciple of Mazzini, Bright, and Gladstone. When a Radical MP declared that 'Whatever is good in the way of self-government for Canada must be good for India', Morley tartly replied: 'In my view that is the most concise statement that I can imagine of the grossest fallacy in all politics.' Morley's dilemma was the ubiquitous 'palimpsest' quality of Indian life: he saw the contemporary scene as 'This transition from the fifth European century in some parts, in slow, uneven stages up to the twentieth.' He recognised the imperative need for reform, but not in the direction of responsible government. In the House of Lords debate upon his reforms scheme, Morley emphasised: 'If my existence, either officially or corporeally, were prolonged twenty times longer than either of them is likely to be, a parliamentary system in India is not at all the goal to which I would for one moment aspire' (17 December 1908).

Morley's aims were limited to offering concessions to the Moderates, the constitutionalists, among the Congress leaders, in order to restore their standing, which they had largely lost to the extremists. One of the most shrewd of ICS officials, Sir Harcourt Butler wrote (March 1907): 'Moderation does not last under the Indian sun. If the Government does not draw them to itself the moderates will turn to the extremists and the pressure of racial feeling will hurry them on their way.' Morley, too, was alive to the dangers of delay. Concerning the labyrinthine consultations of the Viceroy's advisers, he commented: 'Well, I am a great believer in the virtues of collective consultation, and I am all for taking time and giving opportunity to allow men to come round to your own judgment. But time is one thing and eternity is another.'

Controversy has arisen over the actual authorship of the reforms which are jointly linked with the names of Morley and Minto, the Viceroy (1905–10). Contemporary opinion attributed the major part to Morley. For example, the Anglo-Indian newspaper *Pioneer* writes (31 December 1909) of Morley: 'Yielding it may be, a little on this side or that according to the force of the gale or his own instincts, but in the main holding a set course to the haven of political concessions.' The *Pioneer* contrasts this with 'the humiliations of the Indian government, its change of policy, its timidity, its slowness to use legitimate powers, its perplexed handling of constitutional amendments'.

Under the Reforms, the official majority in the provincial Councils was abandoned. The elected element was greatly increased (in all provincial Councils together, from 39 to 135) and in Bengal a majority of the legislature was elected. The central legislature was expanded to include sixty additional members (additional to the Executive Councillors) of whom a majority were to be non-officials, twenty-seven being elected. The greatest innovation lay in the introduction of the principle of communal representation into the Councils, and here it seems clear that the guiding hand was that of Minto. In October, 1906, the Viceroy received a deputation of Muslim notables to demand separate representation for their community. There is no need to question that they were genuinely giving voice to the overwhelming sentiment of Muslims at that time.

However, the proposition that Muslim interests ought to be safe-guarded by creating separate Muslim constituencies in which Muslims alone would vote for the Muslim members took the principle to its logical limit: though there were precedents (as in Cyprus) for this course. The expanded membership of the legislatures continued to be mainly chosen by electoral colleges formed by members of municipalities and district boards. Thus in the United Provinces a majority of the elected members were chosen by local bodies, while in Bombay, nine of the twenty-one elected members were chosen by the Corporation of Bombay, and other local bodies. The landlords, business, and the universities continued to elect their own members. The new Muslim constituencies gave separate, and substantial representation, not only in the provincial legislatures, but also at the centre, where they had six places specially reserved. Because Muslims were also successful in gaining some of the landlord and other seats, they entered the all-India legislature in 1910 with eleven out of the total of twenty-seven elected seats.

It is noticeable that the area which now forms Pakistan remained on the margin of constitutional development. The Punjab was granted a legislature only in 1897, and under the Morley–Minto Reforms, out of a total of twenty-four, only nine were elected. In 1901, six districts were hived off the Punjab to form the North-West Frontier Province. Ruled by a Chief Commissioner, with an administrative elite which continued to draw half of its numbers from the Indian Army, the NWFP had no legislature and no political life. Baluchistan was similarly governed. Sind continued to be administered as a Division of the Bombay Presidency, right out of the mainstream of political development. By contrast, what is now Bangladesh (and was from 1905 to 1912 Eastern Bengal) had a livelier political tradition, and a legislature with a larger elected element.

Burma was given a legislature in 1897, but the share of the indigenous peoples was minute. Even after the Morley–Minto Reforms, out of a total of seventeen members there was only one elected non-official who was chosen by the Burma Chamber of Commerce, a European organisation.

Just as in the 1830s, when Ceylon felt the impact of the Utilitarian reforming movement which, like an earth tremor, agitated South Asia, so the effect of the Morley–Minto Reforms had repercussions in the neighbouring island. The respectful petitions of the Ceylonese leaders for a greater share in the affairs of their country were received with the same patronising suspicion as was the fate of the Congress

Moderates. The Governor, Sir Henry McCallum, described their requests to the Secretary of State for the Colonies (then Lord Crewe) as 'of course the establishment not of representative, but of oligarchical class government'. However, the Morley–Minto atmosphere necessitated some gesture. Although Lord Crewe agreed that the demand for reform came from 'a very small minority . . . of the natives of Ceylon who have assimilated an education of a purely Western type' (the 'microscopic minority' again), he altered the Legislative Council in recognition that 'the possession of Western education must be attended in future by the exercise of popular franchise'. Membership of the legislature was increased to eleven official and ten non-official members. Of the latter, four were elected by 'interests': two by the European domiciled community, one by the Burgher (Eurasian) community, and one by the Educated Ceylonese, so-called. This strange group was distinguished from the (presumably uneducated) six nominated members: one Kandyan, two Tamils, two Low Country Sinhalese, and one Muhammadan.

The Morley–Minto Reforms were at first well received by the Moderates, for whom they had been largely devised. However, the feeling soon grew that these Reforms had not given Indian politics any real sense of direction. The partition of Bengal, which Curzon repeatedly declared to be a *fait accompli*, was a continuing source of discontent, Lord Hardinge, the new Viceroy (1910–16) deliberated with his Council on possible lines of development. A despatch of August, 1911 stated: 'The only possible solution would appear to be gradually to give the Provinces a larger measure of self-government until at last India would consist of a number of administrations, autonomous in all provincial affairs, with the Government of India above them all, and possessing power to interfere in cases of misgovernment, but ordinarily restricting its functions to matters of Imperial concern.' In the House of Lords, the Conservative peers, Curzon and Lansdowne, accused the Liberal government of contemplating a federal form of Home Rule in India. This was denied by the Secretary of State, Lord Crewe (1910–15), but the Under Secretary, Edwin Montagu, took a different line. 'We cannot drift on for ever without stating a policy', he said. Already, in his first speech as Under Secretary in the House of Commons he had challenged the accepted view of Congress as a 'microscopic minority', observing: 'We must remember that the amount of yeast necessary to leaven a loaf is very small; when the majority have no ideas or views, the opinion of the educated minority is the most prominent fact in the situation.' After

Hardinge's despatch, Montagu declared in a public speech: 'That statement shows the goal, the aim to which we propose to work – not immediately, not in a hurry, but gradually.' Even this tentative commitment was too much for Liberal leaders. Lord Crewe stated emphatically that he saw no future for India on the lines of colonial self-government. Lord Bryce, the exponent of democracy in America and Australia, observed at this time that if Britain were to surrender India: 'Its political unity, which depends entirely on the British Raj, would vanish like a morning mist. Wars would break out. . . . To India, severance from England would mean confusion, bloodshed, pillage.[1]

The First World War, with its urgent call upon the armed forces of India, did not inject much urgency into the leisurely search by the government of India for some formula for constitutional advance. A shock was given by the disastrous campaign in Mesopotamia (Iraq) which led to the fall of Kut-al-Imara. A Commission of Inquiry censured the part of the government of India in this debacle. Speaking in Parliament in July 1917, Edwin Montagu insisted: 'The government of India is too wooden, too iron, too inelastic, too ante-diluvian to be of any use for the modern purposes we have in view.' After the debate, the Secretary of State for India, Austen Chamberlain, tendered his resignation. He was succeeded by Montagu (1917–22). The question of a declaration of policy had been agitating Whitehall and Simla. The Cabinet now considered draft formulae. Montagu wanted to have a declaration that India's goal was self-government, but Curzon and others objected and insisted on the use of the phrase 'responsible government'. At last, on 20 August 1917, the British government committed itself to a definite constitutional future for India: 'The policy of HM Government, with which the Government of India is in complete accord, is that of increasing association in every branch of the administration and the gradual development of self-governing institutions with a view to the progressive realisation of responsible government in India as an integral part of the British Empire.'

The announcement went on to indicate that Montagu would visit India to work out a plan to give effect to the pronouncement. The last paragraph stated: 'The British Government and the Government of India, on whom the responsibility lies for the welfare and advancement of the Indian peoples, must be judges of the time and measure

[1] J. Bryce, *The Ancient Roman Empire and the British Empire in India*, London, 1914.

of each advance. . . .' The concept of trusteeship was thus restated. All unknowing, the British had already lost the initiative. Henceforward they could determine neither the pace nor the direction of political change. Yet although the Indian leaders were now to acquire a compelling negative, limiting influence upon events, they were a long way themselves from shaping policy.

8 The Rise of Modern Social, Religious and Political Movements

Social and political movements in nineteenth-century India were essentially movements to reform and renew society and religion. They began with the individual efforts of pioneers, inspired by contact with English institutions to modernise and purify their own community. Their approach implied re-education of those they sought to influence; and education and communication played a vital part in their endeavours. But the greatest departure from older Indian reform movements lay in the emphasis given to organisation. Whereas Kabir, Nanak and other prophets of reform had largely relied upon face to face contacts, upon loose, non-formal links with their followers, the nineteenth-century reformers accepted the techniques of the West, if not Western standards. Sometimes borrowing was conscious, explicit: thus, the founders of the Indian National Congress deliberately adopted the methods of the Anti-Corn Law League which, in the 1840s, carried on a nation-wide campaign for free trade in Britain. Organisation in place of inspired leadership: this was the characteristic phenomenon of the new movements. If the structure of these pioneer bodies appears rudimentary by twentieth-century Western standards, we must base our comparison upon the methods of traditional Asia for a fair evaluation.

The pioneers of reform regarded Europe and Christianity – more particularly, England and Protestantism – as their model. In contrast to the reaching out of the reformers to the West, the traditionalists endeavoured to repel the new forces and to reverse the process of modernisation, returning to traditionalism. The final expression of this feeling came in 1857 when, in the wake of the Sepoy Revolt, the forces of the old order sought to expel the British and restore the former structure of authority. The failure of the traditionalists left a clear field to the modernists: until a second wave of reformers emerged, confident that through the technique of organisation they could reassert the true greatness of Asian religion and social values. These fundamentalists commanded one asset denied to the modernists: because they spoke in the language of tradition they could speak to the mass of the people.

Both the modernists and the fundamentalists began with the mission of reforming their own countrymen. But no reformation could have much meaning unless it could face the problem of foreign rule. The modernists saw themselves as citizens of the British Empire, and their goal was equality with their English fellow-citizens. The fundamentalists saw themselves as heirs to a unique tradition. This raised a dilemma which did not face the modernists: the tradition was essentially based upon religion: Hinduism for the majority, Islam for a substantial minority. Any attempt at synthesis between these two religions inevitably involved the absorption of the minority into the majority. And so the politics of nationalism in India became inextricably involved with the politics of communalism: of alignment according to religion.

The pattern of Ceylon followed much the same lines, except that the reform movement did not fully develop from an individual to an organisational basis: moreover, the fundamentalists did not count for so much, and the mass of the people were scarcely involved in a national movement. In Burma, tradition remained dominant. The forces of modernisation did not acquire an indigenous complexion: modernisation was left largely to the foreigners – Europeans and Indians until after the First World War.

It was from the new middle class – literally, intermediaries, middle-men, who provided the brokers and the agents for the British, in government and in commerce – that the new Indian reform movements derived their founders and pioneers. The great port cities, especially Calcutta and Bombay, were the centres of these movements. Beginning among small groups, their seminal influence spread gradually to the hinterland and then up country to the *mofussil*, the countryside. This effect was foretold by the 'Father of Modern India', the first great reformer, Ram Mohan Ray (1774–1833), who recorded in 1824: 'The native inhabitants of Bengal, in a great degree, follow the example of the opulent natives of Calcutta.' Ram Mohan was born into a high Brahmin (Kulin) caste. His early life was spent in the pursuit of religious truth; he studied Islam at Patna and Hinduism at Banaras, going on to Tibet to seek out the message of Buddhism. In all this searching he was disappointed. At twenty-two he began to learn English and he entered government service, becoming *sheristadar* (head clerk) to the Collector of Rangpur. He retired at an early age and settled in Calcutta in 1814. From

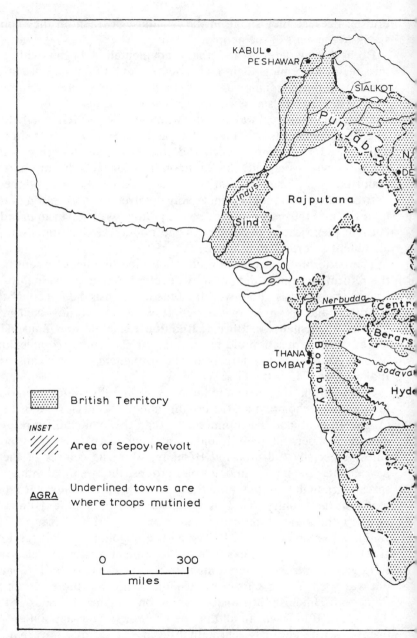

Map 9. The Empire of the Queen, c. 1860. Inset: area of the Sepoy Revolt ('Indian Mutiny') of 1857.

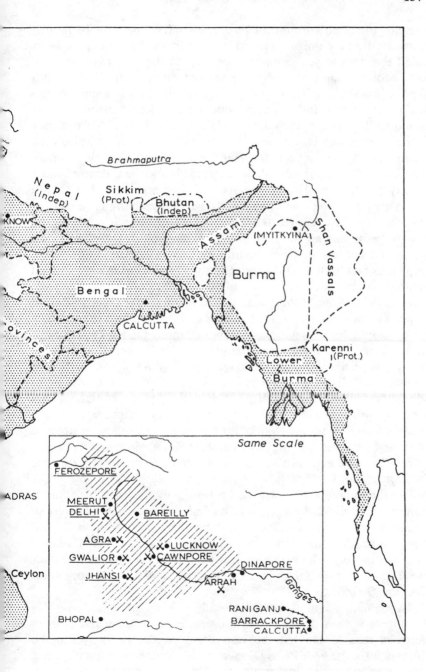

Brahmaputra

Nepal
(Indep)

Sikkim
(Prot)

Bhutan
(Indep)

KNOW

Assam

IMYITKYINA

Shan Vassals

Burma

Bengal

CALCUTTA

rovinces

Karenni
(Prot.)

Lower
Burma

ADRAS

Ceylon

Same Scale

FEROZEPORE

MEERUT
DELHI

BAREILLY

AGRA

GWALIOR

LUCKNOW
CAWNPORE

JHANSI

DINAPORE

ARRAH

Ganges

RANIGANJ

BHOPAL

BARRACKPORE
CALCUTTA

his study of the philosophical *Upanishads* and of the New Testament he evolved a new religious position, and in 1814 he started a body called the *Atmiya Sabha* for the worship of the one invisible God. Ram Mohan found one of his principal disciples in Dwarkanath Tagore (1794–1846). These two played a major part in launching the first great modern independent Indian educational institution: the Hindu College (later, Presidency College). The probable originator of the scheme was David Hare (1775–1842), a Cockney Rationalist watchmaker settled in Calcutta. Hare and Ram Mohan assisted in the founding of the Calcutta Book Society (1817) and the Calcutta School Society (1818). The Hindu College – a high school, rather than a university institution – was financed largely through the generosity of Dwarkanath Tagore and the Raja of Burdwan. Several of the Tagores were among the first pupils. Education in the college was conducted entirely in English, and at first orthodox Hindus were suspicious and hostile. Only about twenty boys were registered, and numbers did not rise to over seventy until 1823.

Meanwhile, Ram Mohan was launching into other enterprises. He began a sustained attack on the abuses of Hinduism, more especially sati and multiple marriage, then common among the Kulin Brahmins. In reply to the Serampore missionaries, he launched in 1819 a newspaper in the Bengali language, *Sambad Kaumudi*, 'Moon of Intelligence.' His religious pilgrimage was taken further in 1828 when he renamed his sect the *Brahma Sabha*, and adopted a congregational form of worship, with hymns, prayers, and scripture readings, modelled on Protestant, Nonconformist lines. His followers abjured caste and accepted monogamy. In 1830, Ram Mohan travelled to England to give evidence before the Committee preparing to revise the Company's Charter (also, paradoxically, he went to plead the case of the Mughal emperor, who bestowed on him the title of Raja). Ram Mohan mingled among the radical and Utilitarian leaders in England, where he remained until he died. His *Brahma Sabha*, though including the influential Tagore family, attracted only a minute following. The orthodox leaders countered by founding their own Bengali newspaper, *Sambad Chandrika*, and their own organisation, the *Dharma Sabha*.

Dwarkanath Tagore – often called Prince Dwarkanath, from his munificent style of living – was more interested in secular than in religious reform. He led the opposition to the Press Act which culminated in the Free Press Dinner of 1835 and the presentation of a petition to Bentinck. He was also the moving force in the foundation of the first medical college and teaching hospital in 1835. He promoted the departure in 1844 of the first four medical students to England to study for the Diploma of the Royal College of Surgeons. He helped to form the Landholders' Society in 1838, the forerunner of the upper class political organisations. While mainly concerned to protect landlord interests, this Society played some part in fostering political consciousness. Like his mentor, Ram Mohan, Dwarkanath visited England in 1842 and again in 1844, when he died at an early age. Dwarkanath's eldest son, Debendranath (1818–1905) inherited none of his father's business acumen and worldly-wise activity. He did follow the religious inquiry of Ram Mohan, and in 1843, he refounded the reformist society as the *Brahmo Samaj*. The Christian elements in doctrine and practice were eliminated. The *Brahmo Samaj*, though never a popular movement, attracted a much wider following among progressive, middle-class Bengali Hindu intellectuals. Almost all the pioneers of the next generation, whether in besieging the British stronghold of the Covenanted Service, or in political agitation, journalism, or the law were, if not Christians, *Brahmo Samajists*. For example, the first successful Indian entrant into the Covenanted Service, and his successors for nearly twenty years; the first Judge of the High Court at Calcutta (Rama Prasad Ray, son of Ram Mahan); and above all Surendranath Banerjea, 'the King of Bengal'.

Development in Bombay was similar though more confined. The role played by Ram Mohan, Dwarkanath, and the *Brahmo Samaj* in Calcutta was largely fulfilled by the Parsi leaders. The Parsi community, which today numbers only 110,000 in India, then comprised only about 30,000 altogether. Yet among them they produced a high proportion – perhaps half – of the pioneers in social reform, politics, commerce, and industry. Dadabhai Naoroji and Pherozeshah Mehta were their political giants; B. M. Malabari dared more than any in social reform; while Jamshetji Tata, India's pioneer industrialist was the greatest of all. While these men were still babies, Western education was being launched in Bombay through the financial backing of the great Parsi merchants Jamshetji Jeejebhoy, Cowasji Jehangir and Framji Cowasji. Together with Elphinstone they established in 1822 the school which later became the Elphinstone Institution. A flourishing press, both in English and in Marathi, developed, while in 1845, the Grant Medical College came into being. As in Calcutta, the 'New Men' were drawn from small, enterprising social groups: the Parsis, and also the Chitpavan

Brahmins from the Western coastal districts. Also, as in Calcutta, the
Brahmins provided the vanguard of reform as well as the rearguard of
orthodoxy. In Bombay and Maharashtriya the Chitpavan Brahmins
were to contribute the first of the reformers and also the stalwarts of
the orthodox.

Throughout India, the only movement to offer even the promise of
popular reform and mass action was that of Protestant Christianity.
The decision of the Serampore missionaries that, following conver-
sion, Indian Christians must renounce caste was revolutionary.
Henceforward, the Brahmin and the Untouchable who became
Christians acknowledged no difference in caste status. The first
Serampore convert was a carpenter: it was no great marvel when his
family broke caste. But when Kayastha converts followed, and then a
Kulin Brahmin who married the carpenter's daughter: this was
revolutionary. By 1830 there were about 27,000 Protestants in India,
Ceylon and British Burma; during the next twenty years, there was a
fourfold increase (1851 = 91,000) while by 1880 there were altogether
nearly half a million Protestant Christians in South Asia. The
long-established Catholic community increased at a slower pace:
from three-quarters of a million in 1851 to well over one million in
1881. The Catholic Church was mainly rooted in south India, where it
formed a recognised separate community. The new Indian Protestant
movement, while drawing many converts from socially inferior
castes, was also attracting some of the leading young intellectuals: for
example, two of the four young medical students who went to
England in 1844. Michael Madhusudan Dutta (1824–73), whom some
consider the greatest Bengali poet of the century, was a Christian
convert. This wave of conversion among the high castes was bitterly
resented, even by those Hindus who called themselves reformers: for
example, the liberal *Brahmo Samaj* leader, Prasana Kumar Tagore,
disinherited his only son when he became a Christian. Hatred of the
Christians intensified because orthodox Hindus suspected (not without some reason in the years before the Mutiny), that the missionaries intended an all-out assault upon caste. In Calcutta, fuel was added
to the flames by the activities of Henry Derozio, a young Eurasian
schoolmaster at the Hindu College, who was in fact a Rationalist, a
disciple of Tom Paine. He started a journal, *The Parthenon*, teaching
that religion was dead. Under his influence, young Brahmins refused
investiture with the sacred threefold thread and partook in beefeating
parties. Dismissed from the college in April, 1831, Derozio soon after
committed suicide, and his coterie disintegrated.

In Bombay, there was some co-operation between Christian and non-Christian reformers. Baba Padmanji, author of *Once Hindu, Now a Christian*, helped to found a secret society, the *Paramahamsa Sabha*, along with Dadoba Pandurang and other Brahmins. The members demonstrated their abjuration of caste by eating bread from a Christian bakery, and worked to abolish caste practices and idol worship, and to permit widow remarriage. This was exceptional. A great agitation took place in 1842–3 over the alleged induced conversion of a Hindu boy in a Bombay missionary school. In South India, the closed ranks of the all-powerful Brahmins held firm against proselytisation: although the degraded condition of the Pariahs and other Untouchables offered an even greater incentive to improve their lot by conversion. The great Tinnevelly riot occurred in December, 1858, when it was proposed to take the corpse of a low-caste Christian convert through the streets of the town. Yet despite all pressure, the sapping of caste by Protestant Christianity led to a beginning of social mobility. In Maharashtriya, Jyotirao Govindrao Phule (1827–90), launched a campaign against Brahmin dominance on behalf of those consigned to low caste status. Although belonging to the humble Mali (gardener) caste he was educated at a Scottish Mission School where he was much impressed by the missionaries' refusal to agree to high caste pressure to exclude untouchables. He organised a programme of social reform, including female education and the uplift of the untouchables. He encouraged the non-Brahmins to conduct religious ceremonies, even weddings, with their own 'priests', excluding the Brahmins. He wrote many tracts, dramas, and other works, and even rewrote history to show that the Brahmins had stolen the birthright of the Marathas (meaning all the other communities of his religion). They had tricked the Marathas into admitting them to the dominant place in a previously equal society.

Phule's efforts to 'reconstruct' history to overcome Brahmin supremacy had a parallel in South India. There, too, the original impulse came from Christian missionaries by whose scholarship the antiquity of the Tamil language, and its independence from Sanskrit was first established. Their thesis was taken over by the Vellalas, the agricultural castes. They also evolved a view of history whereby a casteless Tamil nation was deceived into accepting Brahmin rules of hierarchy. But whereas Phule had tried to evolve a broad Maratha movement including all non-Brahmins the Vellala intelligentsia were not interested in a mass response. In South India, the non-Brahmin movement was an elitist, urban phenomenon.

The reforming impulse had little effect among Muslims. Delhi College was endowed (in 1825) by Nawab Itmut-Dowlah, but in general the community clung to traditional Arabic and Persian education, even after the Courts and the higher administration changed over to the English language. The consequences of this conservatism were not at first apparent: Muslims still retained their privileged position in government service. But in the provinces, where recruitment was by examination, they began to lose ground. For example, in Bengal in 1838, eight of the Principal Sadr Amins (the highest grade of Indian judge) were Muslims: only one was a Hindu. But of those gaining the diploma of Munsif, giving entry to the higher legal profession, out of seventy successful candidates in 1841, only three were Muslims: the consequences of this substitution process were not fully apparent until after 1857.

While the Muslim elite appeared indifferent to their supersession, there was a certain strengthening of the faith among the masses. The puritan Wahabi movement, originating in Arabia (Muhammad ibn-Abd al-Wahhab, 1703–92), spread across the Islamic world, to wean the faithful away from the worship of saints and veneration of tombs back to the One God. Under the influence of Sayyid Ahmad Shahid missionaries toured the Gangetic plains, to recruit soldiers to fight the Infidel. Much of their effort was concentrated against the Sikh kingdom in the Punjab, but a minor consequence of Wahabi activities was the revolt of Titu Miyan in Lower Bengal, 1831–2. More generally, the movement served to turn the Muslims of the countryside away from the participation in Hindu ceremonies and worship and to begin to adopt a more explicitly Islamic outlook.

In Ceylon, the principal agency of intellectual change was the spread of Protestant missionary influence. Under the Dutch, education had been mainly through a medium of vernacular languages. The British and American missionaries who founded schools after 1812 emphasised English education. By 1835 there were 235 Protestant schools, 90 government-controlled schools, and about a hundred Catholic schools. Most of these were situated in the maritime provinces. By government instruction, the American missionaries were required to concentrate their activities in the north, in Jaffna district. Because these Americans were especially pressing with educational work, Western education made great strides among the Jaffna Tamils; and so, almost by chance, this community began to move ahead of the others in educational opportunity. The first

Ceylonese to seek higher education in England were a full thirty years ahead of the Indian pioneers of 1844. When the second Governor, Maitland, returned to Britain in 1811, he was accompanied by two sons of a Ceylonese hereditary official, Mudaliyar de Saram. The two lads studied at Trinity Hall, Cambridge. The English-educated elite, of whom they were the prototypes, were even more assimilated to English ways than the upper class Anglicised elite of the metropolitan cities of India.

The social and educational changes which took place in the outlying provinces of British Burma were insignificant, during the first quarter-century of British rule. By an administrative freak, Persian remained the language of the Courts in Arakan until 1845; totally alien to both rulers and ruled! Such intellectual development as there was flowed from the American Baptist Mission, at Moulmein, with its schools, its printing press, and its linguistic labours. Adoniram Judson and the other pioneers desired to work among the Burmese, but because of the strength of the hostility shown by the Burmese rulers, they turned instead to the backward hill peoples; especially the Karens. Once again, an almost chance development presaged immense historical consequences.

By mid-century the impact of British rule and Western institutions in South Asia was such as to have alarmed and upset the old order without having generated enough dynamism so as to have brought to the front new, forward-looking elements. A relatively small-scale reaction to the British innovations came first in Ceylon, with the Kandyan Revolt of 1848. The former Kandyan kingdom, economically poor and backward, was beginning to feel the pressure coming from new roads and the new coffee plantations, with their imported labour. The rebels were drawn from the ordinary Kandyan country-folk, encouraged (though hardly led) by the old Kandyan nobility. Two kings proclaimed that the old days were back again: one in Matale, one in Kurunegala – a descendant of Raja Sinha. The rebels were joined by robbers and marauders from the maritime provinces. The revolt was over within two weeks, though parliamentary inquiries into the means used in its repression went on for two years.

The great Indian Sepoy Revolt of 1857, was, of course, infinitely wider in its scope. The mutiny of 100,000 trained soldiers, provided with almost all the military *matériel* of a modern army, produced such a foundation for struggle as was not seen again until the Russian army mutinies of 1917. The general character of the revolt was similar to that in Kandy. The leaders were all feudal aristocrats, hoping to recapture the glories which had departed with British rule. The followers were (besides the sepoys) a few country folk, a number of religious leaders, and an assortment of ruffians and professional bad characters. Although the British took nearly two years to quench the revolt, the rebels never held the initiative after the first few days of the outbreak. What was most surprising was the volume of support which came to the British, as soon as they demonstrated that they had the will to overcome. Support came chiefly from the tough warriors of the Punjab (many of whom had only just been disarmed by the British in the wars against the Sikhs, 1845–9) and from the Prime Minister of Nepal, Bahadur Jang, whose people, the Gurkhas, had fought a war of independence against the British but forty years before. Perhaps it was because the British were able to defeat the rebels – representing the forces of tradition – by calling upon other forces of tradition, that British policy after 1857 was aligned in support of the status quo. The initiative in social reform (previously a partnership between progressive British administrators and progressive Indian thinkers) was now left almost entirely in Indian hands.

The new universities were the forcing house of reform. For example, the very first graduates of the University of Bombay included M. G. Ranade (1842–1901) judge and social reformer, B. G. Bhandarkar (1837–1925) historian and social reformer, and Pherozeshah Mehta (1845–1915) local government reformer and Congress pioneer. Speaking in 1867, the young Mehta drew attention to 'the strong Anglicising under-current which has begun through the deeper instincts of Indian students'. Not scornfully, but proudly he predicted: 'There will ere long be produced in India a body of men out-Heroding Herod, more English than the English themselves.' In this development, Bengal outpaced the remainder of India: in the year 1860, there were 40,366 students in the schools of Bengal receiving English-language education, compared to 6,552 in Madras Presidency and 2,984 in Bombay. The universities told the same story: numbers soared, with Bengal maintaining the lead. The numbers who graduated in 1864 in Bengal, Madras and Bombay respectively were 28, 11, and 8. For the year 1885, the totals of graduates were 264, 163, and 72. Of these graduates, the overwhelming proportion were Hindus: in 1885, the all-India total was made up of 473 Hindus, 21 Christians, and only 17 Muslims. Although the best of the new breed – the university graduates – were the pioneers of a new age, the system produced an enormous proportion of failures. Because the Indian universities were examining bodies only, the students worked in hundreds of colleges, public and private, good and bad. Only a small proportion of those who matriculated (entered college) actually obtained degrees: perhaps one-quarter of the total. One reason was the method of instruction. Writing in the 1870s, a distinguished Indian professor, Lal Behari De, observed: 'The students of the present day never open their mouths in the class room. . . . They take down the professor's words, commit them to memory – often without understanding them – and reproduce them in the examination hall. A copying machine would do the same.' This mechanical, memorising pattern took permanent hold of Indian university education. It enabled large numbers of students to be entered: but it led to a wastage of young lives, frustration and failure, which forms the continuing background to Indian higher education.

The liberal, social reform movement was largely nourished from the finest of the graduates of the universities, many of the reformers being university professors. Whereas the first organised pressure groups – the British Indian Association (1851) and its successors – represented the landed upper-class in composition and outlook, the reformers were professional, middle-class in outlook. Almost symptomatic of this shift in emphasis was the change-over in the *Brahmo Samaj* in the 1860s. The leadership of the aristocratic Debendranath Tagore, *Maharshi*, 'the Sage', was challenged by the parvenu Keshab Chandra Sen (1838–84). Keshab Chandra was much more in sympathy with Western, Christian ideas than the *Maharshi*. He borrowed many of the techniques of Evangelists like Moody and Sankey. Visiting Madras in 1864, he founded a counterpart of the *Brahmo Samaj* – the *Veda Samaj*. Three years later, his work in Bombay brought forth the *Prarthana* (Prayer) *Samaj*. To the original fourteen *Brahmo* churches were added seventy-two new churches. A visit to England in 1870 seemed likely to herald the entry of Keshab and his followers into Christianity, but they followed their own course. Keshab secured the passing of the Brahmo Marriage Act in 1872; the first measure to bring Hindu marriage within the cognisance of the law. This ratified monogamy, and laid down a minimum age of fourteen for *Brahmo* brides. Subsequently, Keshab's failure to live up to his own precepts in this respect led to a schism in the movement. But the impetus to reform had been supplied.

Keshab Chandra Sen insisted that he was not interested in 'half measures, like the education of this section of the community or the reformation of that social evil'. He went on: 'If you wish to regenerate this country, make religion the basis of all your reform movements.' His creed, *Nabibidhan Samaj*, the New Dispensation, the Religion of Harmony, had as its ultimate aim 'to harmonise the East and West, Asia and Europe, antiquity and modern thought'. Theosophy, 'The Divine Wisdom', was a similar attempt at synthesis. The Theosophical Society was founded in New York in November, 1875, by Madame Blavatsky and Colonel Olcott. Early doctrine drew mainly upon ancient Egypt, but increasingly Theosophy was influenced by Hinduism and Tantric Buddhism. In 1882, the headquarters of the movement was transferred to Adyyar near Madras, and for a brief while Madame Blavatsky lived in India. Speaking at Banaras she said: 'If the modern Hindus were less sycophantic to their Western masters, less in love with their vices, and more like their ancestors', they would acquire mastery, through occult power. Colonel Olcott particularly interested himself in Ceylonese Buddhism. He wrote a *Buddhist Catechism* (1882) to illumine the ignorance of the day in Ceylon, and to combat the work of Christian missionaries. The *Catechism* was a best-seller. The militant Buddhist movement in Ceylon began early in the 1870s; the scholar Sri Sumangala Thera was its foremost figure. A certain reformation was felt among the monks, the *Sangha*, and an emphasis upon *ayurvedic* medicine and the indigenous tradition provided a counterforce to the predominant Anglicisation of the intelligentsia of Ceylon.

The relations between Indian Islam and the West moved in an opposite direction during this period. The Wahabi militants were virtually destroyed in the 1860s, when the Wahabi leaders were brought to trial at Ambala (1864–5) and Patna (1868–71). Islamic resistance to alien rule seemed to have come to a dead end, but a new initiative was created, largely by the activity of one man, Sayyid Ahmad Khan (1817–98).

The Sayyid came from a Delhi court family, and in 1837 entered the service of the East India Company as a clerk. During the Mutiny he firmly supported the British cause, and was deeply impressed by the resilience of British power during those dreadful days. He rose in the service, and retired as a Sub-Judge in 1876. Meanwhile, he had begun to take up the cause of Muslim education and rehabilitation. He founded a Translation Society in 1864, which enabled Muslims to gain knowledge of Western works, such as Mill's *Political Economy*. He did much to break down prejudice against Islam among Christians. He emphasised the progressive aspects of Islam: for example, he laid stress on monogamy, and he welcomed the new advances of science, accepting evolution as a concept natural to Muslims. He asserted the supremacy of Islam as the one great monotheistic religion, expressing God's will uniquely revealed through the Quran. His Translation Society proved the nucleus for an Anglo-Oriental College at Aligarh (established 1875) where an education of a Western type could be obtained in an Islamic environment. Despite the united opposition of the *Ulama*, Sir Sayyid succeeded in interesting the Muslim princes and great landlords in his enterprise. He also attracted outstanding English educators to work in the College. Writing in 1872, Sir Sayyid observed of 'the two races', Muslims and Hindus: 'It cannot be expected that Mohammedans who are made of much sterner material than the Hindus will adapt themselves so readily to this changing age. Let us have time, let us live, work and wait.' Time: for Muslims to adjust their Perso-Arabic culture to the challenge of the new era of Western education: and meanwhile, Sir Sayyid relied upon the Pax Britannica to hold the balance steady between the 'two races'.

Thus far in the confrontation between East and West, the East had been concerned to hold its own in the face of the superior challenge of Western science and technology. But the acceptance of Western superiority received its first great challenge on the spiritual plane: where Asia had always claimed a higher development than materialistic Europe.

The first movement proclaiming reform – indeed revolution – yet as anti-Western, as ardently Asian, as any of the orthodox movements, was the *Arya Samaj*, or 'Society of the Aryan People'. Its founder, Dayananda Saraswati (1824–83), spent his early middle years as a wandering *sannyassi* in the old tradition of Hindu asceticism. Eventually, he found inspiration through the Vedas, the oldest of all the proto-Hindu texts (*c.* 1500–1000 BC). His spiritual autobiography, *Satyarth Prakash* ('Light of Truth'), was written in Hindi, though Dayananda was himself a Gujarati speaker. He preached a creed which included many of the tenets of the *Brahmos* and other reformers: idols were condemned, priests denounced, widow remarriage was commended, and people of other religions were admitted into the fold of the Aryan faith. Equally important, Dayananda followed the mediating social reformers, as well as other nineteenth-century pressure groups, in setting up a systematic organisation. In place of the old Hindu tradition of the *Guru*, the sage, and his disciples – a personal relationship, even when passed on from one generation to another – Dayananda introduced the concept of structural organisation. The *Arya Samaj*, founded in 1875, had its branches, its regular meetings, its congregational services.

To Madame Blavatsky, Dayananda wrote: 'As night and day are opposed to each other, so are all religions opposed to one another.' In saying this, he was claiming a supreme role for the purified Hinduism of the Vedas. Yet his attitude (and that of his followers, e.g. Lala Lajpat Rai) was dualistic. While challenging Christianity and Islam, he often appeared more in accord with fellow-reformers and believers of other faiths than with secular, debased co-religionists. It appears that he contemplated a unified reform movement, and with that in mind he met leaders, including Keshab Chandra Sen and Sayyid Ahmad Khan in 1877: nothing came of this, because Dayananda insisted that all must accept the authority of the Vedas as the basis of common action. This phenomenon – a desire for harmony, for a common cause, and the insistence that all non-Hindu co-operation must include an acceptance of the Hindu matrix – was to characterise the national movement in India during the years ahead.

Organisation was the hall-mark of the religious revivalist movements; now organisation was about to enter the political field. The new professional men began to find expression in literary and debating societies, such as the Elocution Encouragement Society, founded in 1867 on the Bombay side, or the Triplicane Literary Society of Madras, established in 1874. An active press was emerging as their mouthpiece: the *Amrita Bazaar Patrika* was launched in 1868 by the Ghose brothers, and the *Hindu* of Madras appeared in 1878. Because the Vernacular Press Act bore heavily upon newspapers in the Indian languages, most of these new progressive journals used the medium of English.

The viceroyalty of Lord Ripon witnessed Liberal policies challenged, and to some extent modified, by the reactionary element in the European community in India, organised to express an arrogance that claimed to be above the law. Such a demonstration might have led to a contrary wave of reaction among Indians. The political spirit which did emerge at this hour was moderate, non-racial, liberal. The initiative was taken by A. O. Hume (1829–1912) a retired civilian who had seen the excesses of the Sepoy Revolt as District Magistrate of Etawah: had seen, but had not succumbed to, the hysteria of the hour. Through his long years of service (he retired in 1882) the events of 1857 remained present in his mind. In retirement, he lived at Simla, and interested himself in, among other things, comparative religion: including the Theosophy of Madame Blavatsky. His religious inquiries brought him into contact with *rishis*, holy men, who warned him that India was in extreme danger of an uprising, another Mutiny. Kristo Das Pal, editor of the *Hindu Patriot*, confirmed that at this time the danger of revolution was 'very great'. Hume searched for a constitutional outlet for this anticipated wave of unrest, and decided to issue an appeal and a challenge to the graduates of Calcutta University to give a lead to their country. There were several possible vehicles for the new, professional, middle-class leadership to utilise: especially the Indian Association (1876) and the National Conference and National Fund Campaign. Largely due to the initiative of Surendranath Banerjea (1848–1925), Hume's appeal was given shape in the Indian National Congress, which first met in 1885. The inspired name of the 'Congress' had a European rather than an American connotation: it was intended as a gathering promoted for specific purposes. Nevertheless, it attracted to itself the alternative symbolism of a national assembly, a parliament. The intention of Hume and others among the founding fathers was to make the Congress a platform for social as well as political feeling. This aspect was discarded, because of the overall need to create a feeling of unity: and social questions would immediately divide opinion, even among progressives. The main emphasis was upon the creation of a sense of all-India patriotism. Addressing the second Congress in 1886, Dr Rajendralal Mitter observed: 'For long our fathers lived and we have lived as individuals only or as families, but henceforward I hope that we shall be living as a nation, united one and all to promote our welfare and the welfare of our mother-country.' The second constant theme of congress speeches was that of loyalty to Britain and the British Crown. Again, at the second Congress, Dadabhai Naoroji as President asked rhetorically: 'Is this Congress a nursery for sedition and rebellion against the British government [cries of "No", "No"] or is it another stone in the foundation of the stability of that government? [cries of "Yes", "Yes"].' This feeling was eloquently stated by Pherozeshah Mehta in a speech on the controversial Ilbert Bill (1883): 'If I entertain one political conviction more strongly than any other, it is that this country in falling under British rule has fallen into the hands of a nation than which no other is better qualified to govern her wisely and well.' This view of India's link with Britain as guided by Divine Providence was reiterated by Congress leaders for twenty years on end. Somewhat ungraciously, many British observers dismissed these utterances as lip-service, and suspected the Congress of working to undermine British rule. But there was no subterfuge: Mehta, Naoroji, Banerjea, and their followers were as much men of principle as the British Victorian Liberals they admired and so closely resembled.

The appeal of the Congress was effective in absorbing (to a considerable degree) the separate Bengali, Marathi and Madrassi movements with their appeal to that linguistic and regional 'nationalism' which was later to be known by the unattractive label of 'linguism'. The Congress was much less successful in attracting the Muslim community. Those few Muslims who played a prominent part in the Congress were mainly members of the cosmopolitan trading communities of western India, who were not conscious of being at any disadvantage in relation to the modernising Hindus. For example, Badruddin Tyabji, the President of the third Congress, was a member of an enterprising Bombay clan: his son was the first Muslim to be successful in the examinations for the Indian Civil Service (1885). The prevailing view was voiced by Sir Sayyid Ahmad Khan. He continued to insist that Muslims should not dabble in political associations: more, he argued that English-style representative institutions could not be translated into India, where elections would be contested not on a basis of personalities or parties but purely on community or 'communal' lines. His observations on the 'Present State of Indian Politics' were printed in the *Pioneer* newspaper in 1888. He developed his 'two nations' theory in the following somewhat cloudy imagery: 'I have often said that India is like a bride whose two eyes are the Hindu and the Mohammedan. Her beauty consists in this – that the two eyes be of equal lustre.' It might be possible to interpret the 'two eyes' parable as an acceptance of the integral role of the Muslims within an India where the communities enjoyed parity of esteem. But what of the next passage, which closely followed? 'Suppose that all the English . . . were to leave India. . . ? Is it possible that under these circumstances two nations – the Mohammedans and the Hindus – could sit on the same throne and remain equal in power? Most certainly not. It is necessary that one of them should conquer the other and thrust it down. . . . Probably they [the Muslims] would be by themselves enough to maintain their own position. But suppose they were not. Then our Muslim brothers, the Pathans, would come out as a swarm of locusts from their mountain villages and make rivers of blood to flow from their frontier on the north to the extreme end of Bengal.' Sir Sayyid was speaking to an audience, among whom would be men who remembered the Muslim court of the Nawabs of Oudh at Lucknow – which had lasted until 1856 – or the even grander court of the emperors at Delhi, whose faded pomp was brutally stamped out in 1857. The Muslims of the north had a long tradition of being the ruling race. They were not prepared to become the understrappers to the new Congress politicians. Sir Sayyid's active supporters were all Muslims of the traditional official class; they enjoyed the patronage of the Muslim aristocracy and the princes; but it was they who worked to create organisations. The farthest Sir Sayyid would go towards recognising the new situation of political organisation and agitation was to create a Muhammadan Educational Congress in December 1886 (the term 'Conference' was substituted for the suspect 'Congress' in 1890). In putting forward the Muslim point of view, Sir Sayyid was considerably influenced by British collaborators; especially Theodore Beck of the Aligarh College, and Colonel G. F. I. Graham, his biographer.

Besides lack of success in attracting the Muslim reformers to its ranks, the Congress was unable to maintain the first intention of providing a recognised forum, a 'native parliament' for India. The highpoint of the year was the annual Congress. This was held in the great cities in rotation and always took place in an enormous tent, called a *pandal*. Attendance in 1885 numbered only 72; numbers rose at the second, Calcutta, Congress to 440 (more than half from Bengal), and attendance at the fourth Congress was 1,248; thereafter, numbers declined. The proceedings were elaborately stage-managed by a Reception Committee. The President for the year made the keynote speech and a fervent declaration of loyalty was always carried with acclamation. A series of resolutions were passed, containing proposals for a fuller share for Indians in the higher civil services, and the amelioration of grievances which troubled the upper and middle classes. The annual Congress always took place around Christmas and New Year, when the Courts were closed and the lawyers were free. Years before, in 1876, S. N. Banerjea had said: 'We have a very useful institution among us, the Hindu *Mela*. Now why not make it an Indian *Mela*?' This exactly describes the character of the annual Congresses. They incorporated the ritual, cyclical character of the *Mela*, the Hindu festival; and something of its secondary function as a social excursion: rather like an American convention. For the rest of the year, the Congress was virtually dormant. From 1885 to 1899, there was no formal constitution. Continuity was provided by a small, closed group, among whom A. O. Hume had acknowledged primacy. From 1885 to 1906 he was General Secretary of the Congress and virtually its only full-time official. William Wedderburn (1838–1918) another retired civilian, was the main ambassador for the Congress in England. He formed a British committee in July, 1889. After unsuccessful efforts, he entered Parliament in 1893 as a Liberal, serving till 1900. Other members of the inner group were Banerjea, Mehta, Naoroji, Tyabji, and W. C. Bonnerji (1844–1906), a pioneer among Indian barristers and a Christian. The zeal and energy of this group were outstanding; but these men who were pioneers and progressives in the 1870s or 1880s were very moderate moderates by the 1900s. A great deal of attention was paid to propaganda in England. A journal, *India*, was published at an annual cost of £1,500. Altogether, the English branch cost as much as the annual Congress in India. Funds were partly provided by enlightened Indian princes, such as Baroda, Dharbanga and Vizianagram. Naoroji, Bonnerji, and other Indian Congress leaders toured England, giving speeches and lectures. When the brief Liberal interregnum (1892–5) was followed by the long Conservative hegemony (1895–1905) enthusiasm flagged and the British committee ceased to function as an effective pressure group. In India also, as the years passed and the Congress resolutions were brushed aside by the government of India, there was a sense of disillusionment.

Faced with the challenge of social reform, the Congress leaders were divided. The test came over the controversy about the marriage of girls before the age of puberty. The attack was led by the Parsi editor of the *Indian Spectator*, Behramji Malabari (1853–1912), with his 'Notes of Infant Marriage and Enforced Widowhood' (1884). He believed that this issue – the need to fix a minimum age for marriage by law – would unite members of the Congress from all parts of India. He found little support in any quarter, including the British official hierarchy. The main reaction was one of antagonism, and the main opponent was Bal Ganghadar Tilak (1856–1920), editor of the Marathi-language journal *Kesari* ('Lion'), a Chitpavan Brahmin like Ranade. Some regard Tilak as a reformer, some as a revolutionary, and some as a defender of orthodoxy. In the age of consent controversy he opposed legislation on the grounds that this would open the door to increased government interference in the social structure of Hinduism. At the third National Social Conference, created as an adjunct to the Congress, in 1889, Ranade moved that 'cohabitation before the wife is twelve years old should be punishable as a criminal offence': the Conference passed the resolution, despite Tilak's opposition. Yet the following year, alarmed by the feeling against the proposed Age of Consent Bill, especially in Bengal, Ranade withdrew any direct reference to the Bill from the Conference agenda. This took place against the background of the case of Phulmani Bai, aged ten years, whose death was caused by forcible intercourse with her husband, aged thirty-five: a judge ruled that the law of rape was inapplicable. After strenuous opposition from orthodox Hindu members of the legislature, the Bill became law in March, 1891. But the controversy was not finished: the conservatives threatened to retaliate against the reformers by boycotting the Congress and forming a separate 'Peoples' Congress'. An open split was averted, but a wedge had been driven between the liberal moderates and the Hindu zealots.

Another challenge to the reformers came in 1895. It was the practice to hold the National Social Conference immediately after the Congress in the same *pandal*. That year, the meetings were held at Poona, Tilak's stronghold. He campaigned against allowing the Conference to use the *pandal*, demanding: 'Whose is the Congress? Of the people of the Classes or of the Masses?' In this tussle Gopal Krishna Gokhale (1866–1915) was advanced by the ruling group as the counterweight to Tilak: Gokhale was also a Poona Brahmin, a university professor and a disciple of Ranade. Reason did not triumph over unreason: the reformers decided to make separate arrangements for their proceedings elsewhere in Poona.

Tilak discarded the mild, debating society techniques of the moderates for mass methods. He appealed to traditional Maharashtrian loyalties: he revived the Ganapati festivals, dedicated to the Hindu elephant-god, Ganesh, and he promoted festivals in honour of Sivaji, the Maratha hero in the resistance against the Mughals. In reply, Gokhale and Ranade founded a society, the Deccan Sabha, to give expression to Liberalism and Moderation; its manifesto declared: 'The spirit of Liberalism implies a freedom from race and creed prejudices, and a steady devotion to all that seeks to do justice between man and man, giving to the rulers the loyalty that is due to the law they are bound to administer, but securing at the same time to the ruled the equality which is their right under law.' In the contest for the mind of India, the moderate Congress leaders had to contend with religious prejudice and reaction, on one hand, and with an intensely narrow, nationalistic revolutionary spirit on the other: an impossible task for these men of reason and of law, it might be supposed. But they had certain factors on their side, not least patience, and a sense of the importance of systematic organisation and negotiation.

The first initiative went to Tilak and his politics of emotion.

Opportunity came when Poona was smitten by plague in 1897. Tilak aroused religious prejudice against inoculation and other preventative measures. He organised a celebration of the coronation of Sivaji, and gave a lecture on 'The Killing of Afzal Khan' in which the Maratha was extolled for his carefully planned assassination of a Mughal general, Afzal Khan. A few days later, two brothers shot and killed Rand, the District Magistrate, and Lieutenant Ayerst, who happened to be following him. The brothers Chapekar were young associates of Tilak, and he was brought to trial for 'exciting feelings of disaffection'. Tilak was sentenced to eighteen months' imprisonment.

This was not the first sentence passed on an Indian politician: Banerjea had been sentenced to two months' imprisonment in 1883 for contempt of court. The effect was to make the prisoner a public hero. Tilak continued to emphasise the legacy of the Vedas, like Dayananda before him, and to characterise the Muslims along with the British as *mleccha*: a term which means foreigner, one outside of caste, and therefore one ritually unclean. In northern India, the divisions between Hindus and Muslims were increased by the language controversy which came to a head in 1900 over the substitution of the Urdu, Arabic script by the Deva-Nagari script. But the great explosion of feeling – the challenge to the Congress constitutionalists, the outburst against the autocratic government of India, and the rift between Muslims and Hindus – all this came to the boil in Bengal.

Most advanced in English education, the Bengalis had supplied officials and educators to the North Western Provinces (UP), the Central Provinces and Assam. Bengal, while retaining its own intense sense of Bengali culture, had taken the lead in creating a sense of Indian nationalism. While Tilak barely looked further than Maharashtriya, Bengali thinkers were concerned with India and the World. Bankimcandra Chatterjee (1838–94) was one of the first two graduates of Calcutta University. Between 1865 and 1887 he published fourteen novels, mostly in Bengali, which he developed in literary form. A firm supporter of British rule, he was equally an ardent patriot. He invoked theology, showing that Krishna was superior to Christ; an active force, contrasted with a passive. His best known novel, *Anandamath*, reveals how, in the course of history, British rule provides a foundation for a new Hindu national renaissance. The novel includes the hymn to the motherland, *Bande-Mataram*; which may be understood as an invocation to Mother Bengal or Mother India:

Mother, hail! . . .
Though seventy million voices through thy mouth sonorous
    shout,
Though twice seventy million hands hold trenchant sword-blades
    out,
Yet with all this power now,
Mother, wherefore powerless thou?

The spiritual influence of Bengal was given to an India-wide audience by the mystic Ramakrishna (1836–86) and his great disciple Viveka-nanda (1863–1902). Vivekananda contributed two important ele-ments to the *Vedanta* school: he extended the radius of Indian thought when he dominated the Parliament of Religions at Chicago in 1893, and he institutionalised a philosophy of spiritual liberation through social service by founding the Ramakrishna Mission in 1897. Vivekananda taught: 'The Greek sought political liberty. The Hindu has always sought spiritual liberty'. 'We must conquer the world through our spirituality and philosophy. We must do it or die. The only condition of Indian national life, of unashamed and vigorous national life, is the conquest of the world by Indian thought.' Vivekananda declared: 'I do not believe in politics. God and Truth are the only policy in the world.' This led him to insist upon the dependence of an ideal society upon individual responsibility and voluntary action: 'Every attempt at control which is not voluntary, not with the controller's own mind, is not only disastrous, but it defeats the end.'

Vivekananda's spiritual anarchism (if so we may call it) was a major influence in the growth of the thinking of Sri Aurobindo who rebelled against 'the huge mechanism of the modern state' and inspired the political anarchism of young Bengal. The cross-currents of politics and religion were plunged into a cataract of mass feeling by the partition of Bengal in 1905. The Bengal Presidency – like most of the provinces of British India – took shape by the accidents of conquest and accession. By 1900, its population had grown to 78 millions; larger than that of the USA. Included within its boundaries were vast non-Bengali speaking areas: Bihar, whose speech is a form of Hindi, Orissa of the Oriyas, as well as the hill areas of the aboriginals. Many proposals for administrative redistribution had been made during the nineteenth century. Under Curzon, the arch-priest of the cult of efficiency, the subject was reviewed again.[1] It was decided to separate the eastern districts of Bengal, uniting them with Assam to form an entirely new province. It was possible to argue that difficulties of communication between East and West Bengal, and the predominance of Calcutta at the expense of Dacca, made the change desirable. But British officials made no attempt to conceal that an important consequence of the change was to give the Muslims of Bengal a province where they would be dominant: in many ways, the scheme was a forerunner of the concept of Pakistan.

N. C. Chaudhuri, author of *The autobiography of an unknown Indian*, himself a Bengali, has written: 'It was not the liberal political thought of the organisers of the Indian National Congress, but the Hindu revivalism of the last quarter of the nineteenth century – a movement which previously had been almost wholly confined to the field of religion – which was the driving force behind the anti-partition agitation of 1905 and subsequent years.' Thus, the day on which partition took effect (16 October 1905) was observed as a day of mourning. A large part of the population of Calcutta fasted and went bare-foot. Shops were shut. A ceremony called *rakhibandan* was observed: yellow threads were bound round the arms of the demonstrators as a symbol of brotherhood. The next phase was to urge the people to buy Indian-made, *Swadeshi*, goods. Foreign (especially British) goods were boycotted; the ban being enforced with violence. The Muslims who (apart from a few Calcutta intellectuals) were indifferent to the anti-partition movement frequently suffered ill-treatment, and reprisals followed. Rioting was promoted by the anti-partitionists when the Nawab of Dacca, the leading Muslim landowner, visited Comilla. Then in Mymensingh District in 1907 a Muslim mob desecrated the image of the goddess Durga during the popular festival Vasanti Puja. An assembly of Muslim aristocrats and notables, meeting at Dacca on 30 December 1906, decided to set up a political organisation to represent and protect the interests of their community: this was named the All-India Muslim League.

Although Bengal saw its birth, and the great landlords of East

---

[1] It is often suggested that Curzon invented the partition as a deliberate attempt at *Divide et Impera*. There is ample evidence that the proposal was not originated by him: witness his very Curzonian comment, penned when the matter was put before him: 'Round and round like the diurnal revolution of the earth went the file, stately, solemn, sure, and slow; and now in due season it has completed its orbit and I am invited to register the concluding stage.'

Bengal were among its leading members, the prime impetus came from the Aligarh school and the Delhi-Lucknow Mughal official tradition which they represented. The heritage of Sir Sayyid Ahmad had fallen largely upon Mehdi Ali Khan: or Mohsin-ul-Mulk, as he was invariably known. Mehdi Ali Khan (1837-1907), who came from the United Provinces (the provinces were thus named in 1902), entered the East India Company's service and rose to be a Deputy Collector, in 1867. He then entered the service of the Nizam of Hyderabad, who bestowed upon him the titles of Nawab and Mohsin-ul-Mulk ('Supporter of the State'). He was Honorary Secretary of Aligarh College from 1899 to 1907. In August 1906, he wrote to the Principal of the College (W. A. J. Archbold): 'Although there is little reason to believe that any Mohammedans, except the young educated ones, will join that body [the Congress] there is still a general complaint that we [Aligarh people] take no part in politics and do not safeguard the political rights of Mohammedans.' Mohsin-ul-Mulk went on to propose that a memorial be submitted to the Viceroy 'to draw the attention of Government to a consideration of the rights of Mohammedans.'

A deputation of Muslim notables, headed by the Aga Khan did wait upon the Viceroy, and secured a sympathetic response. One of the Viceroy's intentions was to rally moderate opinion, and to reassure the Muslims that the government would not capitulate to the pressure of the 'Extremists', as they were called. However, this propitiation of the Muslim separatists only added further difficulties to the task of the Congress Moderates, those who were working to create an all-India, secular form of politics. These men were aware that initiative had slipped out of their hands. Hume wrote sadly in 1903: 'Years ago I called on you to be up and doing; years ago I warned you that "Nations by themselves are made".... Can you suppose that a race is to be won by merely looking at the course and talking brilliantly about it?'

It seemed that the day of the Moderates was over when even their patron rebuked them and slighted them: the Extremists sought an opportunity to deliver a knock-out blow to Mehta and the other men who had managed the Congress for so long. The return of the Liberals to power in Britain, after more than a decade in the wilderness, gave the Moderates grounds for hope: but these were disappointed by the announcement of John Morley, the new Secretary of State, that the partition of Bengal would not be annulled. One of the Moderates, Banerjea, wavered, and seemed ready to throw in his lot with the men of physical force. Fuller, the Lieutenant-Governor of East Bengal and Assam, forbade the chanting of *Bande-Mataram* in public. In April 1906, Banerjea led a protest demonstration at Barisal when the forbidden cry was raised in defiance, and Banerjea was arrested.

The annual Congress at Calcutta in December, 1906, was a trial of strength. The Moderates had arranged that the veteran Dadabhai Naoroji would be President, and his great prestige was enough to deflect the probes of those who would transform the organisation. However, circumstances led Naoroji to come out with a clear demand for self-government or *Swaraj*. Perhaps self-government had always been implicit in the thinking of the Moderates; long before, Bankim-candra had declared: 'By reading English, Bengalis have learned two new words, Liberty and Independence'; but now self-government was announced as the explicit goal.

The Extremists laid their plans for the following year: the Congress would be held at Nagpur, a Maratha city, and the presidency would be given to Lala Lajpat Rai (1865–1928), an *Arya Samaj* leader from the Punjab, an exponent of militant Hindu nationalism. The Moderates succeeded in getting the meeting-place changed to Surat, where Pherozeshah Mehta's influence was strong. When the 1,600 delegates met on 27 December 1907, the name of Dr Rash Behari Ghose, an eminent Moderate, was proposed for President. Immediately, pandemonium began. While speakers tried to make themselves heard above the din, a shoe was hurled through the air, hitting both Banerjea and Mehta. Nothing more shameful than shoe-beating can be imagined in India, and the police were called in to clear the *pandal*. The Congress was over. Was this the end?

Men of peace and men of violence were turning away from the political organisation as a public meeting. Gokhale endeavoured to find his goal of an all-India patriotism through the Servants of India Society (founded 1905) open to men of all creeds, and including among its goals the education and uplift of women and the depressed classes. In future years, the greatest of the Servants of India was to be Gandhi.

Violence, also, sought expression through individual action. A philosophy of anarchism was provided by Arabina Ghose (1872–1950), Sri Aurobindo. His writings, such as *New Lamps for Old*, emphasised the role of the individual in society. Later he was to renounce politics, but he followed a course somewhat akin to that of Bakunin, the anarchist. The young men who, in the 1900s, turned to violence have been condemned as terrorists: a more just estimate would be to call them revolutionaries. They came mostly from Bengal, though Maharashtriya had its quota. Most were Hindus: but religion had little or no place in their philosophy. Many carried on their activities in London, New York or Paris; they were exiles; some voluntary, some involuntary. The leader of India House in London was Shyamaji Krishnavarma; one of his associates, V. D. Savarkar, wrote *The Indian War of Independence, 1857* (published in 1909), an attempt to reinterpret the Mutiny in terms of revolutionary nationalism. The revolutionaries embarked upon a programme of assassination of British officials, both in India and in England. To some extent they followed the example of the Irish extremists, the Fenians, and later Sinn Fein. Many of the assassins were captured, but the movement was not extinguished.

A striking feature of all forms of political activity was the absence of participation by the ordinary people. Only Tilak was able to mobilise mass support for his agitations: and then only on a spasmodic basis. Although the first labour organisation, the Bombay Mill-hands Association, was founded in 1890, the trade union movement did not become a force until the 1920s: and then under Congress leadership. Village folk participated in a popular movement on an organised basis for the first time in the Mass Movement, as it was called, which sprang up in south India in the early 1900s. This was an expression of social discontent and aspiration for higher things among the lower castes, and especially the Untouchables. In their thousands they embraced Christianity; the movement spreading like a flame from one Untouchable hamlet to another. Along with Christianity they embarked upon mass programmes of adult education and social uplift. As in the early days of the social reformers, the example of the Christian Mass Movement was taken as a model by later political leaders; above all, by Gandhi.

The Morley–Minto Reforms provided the shaken Moderate Congress leaders with a little political leverage; which they used to full advantage. They had expected much more from Morley and the Liberals; but putting the best face on the situation, they contested elections and took their place in the new legislatures. The British government reacted with severity to the bomb outrages, and the Extremist ranks were disarrayed. Tilak was banished to Mandalay gaol. He had shown his hand, writing in his paper *Kesari*: 'The bomb has more of the form of knowledge than a bullet, it is magic [*jadu*], it is a sacred formula [*mantra*], an amulet [*todga*].' For these views he was sentenced to deportation for six years. B. C. Pal, the Bengali Extremist, went to prison for six months. Sri Aurobindo was acquitted of conspiracy in the Alipur bomb trial (in which his brother was convicted) but he abandoned politics and settled in French Pondicherry. Lala Lajpat Rai also went into exile, living in the United States, 1914–19.

The Coronation Durbar, when King George V visited India in 1911, saw an attempt at conciliation. The partition of Bengal, so often called 'irrevocable', was annulled: a new administrative arrangement reunited Bengal proper, but hived away Bihar and Orissa. Muslim feeling was, supposedly, mollified by the announcement that the capital of India would be transferred from Calcutta to a New Delhi which would revive Mughal glories. But Muslim notables at the Durbar were heard to mutter the wry phrase, 'No bombs, no boons'; meaning that Bengali terrorism had yielded results.

Important elements in the Muslim community were becoming restive. The defeats suffered by Turkey at the hands of Italy and the Balkan powers from 1911 onwards stirred up pan-Islamic sympathy. Dr M. A. Ansari led a medical mission of Indian Muslims to nurse the Turkish wounded. This trend in Muslim politics was accompanied by a change in the leadership of the Muslim League. The landlords and the retired officials, with their dependence upon the government, began to give way to lawyers and other professional men, looking less to the old Mughal inheritance and more to the contemporary dilemma of Islam. The meeting of the Muslim League of 1910, presided over by Sayyid Nabiullah of Lucknow, drew attention to the need for a *rapprochement* between Hindus and Muslims. Negotiations began with the Congress, whose representative at these talks was a Bombay Muslim, Mohammed Ali Jinnah (1876–1948). Jinnah was a member of the Borah trading community, originally converted from Hinduism, whose members retained many Hindu customs. A brilliant advocate, Jinnah became secretary to Gokhale, and was regarded as his political heir. At the 1913 session of the League, a number of Congress observers attended, including the poet Sarojini Naidu (1879–1949); a resolution expressed faith in the need for 'harmonious working and co-operation of the various communities'. From 1915 onward, the Congress and the League actually met in the same city, sharing the same *pandal* for their deliberations. It seemed that the Moderates had, against all the circumstances, pulled back the nationalist movement into a Liberal, secular mould.

When war broke out in 1914, the mood of harmony, co-operation and trust was marvellously fulfilled in a great demonstration of unity and loyalty throughout India. Princes, politicians, and people vied in their unstinted offers of support. An Indian Corps was hastily sent to France, and played its part in stemming the German onslaught. India was denuded of regular British battalions; newly-embodied Territorial battalions took their place; and because of the prevailing spirit of co-operation, this gamble in public security was not tested. A million volunteers joined the Indian Army, whose soldiers took the field in theatres of war in Africa, the Middle East and Europe. Yet while peasant lads were enlisting to serve the King-Emperor, the educated middle class and the political leaders were given no part to play in the war-effort. Gradually, the exultant mood of 1914 turned sour. The joint Congress–League meeting at Bombay in 1915 passed a resolution, moved by Jinnah (since 1913, a member of both the Congress and the League, like many of the progressive, younger Muslims), which called for the formation of a joint committee to draft a scheme of post-war reforms. Next year, at Lucknow, the Congress–League Pact was concluded. Thereby the congress accepted the principle of separate electorates for Muslims and conceded a 'weightage' in their representation in all the provinces where they were in a minority. In return, the Muslims accepted a little less than majority representation in their strongholds, Punjab and Bengal. The Lucknow Pact was the highpoint of Liberal co-operation between the communities: it was virtually a challenge to the British government to go ahead with a scheme of political advance which would incorporate the inter-communal agreement. The British, as we have seen, did not even produce a declaration of intent until August 1917; an actual programme of reform had to wait until after conclusion of the war. Once again, initiative slipped out of the hands of the constitutionalists.

Muslim opinion was disturbed when Turkey joined Germany and Austria against Britain and France. The importance of maintaining the brotherhood of all Muslims was voiced by Maulana Abul Kalam Azad (1888–1958), himself a graduate of the Islamic University, Al Azhar, in Cairo, through his journal *Al-Hilal*. A similar theme was voiced by the Ali brothers, Muhammad Ali (1878–1931) and Shaukat Ali (1873–1937) in their radical paper *Comrade*. All three men were placed under restriction in 1914, and despite plans and plots (to incite Afghanistan to fight Britain, for example), the pan-Islamic movement hung fire.

The later war years saw the nationalist movement straining at its moorings, trying to discover a new direction. Among the old inner group of the Congress, only Banerjea remained. Tilak had observed that 'The Extremists of today will be Moderates tomorrow just as the Moderates of today were the Extremists of yesterday' (1907). He exemplified his own dictum by accepting the moderate Lucknow programme as the answer to all his struggles. Mrs Besant launched a Home Rule League in Madras, committing all the branches of the Theosophical Society in India to its support. Her temporary confinement by the government led to an agitation, and her election as President of the Congress. A flood of new men were coming up in the organisation, such as Chitta Ranjan Das (1870–1925), a fiery Bengali lawyer. At a special session in August 1918, and the annual session in December 1918, the Congress demanded that fuller measures of *Swaraj* be granted immediately. The days of 'mendicancy', of patient waiting, were over. Which element in 'Extremism', the backward-looking Hindu nationalism of Tilak, or the revolutionary anarchism of the Bengali terrorists, would prevail? In the outcome, neither prevailed. The leadership passed to Gandhi (1869–1948).

When he returned to India from his long years of struggle in South Africa, Gandhi was a stranger to domestic politics. His viewpoint was wide. He saw the potentialities of a community of nations, the Commonwealth, in which Britain and India could both find new greatness. A few others shared this vision. Rabindranath Tagore understood that the cult of the nation – the goal (differently understood) of both Moderates and Extremists – was a blind alley. At the very moment when President Wilson was exalting national self-determination as the highest end of man, Tagore wrote (1917): 'The advent of another people into the arena of nationality makes another addition to the evil which contradicts all that is highest in Man and proves by its success that unscrupulousness is the way to prosperity.' In the same vein, E. M. Forster, that intuitively perci-pient recorder of India's dilemmas wrote: 'India a nation! What an apotheosis. Last comer to the drab nineteenth-century sisterhood, waddling at this hour of the world to take her seat. She whose only peer was the Holy Roman Empire, she shall rank now with Guatema-la and Belgium perhaps.' When Gandhi returned to India, early in the war years, it was to Tagore's settlement, Shantiniketan, that he went: and it was Tagore who first recognised him as *Mahatma*, 'Great Soul'. Gandhi defied classification. He took on the social service role of Gokhale, the Moderate, and regarded himself as Gokhale's disciple. He inherited the mass methods of Tilak, the Extremist, and he made his appeal to the people in traditional, religious terms as

Tilak had done. Although a revolutionary in his ideas, Gandhi largely smothered the revolutionary, terrorist movement by his creed of non-violence. The transformation whereby Gandhi moved from his total support for the British in their war effort – right down to 1918 – over to total opposition to the British government in 1920, reflects the breakdown in relations between British and Indian leadership during these years. The government of India reacted to terrorism, actual and potential, by something approaching counter-terrorism. First came the Rowlatt Act, giving the government summary powers; then came the Amritsar Massacre, when a British Brigadier-General met murder by murder; then came the Treaty of Sèvres, which virtually liquidated the Ottoman Empire. Strangely, Gandhi's patience survived Amritsar. He wrote to Tagore, condemning the violence in the Punjab, declaring: 'We must fearlessly spread the doctrine of *satya* [sacrifice] and *ahimsa* [harmlessness].' But his patience broke down before the harsh treatment of Turkey. In the teeth of opposition from important Congress leaders of the new dispensation, such as C. R. Das and Motilal Nehru (1861–1931), Gandhi persuaded the Congress in September 1920, to approve non-cooperation as the means to obtain '*Swaraj* within one year'. Gandhi's vision was able to bring together the many voices in the religious, social and political movements of the nineteenth century in a unified conception of freedom: it was his tragedy that the vision was not to be realised in the actual working out of events.

The Indian social and political renaissance and reformation drew strength from the long debate in which it came to maturity. The process of Westernisation in Ceylon was of much longer growth, but the interaction of new and old ideas was confined to a smaller social group, and the political elite did not reach out to embrace the mass of the people. In Burma, Westernisation was of brief duration, and affected only a minute fraction of the population. Yet because old loyalties burned more fiercely – and indeed were never fully extinguished – the new movement for political reform had a ready-made base in the old feelings of patriotism among the traditionalists and their most articulate spokesmen, the monks. Thus, Burmese political expression, though bursting into life like a hothouse plant, drew nourishment from a richer soil than the politics of sophisticated Ceylon.

During the last quarter of the nineteenth century, Rangoon's population grew from 100,000 to 248,000: in those years Rangoon was transformed from a predominantly Burmese city into something like an Indian city. The Burmese and other indigenous peoples occupied the suburbs and the Indians filled the city centre. To a large extent, Rangoon dominated Burma; and the foreigners dominated Rangoon. The Municipality was controlled by European business interests; the few Burmese members were mainly compelled to take part in discussion (carried on in English) through the medium of an interpreter. When Rangoon College was founded in 1884 to provide higher education for Burma, the majority of the students were Indians and Eurasians. The American Baptist Mission College, its only rival, catered almost exclusively for the Karens, whose leading families had embraced Protestant Christianity. The first Burmese language printing press, the Hanthawaddy Press, was opened by a foreigner in 1888. A small modern vernacular literature, plays and novels, began to develop. The authors were briefless lawyers or minor government officials: and their audience was very similar. The *Thooryah* ('Sun') was started in 1911 as the first Burmese-language daily, followed in 1914 by *New Light of Burma*. The early years of the twentieth century saw the first modern forms of political expression. At the government Rangoon College, a group of Burmese students began to build up a Buddhist social service society, strongly reminiscent of Vivekananda's Ramakrishna Mission. In 1908, they formally named their society the Young Men's Buddhist Association. Among these young leaders, several (e.g. May Oung, Maung Gyee, Ba Pe, Ba Yin and Ba Dun) were to become notable politicians. However, Burmese participation in public affairs was still a thing of the future. The first political organisation was a provincial branch of the Indian National Congress, founded in 1908 with an Indian, Dr P. J. Mehta, as its chairman and general factotum. Only one or two Burmese took any interest in the Congress: one being Chit Hlaing (1879–1952) who was to emerge as the first recognised political leader able to speak for Burma. Chit Hlaing was called to the Bar in England, like most of the small professional elite among the Burmese. Almost all these young Burmese barristers were the sons of officials who had served the old Burmese court and had then transferred to the British service. But throughout Burma there remained among the ordinary people a loyalty to the old days – to 'the Golden Land' of the old kings. Thus, the grandfather (some say great-uncle) of the man who was to lead the fight for Burma's independence in the 1940s – Aung san – was a Burmese official under the kings who rejected British overtures and kept up guerilla operations against the British after the 1885 occupation, until he was killed in a raid. This old guerilla tradition, known in

Burmese as *dahmya*, 'swordblades', was not entirely suppressed under the Pax Britannica.

Because the new politics of representative institutions had scarcely touched Burma, the Montagu–Chelmsford proposals excluded the province: the Report observed that 'the desire for elective institutions has not developed in Burma'. This casual relegation to a second-class status, while the Indians (known to most Burmese only as coolies or moneylenders) received a substantial instalment of self-government, was a galling insult. A special scheme was therefore devised: Burmese opinion would be represented through a series of boards or committees which would advise the Governor. This scheme also was unacceptable to public opinion, which suddenly and unexpectedly exploded in the 'December Boycott' of 1920. The protest centred upon the system of government in the new University of Rangoon which was being formed. Because the new University Senate gave no scope to the Burmese, the hitherto apolitical middle-class sprang into radical action. In India Gandhi was calling for non-cooperation; they, too, would refuse to co-operate. Boys and girls were withdrawn from government schools and colleges throughout the land. In Burma, as in India, 1920 marked a watershed in politics.

Ceylon had to wait until after independence for the politics of participation by the people. The island also moved in the direction of constitutional reform, but the only occasion when the political temperature rose above subnormal – in 1915 – was something of an accident and a freak.

The social and religious movements in India towards the end of the nineteenth century had mild counterparts in Ceylon. Buddhism reacted mildly to the challenge of Westernisation and secularism. There were temperance movements; and in 1905 the Ceylon Social Reform Society was founded and fomented a spirit of resistance to Westernisation among the Anglicised middle class. There was nothing radical about Ceylonese nationalism in this period. When, in 1912, elections to the legislature were held, the 'educated Ceylonese' constituency, the vehicle of the middle class, returned Sir Ponnambalam Ramanathan, a retired Tamil official.

The Kandy riots of 1915 occurred largely because the British administration maintained contact with the people through the hierarchy of hereditary Ceylonese officials. Communal differences between Sinhalese and Muslim Tamils in the Kandy area led to riots which lasted only a few days, but were followed by the arrest of nationalist leaders and the imposition of martial law for three

months. Those arrested belonged to the professional, upper middle-
class, and had taken part in the temperance movement and the
formation of the Ceylon National Association. In the absence of a full
university, many intellectuals had joined the Ceylon Medical College
(founded in 1870) and some of the social and political reformers were
doctors. Among those arrested was D. S. Senanayake (1884–1952),
the architect of independence. However, the leadership of the
political movement after the 1915 affair remained firmly in the hands
of the older generation, notably those of Sir Ponnambalam Arunachalam, a former civil servant and a Tamil, and Sir James Pieris, a
Christian and a member of the Karava or fisher caste. The dominant
Goyigama or cultivator caste and the Buddhist order acquiesced in
this situation. Both Arunachalam and Pieris had contacts with Indian
Moderates, especially Gokhale. The association with Indian nationalism seemed natural at this period. When S. W. R. D. Bandaranaike
(1899–1959), who led Ceylon away from the politics of moderation,
went up to Christ Church, Oxford as an undergraduate, he was – like
Jawaharlal Nehru (1889–1964), who had just left Cambridge – the
heir to aristocratic, Anglicised privilege: he was also a Christian. Yet
in his memoirs he relates how he listened to an undergraduate debate
in which an Indian turned the tables on his English opponent: 'That
night I was proud of being an Indian', observed the Sinhalese
nationalist.

And so, the restlessness which came over Indian politics in the
middle years of the war awakened echoes in Ceylon. A Ceylon
Reform League was founded; and in April 1917, Arunachalam
delivered a lecture to the League on 'Our Political Needs'. Next year
he moved a resolution in the Legislative Council, demanding reforms. Conferences, deputations, memoranda followed; in 1919 the
Ceylon National Congress was founded on the Indian model, with
Arunachalam as the first President. The British government responded in 1920 by enlarging non-official representation in the
legislature. The Ceylon Congress was not satisfied, and agreed to
co-operate in its workings with reluctance: but agree it did. Whereas
before 1920 there was an equal share for Tamils and Sinhalese in the
legislature, after 1920 the Tamils had only three seats to the thirteen
held by the Sinhalese. A rift was soon to open between the two
communities.

The year 1920, then, witnessed a massive movement away from
acceptance of British rule and British institutions among Muslims and
Hindus in the Indian sub-continent and in Burma. But in Ceylon the

politicians continued to work within the existing constitutional set-up; perhaps already uneasily aware that attainment of nationhood might be impeded by internal divisions as much as by Imperial obduracy. Before independence was achieved throughout South Asia, internal divisions were to threaten the national movements everywhere.

9 The Contest for Independence

During the years between 1920 and independence, the cavalcade of history in South Asia, with different groups marching forward at different speeds, quickened into a gallop. At times, so much seems to be happening in different places all at once, that the whole picture looks confused. A pattern can be traced out – somewhat artificially – in the following time-sequence. The decade 1920–30 was a period when the nationalist movements and the British government were pulling in opposite directions. The nationalists were (speaking very broadly) united in the conviction that by struggle and mass action they could overcome the resistance of the British to conceding independence. The British government and British politicians on their side began with the well-established concept of granting self-government by instalments: the formula enunciated by Tennyson:

> And freedom slowly broadening down,
> From precedent to precedent.

By the early 1930s the British were coming to realise that full self-government (still defined as Dominion Status) must be conceded within a limited period. Attempts were made to evolve constitutional formulae acceptable to the national leaders. Sensing the changed circumstances, the nationalists relaxed the struggle against British rule and began to operate the machinery of representative institutions. However, with independence in the air, the broadbased nationalist movements began to divide off, and separate interests and ideological forces started to emerge. The years 1930–9 saw the British commence to think seriously about the transfer of power, while the nationalists began to rule: and also to divide. The war years, 1939–45 were the culmination of the whole process. During these five years, entirely different responses occurred among the forces of nationalism; responses to the tides of war and to the trends in British policy. The moderate political leadership in Ceylon recognised the external threat, and co-operated in the war effort. In India, the Congress attempted to force the issue at an hour of crisis; failed; and paid for failure by three years of impotence. Meanwhile, the Muslim League grasped their opportunity and successfully emerged as a rival to the Congress, entitled to speak for the mass of the Muslims. Alone among the countries in the region, Burma suffered three years of invasion, occupation and violent liberation. Under this experience, the old political leadership was swept aside by new revolutionary forces with a crude appeal to the people.

After the cataclysm of war came the epilogue, when all that remained was to settle the conditions under which the transfer of power from British to national control would be completed. These years brought their own surprises but the issue was not in doubt. In late 1947 and early 1948, independence came to more than 450 million people in South Asia. And although blood was shed in this process, the bloodletting was not between European and Asian: the conflict was between Asian and Asian. The old rulers departed in an atmosphere of goodwill. British Imperialism showed itself capable of handing over an empire, without a war and with all the parts of the Imperial machine in full working order. Unhappily, it was a phenomenon never fully reproduced again elsewhere.

These then are the main episodes in the drama: 1920–30, nationalism versus imperialism; 1930–9, the search for a compromise; 1939–45, the pressure of war; 1945–8, the final reckoning.[1]

The proclaimed goal of Gandhi's noncooperation campaign of 1920–1 was '*Swaraj* within one year'. Gandhi's concept of *Swaraj* was summed up in his formula: 'Real self-government is self-rule or self-control.' But how many of his followers were able to grasp that the purpose of non-cooperation or non-violence, *satyagraha*, was to transform Indians themselves? Part of the declared purpose of the campaign was to safeguard the Khilafat (Caliphate) in Turkey as the temporal leadership of the Muslim world. A Khilafat conference in August 1920 heard the Ali brothers call for the repudiation of British rule, declaring that it was 'wholly unlawful for every Muhammadan at this time to remain or enlist in the English [i.e. British-Indian] army'. Muslims were even urged to leave the land ruled by the Infidel (*Dar-ul-Harb*) and migrate to the land of the Faithful (*Dar-ul-Islam*), that is, Afghanistan. Thousands of Indian Muslims did attempt to follow this injunction: only to be turned back at the Afghan border. The Congress stepped up the pressure in November, announcing payment of land revenue would cease throughout the Bardoli taluka

---

[1] To remind readers of the sequence of events, a chronological table is given at the end of this chapter.

(a revenue sub-district unit) in Gujarat. Violence was increasing. There were riots in Bombay and Calcutta, and in south India there was a rising by a fanatical Muslim community, the Moplahs, whose blood-lust was turned against their Hindu neighbours. When a full-scale conflict between the nationalists and the British seemed inevitable (in February 1921) the crisis suddenly evaporated. A mob in the United Provinces attacked a police station at Chauri Chaura and murdered twenty-two constables with bestial brutality. Gandhi announced that, in beginning the non-cooperational movement when Indians were unprepared for the discipline of non-violence, he had committed 'a Himalayan blunder'; the campaign was called off.

If Gandhi had continued he would certainly have forfeited the support of all the moderate elements in Congress: not only those who had quit the Congress to form the new National Liberal Federation, but also men like Motilal Nehru and C. R. Das who viewed uncontrolled mass tactics with disquiet. But Gandhi's decision had a contrary effect upon Congress–League relations. The Muslims felt they had been let down; and the abolition of the Khilafat in Turkey in 1924 did not end the matter. The custom of holding the annual conventions of Congress and League in the same town and the same *pandal* came to an end; and though co-operation and consultation continued, the sense of comradeship had gone. Indeed, among those who dwelt in towns and cities, Hindu–Muslim relations had never been worse. Communal disputes increasingly degenerated into riots, in which stabbings and murders were common.

After the failure of direct action, the political leaders thought again about the possibility of exerting pressure through representative institutions. The Liberals had decided from the start to enter the new, reformed legislatures. For the first time, direct elections were held on a constituency basis. The electorate was tiny – between 2 and 3 per cent of the population – but the contest was real enough. Ministers were selected in most provinces for their personal distinction rather than for the support of a majority party in the legislature: for the simple reason that only in Madras was it possible to see the emergence of a cohesive party, able to make or break a ministry. Under the Dyarchy system, government in the provinces was separated into the Reserved side and the Transferred side. The Reserved side covered responsibility for law and order, and included control over finance. These functions were administered by two 'Members', one a British official, and one an Indian from public life. The Transferred side covered the 'Nation-Building Services' (education, health, local government, agriculture, etc.) and came under two Ministers, who were politicians. Both sides of provincial government were under the oversight of the Governor: almost always a British civil servant, though Lord Sinha was Governor of Bihar and Orissa, 1920–1. Both Members and Ministers sat in the provincial legislature; but the Members were independent of its control, while the Ministers were supposed to be responsible to the legislature. The majority of the legislators were now elected members, but some were nominated to represent special interests, and a few were British officials – mainly heads of departments. It was a system which could be made to work, given goodwill; but which might be obstructed or even over-ruled in half a dozen different ways. Yet the British government was saying, in effect, 'Make a success of Dyarchy, and then we will see whether India may receive another instalment of reform.'

At the first conference of the National Liberal Federation, the veteran Banerjea gave the keynote as 'co-operate when we can, criticise when we must'. V. S. Srinavasa Sastri (1869–1946), Gokhale's successor as President of the Servants of India Society, started a weekly in 1918, the *Servant of India*. The first issue carried the timeless declaration of Ranade and Gokhale: 'The spirit of Liberalism implies a freedom from race and creed prejudices. . . .' In this spirit, Liberal Ministers took office in Bengal, Bombay and the United Provinces: however, their army was one with plenty of generals but none to fill the ranks. They relied upon the goodwill of independents and the nominated and official members of the legislatures to stay in office. The only province where a situation prevailed akin to that in which ministries usually hold office under a parliamentary system was Madras. There, in the first Dyarchy council, the Justice Party enjoyed a clear majority over all other groups in the legislature, including the officials. The Justice Party had emerged as the weapon of the lower castes against the Brahmins. Constituting only three per cent of the population, the Brahmins enjoyed a monopoly in the public services, the legal profession, and higher education throughout south India. Even the restricted Dyarchy franchise gave the lower castes the chance to topple over the proud Brahmins. Their task was simplified by the decision of the Congress, under Gandhi's influence, to boycott the first elections. And so, in Madras, a ministry led by a 'Chief Minister' was able to carry through a definite party programme. A party system of a kind developed in the Punjab. Of the 71 elected members of the first Punjab Council, 24 were lawyers, and 39 were zamindars, landholders. The outstanding

Punjab politician, Fazl-i-Husain, was a member of both the Congress and the League, like most of the Muslim professional men. He turned to the zamindars to provide support for a National Unionist Party, formed to defend the agricultural communities against the urban, capitalist, interests. Fazl-i-Husain relied mainly upon Muslim backing, but he succeeded in attracting agriculturalists of the other communities, especially Hindu Jats and Sikhs. He attempted to settle the constant squabble over the communities' share of public patronage by prescribing fixed percentages for places in the services and in educational institutions. In the provinces with Liberal Ministers, measures for the reform of local government and expansion in education went forward: but the Ministers were always compelled to deal with the suspicion and even hostility of British officials and Indian conservatives.

Within the Congress ranks, many thought that the boycott of the Councils was a serious tactical error. Their leaders were Motilal Nehru and C. R. Das. At the 1922 Congress, differences came to a head, and those in favour of change formed the cumbrously-named Khilafat-Congress-Swaraj Party, with Das as their president. The Swaraj party contested the second elections in 1923, and their intervention upset the previous precarious party balance. The Unionists in Punjab, and the Justice Party in Madras, survived the Swarajist challenge, but the Liberals, in the words of C. Y. Chintamani (Minister in UP) found themselves 'in the unenviable position of the proverbial earthen pot between two brass vessels': the Swarajists on one side, and the landlords and officials on the other. In the Central Provinces, the Swarajists obtained a clear majority: they refused to take office, and eventually brought about the formal suspension of Dyarchy. The situation in Bengal was only a little less chaotic. Two Muslim ministries managed to keep in office from January to August, 1924, but thereafter Dyarchy was in abeyance. Elsewhere, Ministers were drawn from the conservative landlords or from sectional interests.

While politics was showing fissiparous tendencies in the legislatures, politics among the people was degenerating into communal conflict. A movement was launched by the *Arya Samaj* for the return to Hinduism of those Hindus converted to Islam and Christianity since the days of Aurangzeb. Lala Lajpat Rai was associated with the political aspects of this reconversion movement, known as *Sangathan*, while the spiritual lead was given by Swami Shradhanand in what was called *Shuddhi*. Muslims reacted to this attack by organising the *Tabligh* and *Tanzim* movements as a form of counter-attack. Inevitably, this marshalling of religious forces led to communal tension. Swami Shradhanand was murdered in 1926 by a Muslim, and all over north India communal rioting increased in severity. During this period, although the Muslim League existed in name, it had ceased to exercise influence; the more dynamic Muslims were active in the Khilafat Committee and the Swaraj Party. The confused state of politics was intensified when dissensions sprang up even within the Swaraj Party. Now that the Swarajists had entered the Councils, should they not take the next logical step away from non-cooperation and form ministries, when possible? In 1926, the Swarajist group in the central legislature divided, one group forming the Indian National Party to work for *Swaraj* on the Dominion pattern. In this confusion, the British government restored a measure of unity to the nationalist ranks by announcing the appointment of a Commission, headed by Sir John Simon, to make recommendations on future constitutional advance. The Commission was composed entirely of members of the British Parliament; yet the Montagu–Chelmsford inquiry had included Indian representation among the committee drafting the report. The exclusion of Indians from the Simon Commission was the work of Lord Birkenhead, the ultra-conservative Secretary of State. This insult to India alienated even the Indian Liberals and united all but minority interests in a determination to boycott the Commission.

Representatives of all sections of opinion combined to produce an Indian answer to the Simon Commission. An all-Parties Conference was convened in February 1928, and subsequently a committee was appointed, with Motilal Nehru as chairman, to produce constitutional recommendations. Once again, the question of satisfying minority opinion was prominent. Proportional representation, reservation of seats, and separate electorates all had their advocates. Eventually, joint electorates were accepted. The proposals of the Nehru Report were considered in December at Calcutta, when once again the Congress, the Khilafat Committee and the Muslim League all held their annual meetings together. Within the Congress there was a division between Motilal and the older generation, prepared to advocate Dominion status as the basis for *Swaraj*, and the younger men who wanted independence outside the Commonwealth: their leaders were Jawaharlal Nehru and Subhas Chandra Bose (1897–1945), formerly the lieutenant of C. R. Das, and now emerging as the storm-cock of the Congress. The Muslim discussions hinged upon acceptance or rejection of joint electorates. Jinnah was prepared to compromise on this issue, providing that three amendments were accepted: to continue communal representation in Punjab and Bengal for ten years, and to vest residuary powers in the provinces rather than the centre. Jinnah's demands were rejected: 'This is the parting of the ways', he told a friend. This rebuff had the effect of reuniting Muslim opinion. Immediately after the Calcutta meetings, a Muslim all-Parties Conference at Delhi drafted a fourteen point programme, including a federal form of government, separate electorates and reservation of one-third of the seats in the central legislature for Muslims. The rift between Congress and League in the nationalist movement gave no satisfaction to Jinnah – still more at home among Congress and Liberal lawyers and professors than among the landlords of the League: in 1930 he left India to practise law in London. He announced that he had done with politics for good.

The Congress was passing under the control of the new generation of leaders. The annual session at Lahore in 1929 subscribed to what was in effect a Declaration of Independence, and proceeded to plan a further non-cooperation movement to make this a reality. In February 1930, a second civil disobedience campaign began: with Gandhi as its leader. For neither Bose nor Jawaharlal had superseded the Mahatma. Gandhi announced his intention of defying the law by breaking the salt regulations and making his own salt out of sea water. It was altogether typical of his outlook that he should choose the salt tax – a minute levy, which hardly anybody had noticed before – as the symbol of civil disobedience. The Viceroy – Lord Irwin – was in many ways a worthy opponent to Gandhi: he, too, was a man of deep religious conviction with a desire to see India achieve freedom. Reluctantly he ordered the arrest of Gandhi and almost all the Congress leadership. These events took place while a Labour government was in office in Britain. The Secretary of State from 1929 to 1931, Wedgwood Benn, later Lord Stansgate (1877–1961), was a fervent supporter of Indian self-government. There was a definite desire in London to see India move forward to nationhood, and the Prime Minister (Ramsay MacDonald) summoned a Round Table Conference at which Indians representing the political parties and groups, and the Indian Princely States, were invited to find a solution to the communal problems and to make plans for constitutional reform. The Congress (with its leaders in gaol) boycotted the Conference, which met in November 1930. Wryly, the veteran leader Muhammad Ali addressed the conference chairman, Lord Sankey:

'My lord, divide and rule is the order of the day, but in India we divide and you rule.' It was a sad verdict upon a lifetime spent in promoting Muslim–Hindu unity.

Almost at the same time, at the annual session of the Muslim League at Allahabad, the poet Iqbal called for a separate Muslim state in India saying, 'The formation of a consolidated North-West Indian Muslim State appears to be the final destiny of the Muslims at least of North-West India.' One who heard this call, Choudry Khaliquzzaman, records that Iqbal 'failed to attract the attention even of the intellectual classes, much less of the masses'. The League did not follow Iqbal's lead, even in the time-honoured fashion of Indian political debate by moving a resolution on the matter.

Burma was belatedly brought into the Dyarchy experiment after the December boycott. Whereas Gandhi's non-cooperation campaign lapsed, in Burma the withdrawal of Burmese youth from the government schools led to the establishment of a network of National schools as a permanent feature. Many of the next generation of political leaders were educated at these schools, where the pattern was Burmese and not English. The Young Men's Buddhist Association gave way to a political organisation, the General Council of Burmese Associations, or *Wunthanu*, whose leader was Chit Hlaing. The first elections were held in 1922, and as in India the politicians disagreed over whether to contest the elections. The main body of the GCBA decided on a boycott, but one section, led by Ba Pe, formed the 'Twenty-one Party'. In the new legislature, seventy-nine seats were filled by election. Although there was no Hindu–Muslim problem in Burma, the communal system was introduced, and there were separate constituencies for Karens, Eurasians and Europeans. The Twenty-one Party won 28 seats, while an assortment of independents banded together under Sir Maung Gyee, calling themselves the Progressives. Others called them the 'Golden Valley Party', from the name of the upper class suburb where most of them resided.

Because there were no electoral rolls, the first electorate was composed of men on the tax-list: including some who were eighteen years old. But although the electorate was wider than in India, politics had little meaning for the people. There was no Gandhi to dramatise political issues in terms that the ordinary people could understand. The political leadership, the barrister-politicians, established no mass following, and into the vacuum stepped men of the people, Buddhist monks. Their appeal was traditional yet radical: a call for a return to the good old days, and the expulsion of the foreigners from the Golden Land. Many of the British had been accustomed to entering the promenade or platform of the pagodas wearing shoes, where all Burmese went barefoot. Signs appeared in most pagodas: 'Foot Wearing not Permitted'. Itinerant monks preached against the evil of foreign ways: the most famous, U Ottama, was a member of the Hindu Mahasabha (a communal Hindu political party) but links with India were slender. Indeed, the anti-foreign movement included a growing demand that the continuance of Burma as a province of British India should be ended. There was a certain co-operation between the communities in Rangoon politics: S. A. S. Tyabji (a relation of the Muslim Congress leader) was arrested in 1922. Even in Rangoon, there was a strong under-current of resentment against foreign domination (not until 1924 was a Burman, Dr Ba Yin, elected President of the Municipal Corporation).

The 1920s closed with the *Galon* rebellion in Lower Burma. The rising took the authorities completely by surprise though centred within eighty miles of Rangoon. The revolt spread to twelve of Burma's forty districts, and for its suppression nearly 12,000 troops had to be despatched from India. What was most dangerous was the rallying-power of tradition, as compared to the marginal pull of politics, in Burma in 1930. Saya San, who had been dismissed from government employment as a clerk, proclaimed himself *Minlaung*, of the blood royal, and underwent the traditional coronation ceremony, with the traditional number of eight queens in attendance. He gave his followers magic amulets to protect them against the guns of the foreigners and announced that the days of British rule were over. His followers allowed themselves to be shot down in the open by British machine guns, secure in the magical protecting power of their king. All the politicians disassociated themselves from the rebellion, but some unemployed lawyers made a name by defending the *Galon* rebels in Court, notably U Saw (1900–48) and Dr Ba Maw (b. 1897).

When the Report of the Simon Commission was published, it recommended the separation of Burma from India. To the Burmese representatives at the Round Table Conference this was the main talking point. Many were suspicious: was this another device to fob Burma off with a settlement inferior to that given to India? There was much talk about Burma becoming a Crown Colony. The issue brought about a new alignment of parties, with re-unification among the GCBA groups to oppose separation. Dr Ba Maw emerged as the champion of the anti-separationists. A general election was held in

1932, to sound public opinion, and the anti-separationists came back in a majority: but this did not mean that separation had been rejected.

During the 1920s, Ceylon moved from the nineteenth-century type of Crown Colony administration to the threshold of popular government. The 1920 reforms lasted a bare four years; then in 1924 a further expansion of the legislature gave the elected members a majority. These members were elected on a very narrow base: only 4 per cent of the population enjoyed the vote. Moreover, they were not even offered the partial share in ministerial responsibility provided by Dyarchy in India. The elected members discovered a device to make their importance felt: the non-official members, together with three officials, formed a Finance Committee which could examine the budget. They had the right to call the heads of the departments of government before them, and they proceeded to exploit this right to inquire into and pass criticisms upon the actions of senior British officials. Tension increased: a classic example of the colonial dilemma emerged, with a powerless but vocal nationalist opposition confronting an official regime, constitutionally all-powerful but morally paralysed by nationalist discontent. The situation, frustrating for politicians and administrators, was eased by the appointment of a Commission of Inquiry which visited Ceylon in 1927, at much the same time as the Simon Commission. The Chairman, Lord Donoughmore, had taken part in the Montagu–Chelmsford inquiry. The Donoughmore Report had some shrewd observations upon the problem of introducing representative government in a country where political parties had not become effective. For the Ceylon Congress had lost ground when Arunachalam and Ramanathan withdrew in 1921 to set up the Tamil Mahajana Sabha to protect Tamil interests. The Donoughmore Commission set themselves against communal electorates: which they somewhat naively assumed were the cause of communal feeling. The Commission submitted its Report to an unusual Secretary of State for the Colonies: to Lord Passfield (1859–1947), Sidney Webb, joint founder of the Fabian Society and the London School of Economics. He was ready to accept all the Commission's proposals, and even to go a little further. Communal representation was abolished in favour of a territorial, constituency system, with the franchise open to every man and woman over twenty-one years of age. And so Ceylon obtained universal franchise in 1931: only three years later than in Great Britain, and years ahead of many European countries. In order to get round the problem of giving the legislators both power and responsibility, when there were no real parties to provide cohesion and some discipline to the legislature, the Donoughmore Constitution turned for its model to the London County Council. Instead of the Westminster model of Cabinet, Ministers, government and opposition, all members of the legislature were given executive responsibility through a number of executive committees. On Dyarchy lines the subjects of foreign affairs, law and order, finance, and public services remained under the control of British civil servants. All other subjects were handed over to seven committees: every member belonged to at least one committee. The chairmen of committees were known as Ministers, and sat along with officials in charge of reserved subjects as a Board of Ministers. In recognition that the Donoughmore Constitution was likely to be the last stage on the road to self-government, the recruitment of British candidates into the Ceylon Civil Service was discontinued after 1931.

India's pathway to self-government remained difficult to discern. After the first Round Table Conference, the Viceroy persuaded Gandhi to agree to Congress participation in a second conference. Unwisely, Congress nominated Gandhi as its sole representative. Gandhi, so intuitively right in personal negotiations, was less than successful in the manoeuvres of the conference table. Discussion degenerated into claims and counter-claims by the Muslims, the Princes, and other minorities. Gandhi departed and launched another campaign of civil disobedience; promptly suppressed. With no agreement, the Prime Minister, Ramsay MacDonald, was left to impose a settlement known as the Communal Award. This was subsequently embodied or embedded in a draft Government of India Bill: reputedly the longest piece of legislation ever to be laid before the House of Commons. At this moment, the Labour government gave way to a National government in which (after the 1931 election) the Conservatives predominated. While Labour, Liberals and moderate Conservatives accepted the need for further reform in India, the die-hard Tories, led by Winston Churchill, opposed the Bill to the hilt. A last ditch campaign was mounted, and the Bill became law only in 1935, not coming into force until 1937.

During this period, the internecine dispute in the Congress continued. Bose made a bid for supreme leadership, but despite the appearance of success, he failed to outwit Gandhi. The men of affairs had their way over the men of ideas; and when the Government of India Act brought full self-government under responsible ministries in the provinces, after much hesitation, the Congress decided to contest the elections.

Meanwhile, the Muslims still could not decide whether to play the political game along communal lines, class lines, or nationalist lines. At last, Jinnah was induced to return from London: it is said, as a retort to a remark by Jawaharlal Nehru that Jinnah was finished: not the last of Nehru's casual utterances to have unfortunate results. Jinnah attempted to rejuvenate the League, and he set up a parliamentary board to co-ordinate Muslim politics throughout India. He was rebuffed in the two Muslim strongholds. Punjab and Bengal. In Punjab, Fazl-i-Husain and his successor, Sikander Hyat Khan made it clear that while they would accept the League as the Muslim vehicle in Delhi, in Punjab they would not tolerate interference with their carefully contrived Unionist alliance. Fazl-ul-Haq in Bengal was also not prepared to risk his inter-communal Krishak Praja or Peasant's Party for all-India Muslim purposes. In UP, the centre of the Mughal tradition and of the Aligarth movement, things looked unpromising. The conservative Muslim landlord-aristocrats were aligned with their Hindu fellow-landlords in an 'Agriculturalists' Party. The more progressive, professional men among the UP Muslims were all old Khilafatists and Congress workers, such as Shaukat Ali. In 1933 they formed a Muslim Unity Board to work in co-operation with Congress. When an all-India Congress Parliamentary Board was formed in 1934, five out of its 25 members were Muslims. The situation was unexpectedly transformed by the outcome of the 1937 provincial elections in UP.

The UP Muslims (probably the most politically sensitive section of their community throughout India) contested the elections on the Muslim League platform: but they regarded the Congress as their allies in a joint struggle against the landlord Agriculturalist Party. When the UP results were declared, the League candidates had won 29 of the 36 seats reserved for Muslims, while Congress obtained a landslide victory, winning 134 out of 144 general constituencies. The Muslims now expected to join with Congress in forming the ministry: but the wine of victory went to the heads of the Congress leaders and magnified their sense of their own importance. The Muslim Leaguers were offered a share in the ministry, on condition they signed a document agreeing to dissolve the Muslim League Parliamentary Board, join the Congress, and accept its rulings. The Leaguers recognised this ultimatum for what it was: their death warrant: they refused to sign the required undertaking. Subsequently, prominent

UP politicians from the landlords and the professional classes threw in their lot with Jinnah: among them Nawabzada Liaqat Ali Khan (1895–1951), the first Prime Minister of Pakistan.

Congress won a majority of seats in five provinces out of the total of eleven provinces which received autonomy under the 1935 Act. In three other provinces Congress could obtain a majority by the support of allies and independents. After protracted negotiations, Congress ministries were formed in eight provinces, and functioned until October 1939. Several introduced important social reform measures, but their emphasis upon aspects of militant Hindu nationalism (such as the replacement of Urdu by Hindi, and the singing of *Bande-Mataram* in schools and on public occasions) was resented by the Muslims. Although the League had won only 108 of the 485 Muslim seats throughout India in the 1937 provincial elections, the Congress had captured a mere 26. The Congress governments began a programme of mass contact to win over the Muslim electorate, but the Muslim tide was turning, and flowing ever more strongly in the direction of Jinnah and the League. When the Congress ministries resigned in 1939, in protest at India's being committed willy-nilly to war with Germany, Jinnah and the League celebrated a day of deliverance. When the League next held its annual meeting at Lahore in March, 1940, the federal constitution envisaged under the 1935 Act was rejected, and a new demand was formulated: 'That the areas where Muslims are numerically in a majority as in the North-Western and Eastern zones of India should be grouped to constitute "Independent States" in which the constituent units shall be autonomous and sovereign.'

The press dubbed this Lahore resolution as the 'Pakistan demand', after the scheme invented by one Rahmat Ali, an expatriate Indian Muslim living in Cambridge. The 1940 resolution nowhere mentioned Pakistan, and in asking for 'Independent States' the spokesmen of the League were far from clear what was intended.[1] By emphasising the idea of Pakistan, the press (mainly hostile to Muslim separatism) succeeded in converting a wordy and clouded lawyer's formula into a clarion-call. From 1940 onward, Pakistan, and what it implied, was the great talking point of the Indian independence debate.

Meanwhile, the debate in Burma over separation or non-separation had been resolved. As soon as the Burmese politicians

---

[1] Some at least of the Muslim leaders must have read the Declaration of Independence with its asseveration that the American colonies were now 'Free and Independent States'. Probably the same concept was implied in 1940 as in 1776.

realised that they had to choose for all time, they chose separation. The Government of Burma Act, passed in 1935, also came into force in 1937. Paradoxically, Burma – where there was less experience of political organisation than in India – received a greater instalment of independence. The first (and only) elections under the 1935 Act produced a legislature containing several political parties, as well as several groups based on communal interests. The largest was the United GCBA with 46 members, led by the veteran Ba Pe, but he could not find enough support among the 132 members to form a ministry. Dr Ba Maw's *Sinyetha Wunthanu* ('association of poor men-patriots') numbered only 16, but Ba Maw – besides being a gifted orator – was a first class political manipulator. He assembled together a motley band of allies, and held office for two years. In February 1939 he was defeated, and a new ministry was formed by Ba Pe's party together with a new group – *Myochit* – 'lovers of the nation', led by the ambitious and thrusting U Saw, who managed to manoeuvre himself into the premiership in September 1940. Meanwhile, the leadership of the future was emerging, on the fringe of politics in the *Thakin* or 'master' party. Its members almost all gained their experience in the techniques of agitation at the University of Rangoon in the 1930s. They were all lower middle class, by origin, coming from small up-country towns. Their record in class was abysmal, and their Westernisation was barely skin deep. The only intellectuals among them were Ko ('elder brother') Nu and Maung ('brother') Thant: later Secretary-General of the United Nations, together with an Indian lad, M. A. Raschid. They all absorbed the popular Marxism of the 1930s, and turned the Students' Union into a militant, political organisation. They organised a series of student strikes, forced postponement of university examinations, compelled the reinstatement of expelled student leaders, and then quit college in a patriotic glory. They began working for the Thakin party: Thakin Nu became treasurer: 'a treasurer without treasure', as he dryly observed. The parliamentary wing of the party numbered only three, but the main arena of the Thakins was the street and the factory. They replaced the monks as the exponents of proletarian politics, organising the first strike among oil-workers, and building up a private army, known as the Steel Corps (other private political armies were formed by U Saw and Ba Maw). After Dr Ba Maw's ejection from the premiership, he linked up with the Thakins in a new front called the 'Freedom Bloc'. At the same time (in 1939) a group of Marxist Thakins founded a secret organisation called the Burma Revolution-

ary Party. Amid these bids for leadership, one man increasingly stood
out: Aung San (1916–47). Moody, mercurial, malevolent, he could
impose his will on all sorts and conditions of men. He attended the
Ramgarh session of the Indian National Congress in 1940, and met
Gandhi and Nehru: but like Subhas Chandra Bose (with whom he
had much in common) he rejected non-violence and exalted violence.
The British authorities had long watched the Thakins closely, and as
the wartime scene darkened in 1940, they resolved to place them
under arrest. However, the Thakins had their own plans prepared.
Aung San had built up contacts with Japanese undercover agents,
and had agreed to select young Burmans for military training in
Japan. When a warrant was issued for Aung San's arrest, he slipped
aboard a ship in Rangoon River bound for Canton. Thence he made
his way to Tokyo. In March 1941, he arrived back in Rangoon in a
Japanese ship. He linked up with the Revolutionary Party, and
secretly recruited thirty Burmans, almost all Thakins, for training.
After about six months training, they were sent to Bangkok to form
the 'Burma Independence Army'. In a house in Bangkok, the thirty
leaders carried out the traditional Burmese military ceremonial of
blood-mingling, *thwe-thauk*. They pooled their blood in a silver bowl,
then each drank therefrom, and so sealed their comradeship until
death. The Thirty Comrades, as they were now called, assumed
high-sounding titles: Fire General, General Victory, Right Hand
General, General of the Flying Weapon. One Thakin, Shu Maung, a
Sino-Burman, called himself *Bo Ne Win*, or 'Sun of Glory General':
under that title he was twenty years later to become the supreme
leader of Burma. Meanwhile, it was Aung San or *Bo Teza* (Fire
General) who commanded and inspired the swelling ranks of the BIA
as they awaited the Japanese signal to invade Burma, during the last
days of 1941.

Ceylon also underwent a testing time under the threat of Japanese
attack. The Donoughmore Constitution provided the framework for
Ceylon politics for fifteen years. A Professor of Mathematics at
University College (a Tamil, strangely) showed D. S. Senanayake
and his friends how they might secure control over all the executive
committees by distributing their supporters according to a mathema-
tical formula. After 1936, the Board of Ministers comprised only
Sinhalese members: the Tamils and other minorities were totally
excluded. Most of the Ministers were related in some way to the
Senanayake family and belonged to the highest caste, the Goyigama.
This caste network of power formed the only substitute for a ruling

political party. On the Left, parties of Marxist ideology were beginning to emerge, led by Philip Gunawardena and N. M. Perera. The Lanka Sama Samaja or Socialist Party was founded in 1935. With the advent of hostilities in the Far East, emergency regulations were imposed. The Ceylonese political leaders gave their support to the war-effort, and those who were Ministers were given added responsibilities. They functioned almost as a Cabinet, under the direction of the British Governor. With the fall of Singapore, Trincomalee became the advance base of the Royal Navy in the Indian Ocean, while after the formation of South-East Asia Command (SEAC), Lord Louis Mountbatten set up his supreme headquarters in Kandy. Senanayake and his colleagues adjudged that Ceylon's loyal co-operation deserved some mark of recognition from the British government. A Commission, led by Lord Soulbury, visited the island in 1944 and recommended full internal self-government. Guided by the shrewd constitutional advice of (Sir) Ivor Jennings – who was to become the first Vice-Chancellor of the University of Ceylon – Senanayake obtained a constitution which restored a parliamentary, cabinet form of government, without communal representation. The Soulbury Commission's Report was not published until October, 1945: by then, even the broad advance therein advocated had been outpaced by the abrupt ending of the war with Japan, the outlook of the new Labour government, and the stormy struggle for power in India between Congress and League.

The decision of the Congress Working Committee (the 'high command') to instruct all the Congress ministers to resign, after the outbreak of war in September 1939, was a tactical error – a mistake which probably cost them their control over a united India. In Madras, C. R. Rajagopalachari, the far-sighted Chief Minister, recognised how short-sighted was this decision, and resisted the high command for some time. With the Congress ministries out of office, the Governors took back their powers in eight provinces. What could Congress do to regain the lost political initiative? Gandhian non-violence had been rejected by Subhas Chandra Bose, now attempting to raise Indian forces to fight Britain, first under German patronage, and later under the Japanese. Non-violence had never fully appealed to Nehru, who once wrote to the Mahatma, 'For myself, I delight in warfare.' The Socialist wing of the Congress, led by younger men, such as Jayaprakash Narayan, were ready for a direct challenge to the British. The high command hesitated. A last chance for constitutional compromise was offered by the Cripps Mission. The Japanese invasion of Burma rapidly swallowed up Lower Burma, and the British evacuated Rangoon. (Map 10). With a threat developing against India's borders, the Churchill government despatched Sir Stafford Cripps (as a Socialist, a recognised friend of Nehru) to try to associate the Indian political parties with the British cause, in return for the immediate implementation of independence at the war's end. Cripps valiantly attempted the impossible task of satisfying the Congress, while at the same time offering the League something not dissimilar to their 'Independent States'. Also, the Indians were increasingly dubious about Britain's chances of winning through to honour any undertaking: Gandhi, never a cynic, described the Cripps offer as 'a postdated cheque on a failing bank'. Cripps returned to Britain, and Churchill announced that the offer must now be considered withdrawn.

The Japanese attack was halted in April and May 1942, and thereafter, though the Japanese radio might publicise Bose's 'Indian National Army' and talk of 'the March on Delhi', the threat or promise of Japanese intervention in India was slender. What now should the Congress high command decide? Non-violence had been discarded, negotiation was ruled out. Rajagopalachari saw that India must put its own house in order, and recommended that the high command should at once meet the Muslim League's demand for separation and should initiate discussions with the League to set up a government of national emergency. The high command indignantly rejected these proposals. Gandhi now called upon the British, in his paper *Harijan*, to 'Quit India'. Meeting at Wardha in July 1942, the high command called on the British to end their rule immediately. Gandhi called upon his countrymen to 'Do or Die'.

The government of India responded by interning Gandhi, Nehru, and almost all the high-ranking Congress leaders. This did not prevent a mass rising in the eastern districts of UP and Bihar – planned as a national rising, and having repercussions even among Indian troops defending the Assam–Burma border against the Japanese. In the affected districts, a well-planned campaign of assault and sabotage was carried out: but within six weeks the main threat was over, and British authority more secure than before. Congress was silent; while Jinnah and the League built up support, and while the Communist Party – previously unimportant – increased its membership from 5,000 in 1942 to 53,000 in 1945.

While politics remained almost in a state of suspense in wartime India, Burma under the Japanese occupation became (if in name only) an independent state. Under Japanese patronage, Dr Ba Maw resumed the national leadership. His main supporters were the Thakins, and political groups were merged into the *Maha Bama Asi-ayon* or 'Greater Burma front'. On 1 August 1943, the independence of Burma was recognised by Japan and the other Axis powers. Ba Maw became *Naing gan daw Adipati* or generalissimo. Among his Cabinet of sixteen ministers, Aung San was Minister of Defence, Thakin Nu was Foreign Minister, and the Communist Thakin, Than Tun, became Minister of Agriculture. One group of Communist Thakins refused to truckle to the Japanese and made their way to India to organise a resistance movement; among them was an irreverent mocker of the monks, Thein Pe, known as *Tet pongyi*, from the name of a satire against religion he had written. Another Communist, Thakin Soe, actually went underground and fought the Japanese in the delta area, from 1942 onward. The largest wartime resistance movement in Burma was that of the Karens. Some were civilians, some former members of the Burma Rifles. Cruel reprisals were inflicted upon Karen villages, not only by the Japanese, but also by the forces of Aung San, the Burma Independence Army – later renamed the Burma National Army. The bitterness which developed between the Karens and the BNA was to have endless political repercussions.

Meanwhile, the Burmese were thoroughly disenchanted with Japanese 'Independence' which had brought nothing but ruin to the country. Some time late in 1944, Aung San and the Thakins began to plot how they might get rid of the Japanese. A secret understanding was reached between the BNA leaders and all political groups of any consequence (including the leaders of the Karens) to form a united Anti-Fascist Organisation. Than Tun 'went underground' and helped to organise the resistance in Middle Burma at about the same moment that the British Indian Army was celebrating one of its greatest feats of arms: the capture of Mandalay on 20 March 1945. Seven days later, the BNA decided to show their hand. They vanished into the jungle, and Aung San issued a general order, 'We are now at war.' By now, the Japanese were on the run, and they evacuated Rangoon ahead of the British spearhead which occupied the city on 3 May. British official opinion was divided as to how the former collaborators in Dr Ba Maw's government should be treated. The exiled civil government of Burma wished to have no dealings with Aung San and the BNA, and to restore to power those politicians who had remained faithful to the British cause. Admiral

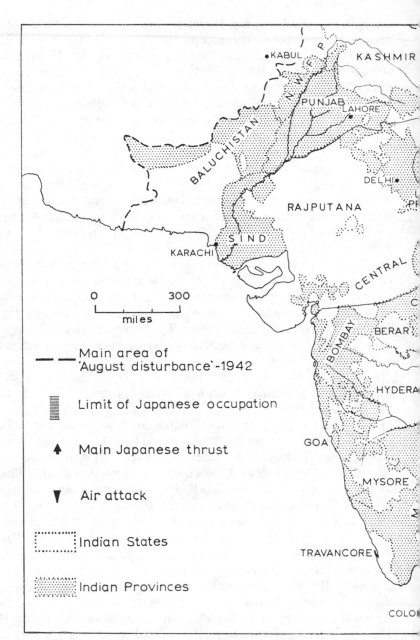

Map 10. The Empire under pressure, 1942–5.

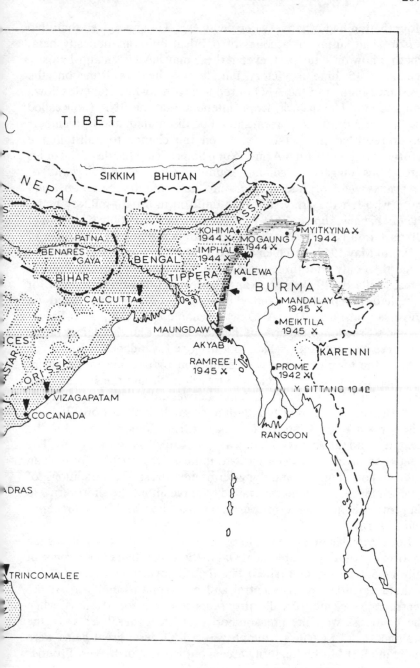

Mountbatten had other very decided views. He announced that: 'No person shall suffer on account of political opinions honestly held, whether now or in the past, even if these may have been anti-British.' When on 15 June a Victory Parade was held in Rangoon, the resistance-banner of the AFO (a red flag with a white star) was flown alongside the Union Jack. It was intended that the BNA (now called the Patriotic Burmese Forces) should be disbanded, and its members either resettled in civil life or given the chance to enlist in the reformed regular Burma Army. Aung San resisted the dispersal of his forces: his biggest bargaining counter. Some of the *Yebaws* or Comrades were drafted *en bloc* into new infantry battalions, and those who left the army still wore uniform in a para-military body, *Pyithu Yebaw Ahpwe*, known in English as the People's Volunteer Organisation (PVO). The British government issued a statement of policy in May 1945, which envisaged a return to the 1935 constitution – and then only after three years of military government. In reply, at a mass rally on 19 August, Aung San came out with a demand for complete independence and the holding of elections based on universal suffrage. The AFO was renamed AFPFL, Anti-Fascist People's Freedom League – perhaps as a sign that the defeat of the Japanese was only the prelude to a struggle for independence.

With the termination of war, politics in India came to life again. The question now was when, and to whom should the British hand over power? The tripartite dialogue between the Congress, League, and British was conducted within a small circle. Lord Wavell, Viceroy since 1943, spoke for the British, Jinnah spoke for the League, and at first Gandhi was the Congress spokesman. The discussion divided between short-term measures (such as forming an interim government) and long-term measures: the conditions of independence. As the parties failed to agree about the short-term, so they switched to long-term considerations, then back to short-term, and so forth.

Lord Wavell's first attempt to bring together Congress and League to form a provisional agreement was made at the Simla Conference of July 1945. This attempt failed. The British government then decided to hold elections for the central and provincial assemblies. At the centre, the League won all thirty seats reserved for Muslims, while the Congress won the great majority of the general seats. In the provinces, the League's triumph was a little less: great gains were made in most Muslim majority areas, but in the North-West Frontier Province the Congressite Red Shirts still stood up to the League.

Flushed with victory, a convention of the new central and provincial League representatives met at Delhi in April 1946. Going beyond the Lahore resolution of 1940 they demanded 'that an unequivocal undertaking be given to implement the establishment of Pakistan without delay.'

Meanwhile, a Cabinet Mission arrived in India in March, 1946, comprising Lord Pethick Lawrence, Secretary of State for India, Sir Stafford Cripps, and A. V. Alexander. It soon became clear that Congress and the League were poles apart, so the three Ministers evolved their own plan, the 'Three Tier Proposal'. This envisaged a central government with vestigial powers, and provincial governments enjoying all residuary powers. The provinces would have the option of forming groups. Group A comprised the Hindu-majority area: Madras, Bombay, United Provinces, Bihar, Central Provinces and Orissa. Group B was composed of the predominantly Muslim north-west: Punjab, North-West Frontier, and Sind. Group C, Bengal and Assam, would have a slight Muslim majority. To the League, this offered the maximum area of the Pakistan demand, within a total Indian unity: still not unattractive to many Leaguers. To Congress, the scheme offered the survival of the outline of the Indian unity. Both Congress and League guardedly accepted the plan. Next it was proposed that an interim government be formed, with five Congress Ministers, five Leaguers, and two minority representatives. Negotiations foundered over the composition of the proposed Ministry, while Nehru went out of his way to observe that: 'The big probability is . . . there will be no grouping.' The Cabinet plan wilted and died in this atmosphere of intransigence. The League refused to join any interim government.

The Viceroy attempted to loosen the log-jam by forming a government without the League. It was at this point that control over the direction of events was wrenched out of the hands of the lawyer-politicians by the action of the mob. As a riposte to Congress, Jinnah proclaimed 16 August 1946, as 'Direct Action Day'. On 16 August Calcutta experienced the worst communal rioting in the torrid history of the city. Bengal, where leaders had always thought of themselves as Bengalis, was tearing apart into two nations, Hindus and Muslims.

Six weeks later, Jinnah abandoned Direct Action and League representatives joined the interim government. Almost alone, Gandhi realised the urgent need for reconciliation. He issued a joint statement with the Muslim Nawab of Bhopal in October, declaring,

'It is understood that all the ministers of the Interim Government will work as a team for the good of the whole of India.' Unfortunately, exactly the opposite was in their minds. In the bickering over portfolios, Congress refused to give up the most important – Foreign Affairs, Defence, the Home Department – but they agreed to hand over Finance, at the suggestion of Sardar Patel, because any Muslim would 'make a fool of himself' in this post (according to Abul Kalam Azad). The aristocratic Liaqat Ali Khan, the League nominee, was advised by Muhammad Ali, a shrewd Secretariat Accounts official, who demonstrated how the whole circus of central power could be made to heed the crack of the Finance whip. Liaqat was able to intervene in New Delhi and beyond. Moreover, he introduced a budget aimed at big business – predominantly Hindu, and supporters of Congress. It was not easy for men who called themselves Socialists, like Nehru, to oppose such a budget.

Returning to the long-term problem, Lord Wavell called on Congress to accept the Cabinet plan without reservations. In reply, on 13 February 1947, Nehru announced the intention of Congress to withdraw from the government unless the League Ministers were dismissed.

The Congress might suppose that time was on their side. Yet despite bold words, Congress was not prepared to try another bid for power by violence, as in 1942; while non-violence – and Gandhi – had been relegated to the sphere of the ideal. On the other hand, Jinnah whose whole inclination was to negotiate, had now concluded that no agreement was possible with an adversary who shifted his ground every time agreement was in sight. Jinnah, the constitutional lawyer, had therefore arrived at the point where force was his final argument.

Lord Wavell was prepared to carry on, as he had done for so many years, patiently working for a solution; but the Labour government had many problems to solve. The Prime Minister announced on 20 February 1947, that Wavell would be replaced as Viceroy by Mountbatten – the man who, in wartime South-East Asia, had never taken 'No' for an answer. Attlee made it clear that, come what may, Britain would withdraw from India by June 1948. By this shock treatment, Attlee hoped to force the Indian leaders to discard some of their illusions and face reality.

Attlee made his announcement against the background of a settlement of Burma's future, concluded on 27 January 1947. When Sir Reginald Dorman-Smith returned to Burma as civil Governor in October 1945, he first appointed as leader of the Executive Council

Sir Paw Tun, who had accompanied the British into wartime exile. The other members were also pre-war legislators. Aung San replied by building up the PVO and other militant forces. U Saw, the pre-war Prime Minister, had been interned by the British for intriguing with the Japanese; he was released in January 1946, and began to organise a strong-arm following for a trial of strength with Aung San. In July 1946, the more ruthless Communists (those led by Thakin Soe, the first resistance fighter) 'went underground', in contemporary parlance, and returned to a guerilla war; this time against the British. They were known as the Red Flag Communists. On 31 August, Dorman-Smith was replaced by Sir Hubert Rance, known for his ability to get on with Aung San and the former BNA leaders. Six days after his arrival, the police went on strike: their grievances had been building up for months. Aung San used the opportunity to demonstrate the hold of the AFPFL over the country: the strike became general in the public services and in schools and colleges. The Governor was reluctant to use the Indian troops garrisoning the country for internal security – he had but one British battalion at call. He decided he must come to terms with Aung San. On 26 September 1946, a new Executive Council was formed. Out of nine members, six were AFPFL nominees, while one was U Tin Tut, a senior civil servant. Aung San was Prime Minister in all but name, with Tin Tut as his *éminence grise*. In appointing his Ministers, Aung San picked one Communist, *Tet pongyi* Thein Pe, but passed over Than Tun, the chief Communist leader. The omission was deliberate. Aung San and Than Tun had been very close: they had married two sisters. But Than Tun was the one strong man capable of challenging Aung San, with the backing among the rural masses to give him a power-base. The challenge was deliberate: and Than Tun took it up. He demanded a larger share of power. Aung San stood firm. Than Tun now declared a general strike: against the AFPFL government, not the British. Aung San expelled the Communists from all offices within the AFPFL and the trade unions. Than Tun was content to lay low and bide his time. Having shown himself master of the politicians and the administrators, Aung San now presented a demand for immediate independence. On 20 December 1946, Attlee announced a new policy: a Burmese delegation would be invited to London to discuss the terms for transfer of power in Burma. Aung San came to London in January 1947, and with Tin Tut at his elbow succeeded in securing all that he wanted. On 27 January a document known as the Attlee Aung San agreement was signed. Its import was summarised by Aung San as 'Full independence within one year'.

This agreement confirmed Aung San's standing with the Burmese, but there remained the minority peoples to be reassured. A meeting was staged at Panglong in the Southern Shan States, at which Aung San succeeded in winning over the Kachins and Shans by promises of statehood. However, the Karens, the largest minority group, remained aloof. They had not forgotten the violent deeds of some sections of the BNA against their villages, and they mistrusted the PVO with their displays of force. The next step, under the Attlee–Aung San agreement, was the holding of elections for a constituent assembly. These took place under AFPFL auspices.

There were 182 'general' seats, of which AFPFL won 176; the 'White Flag' Communists led by Than Tun contested 14 constituencies but won only six (giving twelve representatives). The Karens were in disarray, and the main organisation, the Karen National Defence Organisation (KNDO) ordered a boycott: their 24 MPs were therefore returned virtually unopposed by the pro-AFPFL Karen Youth Congress. A majority of the new members of the constituent assembly belonged to the PVO or the Socialist Party. Before the assembly came together, the AFPFL held a General Convention which largely determined the form of independence. Burma would be an independent sovereign republic, outside the British Commonwealth. (At this stage no one had considered the possibility of a republic remaining within the Commonwealth.) The constituent assembly met in June, and unanimously chose Thakin Nu as its President: Nu had made up his mind to leave politics and devote his life to literature, but he was persuaded by Aung San to be a member of the assembly.

Then came the event which still dominates the political life of Burma. At 10.40 am on 19 July 1947, four youths dressed in army uniform entered the room where the Cabinet was meeting. They sprayed the room with sten gun fire: then, still unchallenged, they left. Dead or dying lay Aung San and six other Ministers. In this hour of crisis, Sir Hubert Rance called upon Thakin Nu to become premier, and the next day he took up office. The murderers were traced to the home of U Saw. One of Aung San's henchmen had already tried to assassinate U Saw, and he calculated that as leader of the opposition he would be called on to form a government if Aung San was killed! U Saw was tried and executed on 8 May 1948. His plans were foiled by the steadiness of Governor Rance and the resolution of Thakin Nu who now (with genuine reluctance) prepared to lead his country towards independence.

Aung San had faced the British and the Communists, and within a few months he had made himself Prime Minister and had obtained a constitutional agreement which gave Burma independence in the form he wanted, many years ahead of the time-table laid down in British policy. It was a triumph of will: despite the alacrity with which the Labour government acquiesced in his demands, heedless of the pleas of the heroic Karen resistance leaders. In India, there was no such assertion of will by the leaders of the Congress. In the end, they accepted a solution and a time-table largely prescribed by the British and by Jinnah.

When Mountbatten arrived as Viceroy, he made it clear that he would press ahead with the transfer of power: a transfer to provincial governments, if no agreement was forthcoming at the centre. Gandhi made one last effort at reconciliation. He urged the Viceroy to dismiss the existing Cabinet, and ask Jinnah to form his own. This might consist of Muslims – or whoever he chose to appoint. Jinnah would be free to work for Pakistan if he chose: 'Provided that he was successful in appealing to reason and did not use force.' This offer was repudiated by Congress, and Gandhi announced that he would take no further part in negotiations. The drift towards communalism and violence continued. Nehru and the men of action in Congress shrank from appealing to force, as Aung San had done. It seemed that India would become a congeries of provinces: a South Asian Balkans. The situation was largely retrieved by Sardar Patel who realised the dangers of drift: the growing threat of communal chaos and the opportunities opened to the Princes to 'go it alone'. He saw the need for a rapid transfer of power, and constitutional experts showed him how this could be achieved. He succeeded in convincing the Congress leaders that Pakistan would be preferable to Balkanisation. Moreover, if it was accepted that Pakistan was being separated from India, as Burma had been in 1937, this would not be partition: the essential India would remain. To these constitutional arguments, Mountbatten added his own personal, persuasive charm. Nehru acquiesced. To facilitate the transfer of power, it was agreed that the new states should function as Dominions, owing allegiance to the Crown, under the framework of the 1935 Act. And so, independence was obtained under a constitution which Gandhi once described as 'Satanic' (though he admitted he had never read the 1935 Act).

Jinnah had obtained Pakistan: but the arguments which had been employed (the 'Two Nations' theory) to obtain self-determination for the Muslims could be applied to the two great provinces of Punjab and Bengal, with their immense non-Muslim minorities.[1] Assam (which would have joined the Muslim-majority group B under the Cabinet plan) included only one largely Muslim district: Sylhet. So Jinnah was required to accept what he had often scornfully called a 'motheaten' Pakistan.

The new plan was announced by the Viceroy on 3 June 1947. He added that the actual date of the transfer of power would be advanced to August 1947, because of the deterioration in communal relations and the uncertainty in the public services. Just two months remained to partition the Indian sub-continent.

It was realised that partition must bring great strain, and possibly bloodshed. The actual boundaries of Pakistan had still to be drawn. The task was given to a judicial tribunal of five: two Muslims, two non-Muslims, with a British chairman. The Muslim and non-Muslim boundary projections disagreed so completely that it was left to the English chairman, Lord Radcliffe, to make his own award: which would be announced after 15 August, Independence Day. Wherever the boundary came, it must fail to satisfy. The new East Pakistan province would be much the same as the Eastern Bengal of the 1905 partition: and the majority of town-dwellers in the East, together with almost all the professional and trading classes, were Hindu. But the main problem was Punjab. The northern districts were populated by Muslim cultivators. The southern districts had a mixed Hindu and Muslim population, with the former in the majority. The middle districts, the *Manjha*, were the country of the Sikhs. The older areas of cultivation included a number of petty Sikh states, while away to the west stretched the canal colonies – those former desert wastes, brought into fruitful prosperity by pioneers, among whom some of the most enterprising were Sikhs. Somewhere in this belt of territory the new frontier must be drawn. When Pakistan had first been mooted, some had urged a Muslim–Sikh *rapprochement* on a basis of agricultural interests on something like the old Unionist basis. But to gain control of Punjab, Jinnah had set out to smash the Unionist Party and all it stood for, and as independence and the moment of truth came nearer, the Sikhs flung in their lot with Congress against the League.

---

[1] According to the 1931 Census, in Punjab there were 16,217,242 Muslims and 12,201,577 non-Muslims, while in Bengal there were 33,005,434 Muslims and 27,301,091 non-Muslims.

To guard against violence in the Punjab, a special Boundary Force was provided by the superb 19th Indian Division which had captured Mandalay. The communal rioting which had already cost the lives of thousands had originated in Calcutta: thither proceeded what Lord Mountbatten called the 'one man boundary force': Gandhi. As 15 August drew nearer, officials in Delhi tried to divide up the financial and material assets of the government of India. The great Indian Army, fresh from triumph in the Second World War in the Middle East, Italy, Burma and the Far East, was laboriously separated into Muslim and Non-Muslim units. Muslim civil servants were given the option of staying in their own provinces or proceeding to Pakistan. The residuum of British civil servants – no more than 600 now – continued to take the strain of supreme responsibility, while the old loyalties were dissolving and strange new loyalties were emerging. An air of unreality hung over all: was this British Empire of nearly two hundred years really about to disappear? Even the pronouncements of the leading politicians seemed to be directed more to the old object of assailing the British than the new goal of building a nation. Meanwhile, in the back streets of city bazaars, and even in little country towns, men spoke words of foreboding, and the rowdies and fanatics looked to their weapons. When the appointed day arrived, smoke was already beginning to rise from burning villages in the 'Land of the Five Rivers', Punjab. During the following weeks there was a mass exodus of Hindus and Sikhs from what had become West Pakistan, and an even greater flood of Muslims from Delhi and East Punjab into the new state. It has been calculated that about six million moved east and eight million moved westward. Perhaps as many as 200,000 did not get to journey's end, but were massacred. It was a horrific start to relations between the two great neighbours.

When independence came to Burma, on 4 January 1948, violence was also loose in the land. Burma's constitution was drafted with great speed and adopted on 24 September 1947. Nu insisted that this was a Leftist constitution, but although declarations in favour of a welfare state were included, the familiar structure of parliamentary government and independent courts of justice provided the foundation. All that now remained was to legitimise the break with Britain. This came with a Treaty concluded on 17 October 1947, between Great Britain and 'the Provisional Government of Burma'. Thakin Nu gracefully acknowledged the goodwill shown by the departing Imperial power: 'From beginning to end, the British government were at pains to win our goodwill rather than our treasure.' The

Communists launched a big propaganda campaign against the Treaty. Concentrating upon the defence agreement (concluded at Burma's request) the Communists tried to show up the Nu government as British stooges. In reply, Thakin Nu made wholehearted efforts to bring back the extreme Left into the AFPFL fold. He was again rebuffed. When the new Union flag was hoisted at the hour pronounced propitious by the astrologers – 4.00 am on 4 January 1948 – some insurgents were already in the field to challenge the new government. All around, others awaited the moment to strike.

By contrast, when independence came to Ceylon on 4 February 1948 – exactly one month after Burma, and less than six months after India and Pakistan – the event was celebrated as a public holiday, a kind of festival, and little more. When the brother of King George VI handed over the instruments of independence in a great pavilion at Kandy, there was little constitutional innovation. Ceylon remained a Dominion of the Crown (as it remained until 1972) and the last British Governor under the Colonial Office became the first Governor-General of Ceylon. When he departed, it was to hand his office over to Lord Soulbury, who remained as representative of the Crown at King's (later Queen's) House down to 1954. The Soulbury Commission's recommendation for internal self-government, made in 1944, was carried further by the press of events. Jennings and other advocates urged the British government that it would be ungracious and downright unjust to delay giving full independence to a Ceylon which had played a full part in the war effort, through the decision of her political leaders, when independence was granted to an India whose leaders had been at best neutral and to a Burma where the 'Freedom Fighters' had been fighting alongside the Japanese. The point was grasped by the Labour government, and the constitutional draft was amended to concede full independence. And yet the means whereby this was implemented – by Orders in Council, a mere official notice instead of the Acts of Parliament for India and Pakistan, and the Treaty signed with Burma – seemed to indicate the difference in the nature of the independence which was being achieved.

It was not until 1947 that D. S. Senanayake decided to create a political instrument for his system of personal politics. The United National Party brought together his Sinhalese associates from the State Council, the old Ceylon National Congress, a number of Tamils, the Ceylon Muslim League and S. W. R. D. Bandaranaike's *Sinhala Maha Sabha*: in fact, all political elements except the extreme Left. From this impressive basis of unity, Mr Senanayake surveyed the task ahead. Contemplating an island that was prosperous, cosmopolitan and devoid of political or religious fanaticism, he must have been well pleased with the contrast to the divisions and bitterness which were tearing at the newly-independent neighbouring countries of South Asia. Yet, in a few short years, Ceylon was to be plunged into a time of testing trial with all the rest.

CHRONOLOGY OF EVENTS LEADING TO INDEPENDENCE

1917: Montagu's declaration preparing first moves to Indian self-government.
1919: Gandhi's first civil disobedience campaign; Amritsar massacre; Government of India Act.
1920: Elections for Dyarchy provincial Councils; Burma excluded.
1921: Ceylon legislature enlarged.
1922: Gandhi's second campaign: Congress split, with some adopting 'Council entry'.
1923: Burma brought into Dyarchy scheme.
1924: Elected majority in Ceylon legislature.
1927: Simon Commission advises on political development in India and Burma; Donoughmore Commission given same task in Ceylon.
1929: Viceroy's statement on Dominion Status fails to satisfy Gandhi.
1930: 1st Round Table Conference on India; anti-Indian riot, Rangoon.
1931: 2nd Round Table Conference attended by Gandhi; November, RTC on Burma.
1932: Elections in Burma on issue of separation from India.
1933: Gandhi fasts against untouchability.
1935: Government of India Act foreshadows federation; Government of Burma Act.
1936: December, Burma election results in Ba Maw becoming Premier.
1937: 1 April, Burma separated from India; provincial elections, India, Congress ministries in seven provinces.
1938: July, anti-Indian riots, Burma.
1939: September, on outbreak of war, Viceroy announces India at war with Germany; October, Congress ministries resign.

1940: March, Muslim League's resolution – 'Pakistan'; August, Viceroy makes offer on postwar independence.
1941: December, war between Britain and Japan; invasion of Burma starts.
1942: March, Rangoon falls, Indian exodus; 23 March, Cripps in Delhi with new offer; 10 April, Congress reject Cripps offer; May, British forces leave Burma; 8 August, Gandhi tells India, 'Do or Die'; 9 August, Congress leaders interned.
1943: Famine in Bengal; 1 August, Japan declares Burma independent; October, Wavell arrives as Viceroy.
1944: Japanese advance into India repulsed; November, British advance begins; December–April 1945, Soulbury Commission tours Ceylon.
1945: 3 May, British reoccupy Rangoon; 17 May, British announcement, no political advance in Burma for three years; June–July, Simla Conference, no agreement; 14 August, Japanese surrender; December–January 1946, elections throughout India.
1946: 23 March–29 June, Cabinet Mission in India; their plan gains equivocal acceptance; 10 August, Interim Government under Nehru; 16 August League Direct Action Day, Great Calcutta Killing; November, police strike, Burma, Aung San and AFPFL given majority in Governor's Council; 20 December, Attlee announces speed-up of Burma's independence.
1947: January, Burmese leaders visit London; Aung San announces 'Independence Within One Year'; 20 February, Attlee announces Britain to leave India by June 1948, with Mountbatten as new Viceroy; March, Senanayake demands full Dominion status for Ceylon; April, AFPFL victory in Burma elections; May, AFPFL state Burma will be republic; 3 June, Mountbatten announces Congress–League agreement on partition scheme; 18 June, parliamentary statement 'Immediate Steps' to full self-government for Ceylon; 19 July, Aung San assassinated, Nu takes over in Burma; 15 August, independence for India and Pakistan; 17 August Partition Award announced; 17 October, Treaty, Britain and Burma.
1948: 4 January, Burma independent; 4 February, Ceylon 'independent'.

10 Independence: the Springtime

The concluding section of this book is divided into two chapters whose titles attempt to reproduce the atmosphere of the times with their suggestion of hope and disillusionment. Of course, there was no definite moment at which the hopes and dreams turned sour. There can be no doubt that the first decade of independence was one of optimism shared by almost all:

> Bliss was it in that dawn to be alive
> But to be young was very heaven.

So wrote the young Wordsworth of the early days of the French revolution. By the late 1950s there were signs that independence had not liberated the people and their leaders from their constraints and frustrations, as all who were politically active had expected. Perhaps the legacy of colonialism could be blamed for many problems. However, when differences between India and Pakistan over Kashmir degenerated into warfare in 1965 there was a realisation that these problems were not going away: they would not be easily resolved. Peaceful Co-Existence, or Non-Alignment as India preferred to define it was not the complete answer. When war broke out between two states and peoples whose destinies had been shared for centuries this was indeed a turning point in history. Thereafter fissiparous pressures began to grow into critical proportions; both in national politics and between peoples and cultures.

These two chapters will be separated in the mid-1960s: not that everything which followed was 'downhill all the way'. And to focus upon the outstanding events may entail missing unspectacular improvements. However, the unfolding of 'the Asian Drama' does reveal a gathering cycle of crisis and violence which is still escalating in the 1980s. If one had to choose one year when South Asia 'lost its innocence' it would be 1962 when China launched an attack on the north-eastern border of India (invariably described as an 'invasion'), when the second military coup in Burma removed a civilian government elected by an overwhelming majority two years earlier, and when an attempt was made to launch a military coup in placid

Ceylon. The year also saw the introduction of 'Guided Democracy' in Pakistan; certainly not among the most momentous events in that country's turbulent history, but a claim that an authoritarian system could provide an answer to the failures of parliamentary democracy.

In 1964 the death of Nehru marked the passing of an era, while the following year when the unthinkable happened: war between India and Pakistan this was also in a different way a watershed. We shall close this chapter with those years and begin again with the accession of Indira Gandhi to supreme office, a development which opened up another phase in the history of South Asia.

The lands that had become four soverign states had gained their freedom from colonial rule through the personality and prowess of their major leaders, backed by political organisation which gave the appearance and perhaps the substance of mass support. Much now depended on the leaders. India was fortunate in her prime minister; Nehru had the rare distinction evoked by that overworked term *charismatic*. Amid the challenges which in the early days could have swamped a lesser man he rose magnificently to every occasion. Moreover, he remained at the helm throughout most of the first two decades. In the early days he had as his coadjutor Sardar Patel whose practical realism and business ability admirably complemented the more mercurial qualities of Nehru. Besides the outstanding ability of its top leadership, India had evolved a super-party, the Congress, which adjusted rapidly from the requirements of agitational politics to those of government. For most of the first two decades Congress provided a political framework throughout the Indian Union.

None of the other new nations enjoyed similar advantages. Pakistan, in Jinnah, also had a venerated leader but he was already a sick man and survived only twelve months after independence. His lieutenant, Liaqat Ali Khan, lacked his charisma and then only outlived his chief by three years. The challenge of winning the Muslim vote in the 1945–6 elections galvanised the Muslim League into fighting a popular campaign; but thereafter the League relapsed into what it had been before – a set of power-brokers. In Burma, Aung San, the nation's hero was already dead. His successor, the mild and modest Thakin Nu was to show that he possessed courage: but not the ruthlessness which had enabled Aung San to outface the British and outwit his adversaries. As for political organisation: the AFPFL had begun to crumble at the edges even before Aung San's death and it was soon to lose other adherents, even though it survived (more or less) until 1958. Finally, Ceylon's middle-class politics had not needed the active support of a mass organisation: the party of government, the United National Party (UNP) was not actually created until after the formal transfer of power. Don Senanayake was an effective and efficient leader, though he did not aspire to be a Nehru or a Jinnah. He died in 1952, leaving a vacuum at the top.

The new nations had two immediate tasks to tackle in order to implement independence: one was to establish the integrity of their territory and the second was to work out a constitution which would create a setting in which national needs and aspirations could be realised. There were varying responses.

As an island with a long-established administration there were no questions about Ceylon's territorial integrity. Also, because constitutional evolution had progressed so far before the transfer of power, the United Kingdom Order in Council which set up the new Dominion seemed to suffice: after all, universal suffrage, a great novelty elsewhere in South Asia, was already long familiar. Burma adopted its constitution before independence. There did not seem to be any pressing territorial problems, though it was known that China had historic claims to sections of the north-west borderland. As for internal claims, the Shans and Kachins had been awarded their own states in the constitution. The only minority still restless and dissatisfied were the Karens; and Nu was prepared to discuss alternatives with more generosity than Aung San had shown.

India had to handle the 582 former Princely states which the British had treated with such care. The vast majority were induced by Mountbatten to accede to the Indian Union on the eve of independence in return for recognition of their rulers' privileges. There were three recalcitrant rulers. The small Hindu-majority state of Junagadh had a Muslim ruler who announced he would join Pakistan though his little state was surrounded by Indian Kathiawar. He was very rapidly disabused. The only two remaining uncommitted were the biggest fish in the princely ocean: Hyderabad and Kashmir. The former had a largely Hindu population and was situated in the heart of India; nevertheless, the Muslim ruler, the Nizam, planned to launch out on his own (Hyderabad was larger than many European states). For a year he prevaricated; then Patel (responsible for liquidating the princely domains) sent in the Indian Army in September 1948. After a brief resistance the Hyderabad forces capitulated.

Kashmir presented the contrasting paradox of a Hindu maharaja with a predominantly Muslim population in a state contiguous to the new Pakistan. If the principle of 'like with like' acknowledged in the division of the provinces of Punjab and Bengal was followed, Kashmir must certainly join Pakistan. Mountbatten (still Governor-General for ten months after independence) urged the Maharaja to do so; but he procrastinated and very unwisely Jinnah and his minions decided to make up his mind for him by sending in tribal levies, *lashkars*, from the North West Frontier. Totally undisciplined, their advance was delayed by looting and killing. The Maharaja fled to Delhi to ask to join the new India. Mountbatten reluctantly accepted, and an Indian battalion was flown to restore order. They halted the tribesmen and began to drive them back. Subsequently, Pakistan sent in elements of the army in plain clothes, and a civil war threatened. India invoked the authority of the United Nations and a cease fire was agreed in January 1949. (Map 11). A UN plebiscite was supposed to determine the wishes of the Kashmir people, but this was never held. Apart from a sliver of contiguous territory occupied by Pakistan, Kashmir had effectively become part of India.

Tiny portions of the Indian coastline had remained in French possession since the eighteenth century. France graciously accepted their incorporation into India conditional on the preservation of French culture (so that still in the 1980s in schools in Pondicherry teaching is in French as the 'native' language). Portugal showed no disposition to give up its larger possession, Goa, with consequences that followed much later.

Meanwhile, India proceeded to deliberate upon its new constitution. Although the source is not acknowledged, its main provisions flow from the 1935 Government of India Act. There is a federal structure, with State governments throughout the country. Their powers are more limited than the States of America. Each state has a legislature with a Chief Minister who must have an elected majority. At the centre, the Prime Minister is invariably the leader of the majority party in the Lower House of Parliament (*Lok Sabha*). He or she chooses the Cabinet. The President is largely a ceremonial Head of State though exercising emergency powers on the advice of the Prime Minister, at the centre or in any of the states. This constitution, adopted in November 1949, has survived all the strains of the last forty years. Amendments have been introduced, but its essential structure remains unaltered.

The experience of Pakistan could not have been more different. Former princely states, including Kelat and Bahawalpur were absorbed; but three ministates on the northern border (Amb, Dir, Chitral and Swat) were left alone. The Indian seizure of Kashmir, as it was perceived, remained a major irritant and grievance. The 'K' was an integral part of Pakistan: it was inalienable.

The adoption of a constitution was delayed because two outstanding problems defied solution – and were in conflict – these were religion and regionalism. In his inaugural speech in August 1947 Jinnah called eloquently for a common citizenship in a secular state. Inevitably, others asked why, then, fight for Pakistan? The principal Islamic theologian, Abul Ala Maududi denounced the new state as *Kufr*, unlawful. After much debate the Constituent Assembly adopted an Objectives Resolution which ambiguously affirmed 'Sovereignty over the entire universe belongs to Allah Almighty alone' and then went on 'The Constituent Assembly ... have resolved to frame a constitution': thus, in the view of Supreme Court Judge Munir trying to abrogate God's prerogative. The Hindu minority in the Assembly opposed the resolution; from March 1949 to December 1952 a basic principles committee wrestled with the dilemma.

Regional differences and inequalities provided even more of a sore and sensitive grievance. East Pakistan contained a majority of the total population, yet the capital and the government were in the West and Westerners almost monopolised positions of power and influence. When Jinnah died, Nizammudin of Bengal became Governor-General, though without the Qaid-i-Azam's overarching authority. After Liaqat Ali was shot, Nizammudin stepped into the premiership and a former official, a tough Punjabi, Ghulam Mohammad became Governor-General. In 1953 a crisis blew up in which the members of the Ahmadiyyah community, unorthodox Muslims were attacked in riots in Lahore and other cities. The pious Nizammudin vacillated, and Ghulam Mohammad dismissed him from office though he still commanded a majority in the Assembly. The move was unconstitutional, and there were protests in the Assembly which was subsequently dissolved by the Governor-General.

All this was particularly resented in East Pakistan where elections were held for the provincial legislature in 1954 (the only elections conducted under a popular franchise). The Muslim League was ignominiously defeated, winning only ten of the 310 seats. The winners formed a heterogeneous coalition led by the veteran Fazl Huq and the newly-returned Suhrawardy. This volatile situation was stifled by sending Major-General Iskander Mirza, a wily former Political Officer as Governor. He rapidly dispersed the coalition and substituted martial law. Ghulam Mohammad, now ailing, designated

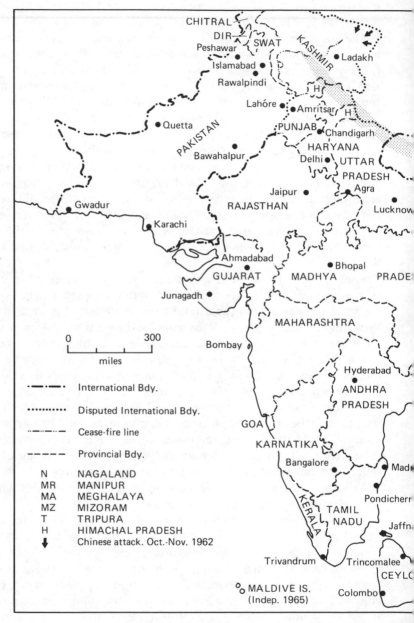

Map 11. Independence and after. States identified by names in use in 1970s and 198(

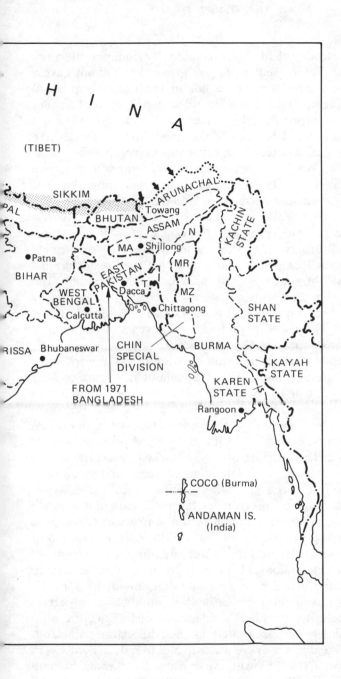

him his successor.

A second Assembly had been created by indirect election. Although the League formed the largest group they did not have a majority. The Assembly convened, not in the intensely political atmosphere of Karachi but in a remote hill station, Murree. Iskander Mirza brought in a former Punjabi civil servant (he had guided Liaqat Ali) as Prime Minister: Chaudhri Muhammad Ali. He tackled the problem in two parts. Whereas East Pakistan was merely the residual part of Bengal, the West was composed of four major administrative units: Punjab, Sind, the Frontier and Baluchistan (plus the four ministates which were not affected). In 1955 the four provinces were amalgamated as West Pakistan: much to the disgust of Pathans, Sindhis and Baluchis. Then the Chaudhri went ahead with a constitution, enacted in February 1956. This document began by reaffirming the 1949 Objectives Resolution, and stating that the President must be a Muslim while the state was designated an Islamic Republic. The differences between the two wings were supposed to be settled by giving each equal representation (150 MPs each) with ten additional seats for women. This constitution had been 8½ years in gestation; it was to be entirely scrapped in October 1958.

Relations between the nation-states of South Asia were most cordial in the early and mid-1950s. Throughout the years of Nu's premiership in Burma he enjoyed close personal relations with Nehru and the two men consulted frequently. India and Pakistan remained on distant terms over most of the decade. There were periodical meetings between Nehru and the various Pakistani prime ministers, but these always lacked intimacy and were marked by a certain sense of inferiority on their side as prime ministers came and went while Nehru seemed to go on for ever. India's relations with Ceylon mainly hinged upon the unsolved problem of the thousands of tea estate workers and other labourers of Indian descent who were not accepted as citizens, deprived of civic rights. At a conference in London in 1953, Dudley Senanayake produced a formula which was to form the basis of all future negotiations. He proposed to divide them into three categories. The first would be registered as citizens of Ceylon; the second were not qualified for citizenship but would be given permanent residence permits; the third would qualify for Indian citizenship and would gradually be repatriated to their ancestral homeland. Negotiations broke down over Nehru's attempt to reduce numbers in the third category. The following year when Kotelawala became premier it appeared that they were in agreement; but this also turned out to be an illusion in practice.

South Asia remained in the sterling area and in general the four countries followed common economic policies: although when Britain devalued in 1949 and South Asia followed suit, Pakistan held out, calculating that its jute exports could sustain the old exchange rates. In 1951 the finance ministers gathered at Colombo along with certain white members of the Commonwealth and subscribed to the Colombo Plan for economic co-operation. Burma joined in 1952. The plan was a major stimulus in those early days but later waned in importance as the United States became the principal donor in the area.

The leaders of the four South Asian states met with Sukarno of Indonesia in April 1954, also in Colombo. This meeting began the initiative which led to the Asian-African Conference at Bandung in 1955. The earlier spirit of co-operation was somewhat dissipated at Bandung where Kotelawala proposed an amendment to a resolution on colonialism by referring to Soviet domination in Eastern Europe. Nehru responded indignantly.

That was a passing difference, but the cloud over India's relations with Pakistan was further darkened when John Foster Dulles brought that country into his network of military containment organised around the Soviet Union. Beside bilateral military arrangements, Pakistan was persuaded to join the United States, Britain and other nations, western and Asian in signing the Manila Treaty which inaugurated the South East Asia Treaty Organisation (SEATO). As a result, Pakistan received a sizeable supply of military hardware, including modern tanks and jet fighters. The military balance between Pakistan and India was decisively affected.

The enhanced importance of the military in Pakistan, combined with the machinations and manoeuvrings of the top politicians were important factors in contributing to the impotence of the public in participating in the affairs of their country. Elsewhere, a good start was made in operating democratic institutions by involving the people in periodic general elections. The earliest were held in Burma, though because of continuing unrest in the districts it was necessary to stagger the first election from June to October 1951. The AFPFL had suffered many defections during the first critical years. The Communists had gone underground, and took no part. The Socialists had deserted Nu in 1949, making overtures to the Communists, but they were back in the AFPFL in 1951 though behaving almost as a separate party. The hill peoples gave Nu loyal support though running their own political organisations. The AFPFL and its adherents gained 85 per cent of the seats on 60 per cent of the popular vote. There was a minute Right Wing opposition and to the Left the Burma Workers and Peasants Party (BWPP) a Socialist splinter group having links with the underground Communists. In 1956 it was possible to hold all contests simultaneously, though ten constituencies were still too disturbed for elections. The opposition coalesced round the BWPP to present a United Front. The AFPFL won a comfortable majority but the United Front managed to gain 47 seats, mostly in middle Burma, the Communists' power base.

Nu retired from the premiership to purge the AFPFL of corrupt elements, while the bombastic Socialist Ba Swe became premier for a year. After Nu's return, the Socialists turned against him. He survived a no-confidence motion, but decided to make another appeal to the country. The Socialists conferred with the army commander, and in response General Ne Win applied pressure. Parliament was convened in October 1958 to sanction a handover to the General. He ruled the country for eighteen months, employing a favourite military formula 'to clear up the mess'. He then announced another election and gave open support to the Socialists. It seemed they must take power, but the country decided otherwise. Against all the heavyweights, Nu launched into a Roosevelt-style campaign, ably supported by Aung San's widow, Daw Khin Kyi. To general surprise, Nu's group, who now took the name *Pyidaungsu Ahpwe-Gyok* (in English, referred to as the Union League) were the winners. In the Lower House they had 166 seats; the Socialists only 38, with 22 going to others. Nu's promises included recognising Buddhism as the main religion and granting regional autonomy to the minorities. These promises seemed rash to critics.

India seemed to justify the reputation as 'the model democracy' which it acquired in the 1950s. Congress enjoyed an impregnable majority in parliament, yet Nehru took care to emphasise its importance as the forum of the nation. He attended its sessions regularly, enduring with a patience alien to his nature the verbose and vapid speeches; trying to ensure that the opposition was treated with respect.

The first election, held in 1952 was to choose 489 MPs in the *Lok Sabha* and 3,373 representatives in the state legislatures. Nehru towered over all others, travelling thousands of miles electioneering. At the Centre, Congress won 362 seats on 45 per cent of the total vote. The Communists – whose strategy was to concentrate resources where most effective – won 23 seats on 3 per cent of votes, while the Socialists won 12 though receiving nearly 11 per cent of the vote. The result was a reflection of the lopsided 'First Past the Post' system which was everywhere taken over from the British practice. At the state level, Congress formed all the ministries though opposition proved strong in Travancore-Cochin (later Kerala) in Madras and in the Sikh-dominated areas of Punjab.

The second election in 1957 found Congress just as strong at the Centre: 494 seats were now at stake, and they won 366 on 46 per cent of votes. The Communists won 29 (10 per cent) and the Socialists 24 (15 per cent). A new phenomenon was the Jan Sangh (People's Party) a Hindu communal party: they won only four seats on 6 per cent of the vote, concentrated in areas where refugees from Pakistan nursed grievances. In the states, the most unexpected result came in Kerala where the Communist Party of India (CPI) won 60 of the 124 seats and Congress won only 43. Independents supporting the CPI won 5; the Muslim League won 8, and there were 10 others representing various splinter groups. Kerala had the highest percentage of graduates of anywhere in India – and the highest rate of unemployment. Nehru accepted the formation of a Communist state government, though a sharp watch was kept. When the Communists encouraged militancy in the trade unions, the Centre intervened and President's rule was imposed: the first time this power was exercised. When another election was held in Kerala in 1960, the Congress was able to form the government: partly because the Roman Catholic church exerted influence among the large Christian population.

At the third general election in 1962 all the parties were improving their organisation and their techniques. Congress won 355 seats at the Centre; the Communists won 29 and the Socialists 17. Congress still controlled all the state governments though in Madras the party of Tamil separatism, the Dravida Munnetra Kazhagam (DMK) nearly broke through. In most of the states the Congress was plagued by factionalism and the powerful Chief Minister of Madras, Kamaraj, proposed that a number of leading figures – Chief Ministers and Cabinet Ministers – should step down and clear the air. It was significant that this move to purify the organisation came not from Nehru but from one of the new breed of politicians whose power base was established not at Delhi but locally. Factionalism remained a major threat still at the time of Nehru's death in 1964.

It was in Ceylon that ethnic and religious forces assumed the most virulent form. Even before independence, the British Governor wrote of Don Senanayake and his arch-rival S. W. R. D. Bandaranaike, 'These two Ministers are rivals in the race for political leadership of the Sinhalese and think that he who displays the greater degree of xenophobia will be the winner'. In the election held immediately before power was transferred, Senanayake was leader of a loose coalition which gained 41 seats out of a total of 95. With the support of six nominated members he secured a majority. The rights of the Indian Tamils were already being squeezed but there were seven plantation seats where members of the Ceylon Indian Congress were returned. It was estimated that in twenty other seats Indian voters had helped Leftist candidates to win. In 1949 Senanayake introduced the Ceylon (Parliamentary Elections) Amendment Act which effectively removed voters of Indian origin from the electoral roll and put seven Kandyan plantation seats into Senanayake's pocket.

He was largely a self-made man, but Bandaranaike was the son of Ceylon's leading Establishment figure; he was educated at Oxford and held vaguely Leftist views but until 1951 he was UNP Minister of Health. He resigned, went into opposition, and founded the Sri Lanka Freedom Party (SLFP). At the 1952 election, although he was returned his new party could not oust the now secure UNP. Then Senanayake died. He was succeeded by his son Dudley, whose temperament was unsuited to the premiership. He handed over to Sir John Kotelawala, another relation (not for nothing was the UNP called the 'Uncles and Nephews Party').

At the 1956 election, Bandaranaike ran a sensational campaign to arouse the resentment of the rural Sinhalese against the Tamils who were alleged to have 'stolen' all the posts in the administration. Although he was an agnostic he made great play with Buddhism as the only national religion of Ceylon. This populist, chauvinist appeal succeeded; militant monks turned out in support and the UNP was shattered retaining only eight seats. Now the new prime minister had to satisfy his Sinhalese supporters. A Bill was immediately introduced making Sinhalese the sole national language. The Ceylon Tamils had stood aside when their Indian cousins lost their rights; now they took fright. In 1958 Bandaranaike concluded a pact with the leader of the minority Tamil Federal Party; and then repudiated the pact under intense pressure from within his party. Communal rioting ensued, lasting throughout May and June 1958, causing the Governor-General to intervene. He declared a state of emergency which was not lifted until March 1959. The Sinhalese extremists remained dissatisfied and in September 1959 a disgruntled monk shot the prime minister.

After a short time, his widow, Mrs Sirimavo Bandaranaike was prevailed upon to take her husband's place. When an election was called in March 1960 the result was indecisive; but Dudley Senanayake was able to form a minority UNP government with Tamil support. He failed to satisfy their demands and they switched sides. In July 1960 Mrs Bandaranaike came to power as the world's first woman prime minister. She produced a welfare programme whose benefits went mainly to the Sinhalese. Within the SLFP the right wingers became concerned at the influence exerted by their electoral partners, the Marxist Lanka Sama Samaj. When the next election became due in 1965 Dudley Senanayake returned with a stable UNP majority. These swings from Left to Right and back did not in actuality represent large shifts in public opinion but were caused by minor fluctuations under the 'First Past the Post' system: but then, no other was approved in South Asia. How can one account for the very different consequences in India, Pakistan and Ceylon?

In Pakistan until two years before independence the traditional leaders had not supported the Muslim League which was in the hands of urban lawyer politicians. When the great landlords of Punjab and Sind, the Khans of the Frontier and the Baluchi chiefs had intervened into pre-independence politics their motives were to preserve their own class interests. Their power lay in their capacity to deliver the votes of their followers. On the eve of independence they jumped on the Muslim League bandwaggon; but their politics remained primitive. As the rulers of Pakistan looked around for capable instruments they turned increasingly to their senior civil servants, particularly the district officers, to orchestrate the popular response. Inevitably, the Pakistan civil servant increasingly assumed an active political role; particularly when Ghulam Mohammad as Governor-General set the example.

The highly educated professional elite in Ceylon were so westernised that they habitually spoke English, at home and at work. Their links with the ordinary people were not much closer than those of the old British bureaucrats. Bandaranaike was utterly westernised, but he deliberately set out to create a different image. Although he had always worn elegant Western clothes he now adopted a 'National Costume' of his own invention: a collarless shirt, a *loongyi* or sarong, all in white with a muslin scarf draped round his neck. It was all as synthetic as his cultural nationalism.

Although Bandaranaike conceived the strategy of mobilising the monks he made no effort to build up a grassroots organisation. Almost the only politicians with genuine proletarian links were the Marxist leaders (themselves impeccably middle class) and their contact was almost wholly with the industrial workers. Hence, as the people exercised their votes at each election there was no feedback; and next time round some would try the opposition.

The civil disobedience campaigns of Gandhi and of Nehru had involved the mass of the people in political action, especially in the Gangetic plain and in Gujarat. Although the top leadership in Congress belonged to the English educated class (mainly lawyers) others had risen to positions of secondary importance. After independence, as the lessons of the general elections were absorbed it was realised that the rural masses represented the most reliable 'vote bank' for Congress. Time after time, the largest Congress majorities were in the countryside. A rural leadership, capable of appealing to the country folk in their own language – both literally and metaphorically – became essential. Otherwise the Communists might make a greater appeal with their programme of land redistribution – as they did in certain areas.

A new political class emerged; the prosperous farmers, who lacked education in English but were shrewdly alert to the social and economic realities of their districts. They had little or no interest in social justice or ideology, and no clear understanding of national problems: but they knew all about their own problems. Nehru's commitment to a 'Socialistic pattern of society' made virtually no impact. When land reform was introduced, designed to redistribute land to the landless these rural capitalists were able to adapt the whole programme to their own advantage. The great landlords were deprived of their estates, but the rural poor obtained no benefit. At most they received barren outlying strips, impossible to irrigate. An attempt to re-emphasise Gandhi's vision of a co-operative rural community was initiated by a highly respected Gandhian, Vinoba Bhave. Following the example of the Mahatma he trudged the countryside calling upon the wealthy to donate fields – even whole villages – to the rural poor. Bhave was joined in his pilgrimage by the former militant, Jayaprakash Narayan, who had once scorned non-violence but now became the advocate of sacrifice and service. This *Bhoodan*, Land Gift movement, was highly publicised but there were few real improvements.

Gandhi had symbolised his identification with the poor by wearing their dress. So for a time did Nehru, but when he became Prime Minister he adopted a more elegant costume. He always wore the Gandhi cap (so called because the Mahatma adopted this item of gaol uniform in South Africa). But Nehru's tunic was an *achkin*, the tight-fitting Muslim jacket. Almost all Congress workers wore the Gandhi cap and homespun clothes, *khaddar*, which Gandhi had made a central part of his programme of social uplift. The issues which were important to these politicians were those which dominated the outlook of their supporters: religion, language, caste, whereas Nehru's priorities reflected the modern world – socialism, international cooperation, parliamentary democracy, rapid industrialisation. He could barely understand those clinging to the values of the past.

If religion held up political development in Pakistan, Nehru was determined that in India it would not be recognised in politics: India was a secular state. Partition had not separated the Muslims from other Indians: 40 million remained in India after the traumas of partition. Yet to many, especially the militant Hindus, they could not be loyal citizens of the republic. Nehru tried to combat such views by including Muslims in the government, and his successors did also. Muslims responded by voting Congress. Religion remained, to surface frequently, often in violent form. Language almost at once became a heated subject of controversy.

Congress had long been committed to *Antar Bahasha*, the national language: and this had to be Hindi as the lingua franca. This might have been accepted had not those labelled Hindi fanatics tried to purge the language of all non-Sanskritic terms which it had absorbed through the centuries. There were strong objections to the adoption of Hindi by those with a different mother tongue. The Bengalis with their poetical literature and musical speech regarded Hindi as undeveloped, while those who spoke the Dravidian languages of the south would have nothing to do with it. The debate became heated after a Telugu speaker, Potti Sriramalu carried out a fast (as Gandhi had so often done) which ended in his death. Nehru had to yield; a States Reorganisation Commission was appointed and virtually redrew the map of southern India. The former princely states, Hyderabad and Mysore were to disappear; four new states were created. This concession to 'linguism' in the south stimulated other demands and controversies. A long dispute followed over the city of Bombay. Maharashtra formed its hinterland, and many of the workforce were Marathi speakers. Yet Gujaratis were also numerous and claimed to have made a much greater economic contribution to the city. The first solution attempted was a bilingual Gujarati–Marathi state; but Congress found that they were losing power, both at the city and the state level. In 1960 Bombay city was included in a monolingual Maharashtra.

Thus far the map of northern India was not affected, but in the state of Punjab, with its prestigious modern capital Chandigarh, designed by Le Corbusier, partition was proposed on the lines of Hindi-speakers and Punjabi-speakers. Presented as a linguistic demand this was really a claim by the Sikhs for a state which they could control. In the Punjabi Punjab they could expect to have a small majority over the Hindus. Nehru absolutely rejected the plan. A Sikh religious leader, Sant Fateh Singh began to fast unto death. He lacked the determination of the Andhra martyr and after 21 days broke his fast. Then the most famous Sikh leader, Master Tara Singh began to fast within the sacred Golden Temple in Amritsar. Bulletins told the outside world of his physical deterioration. After 47 days the fast was abandoned. Tara Singh chose to interpret some delphic words of Nehru as signifying concessions. This was humbug. Yet the agitation was renewed, reaching a peak during Mrs Gandhi's first months in office when three Congress leaders were burnt alive in the historic town of Panipat. She decided to partition Punjab, and the Hindi districts became the new Haryana. What of the prestigious Chandigarh? Mrs Gandhi decided it would become the joint capital of the two states, and the line of demarcation was conveniently sited so as to give the city to neither state.

These were the major conflicts, but everywhere in India the age-old rules of caste inequality were demonstrating that instead of losing their hold they were reaching a new intensity. In the cities, distinctive dress and eating habits might go, but marriage was still contracted according to the dictates of caste (apart from a tiny enlightened upper class minority). Most important was the realisation that caste could be mobilised as a political force. Almost every caste wanted to improve its status: which could only be achieved at the expense of others previously superior. Though powerful, the Brahmins were few; in politics they gave ground to the agricultural castes, though finding compensation in the professions and business. Castes which did not own land exerted what pressure they could through the ballot box. At the bottom of the pile were the Untouchables, whose sub-human status had been legally abolished by the constitution. They had a generous quota of constituencies 'reserved' for their representatives: though the electorate consisted of the whole population so that Congress almost always won these seats. The Untouchables were still denied basic rights by the clean castes. They could not draw water from the village well; they were still restricted to degrading occupations and were almost everywhere excluded from landholding, or if granted land received only barren and waterless soil. Where Untouchables endeavoured to assert their supposed rights they were violently put in their place. Forty years after independence, though a tiny minority had advanced up the ladder of politics (because of the reserved constituencies) and an enterprising few had migrated to the cities and escaped their disabilities, most of the Untouchables remained stuck at the bottom of the heap. The 'palimpsest' nature of Indian society characterised by Nehru still persists: the past dominates the present.

Ceylon became immersed in a version of the past which bore little resemblance to the historical record. From the time the Portuguese arrived in the sixteenth century the country became increasingly cosmopolitan and European influences and cultures were intermingled with those of the island. Apart from the jungle dwellers, most people had a mixed genetic inheritance: Bandaranaike was partly of Tamil descent. In the 1950s and 1960s they were encouraged to believe that only those who were Sinhalese Buddhists were truly indigenous to Lanka. In reality, the Tamils had arrived two thousand years before, while the Sinhalese also originated in India (some speculated about Orissa as their original home). The emphasis upon Buddhism was exclusive, denying Hindus, Christians and the so-called Moors a full place in the social and political order: even though Bandaranaike's family had been Christian since the Dutch time. The former easy-going relationship between the communities became increasingly competitive and abrasive.

It has been seen how religion and language became the sometimes contradictory determinants of politics in Pakistan. To the top politicians and bureaucrats who tried to keep the system from collapsing these became themes to be manipulated. To anyone familiar with Mughal administration it might have appeared that this was the model for Pakistan in the late 1950s, with senior officials issuing orders and military might as the real foundation of authority. The cavalcade of prime ministers passed, at a trot and sometimes at a gallop. Dr Khan Sahib, once the pro-Congress Premier of the North-West Frontier Province made a comeback as Premier of unified West Pakistan. He was strongly supported by President Mirza, but early in 1958 he was assassinated. In the Assembly in East

Pakistan the opposition managed to have the Speaker certified as insane. In a brawl in the Assembly in September 1958 the Deputy Speaker was killed by assailants. Mirza had already publicised his belief that only a presidential system would suit Pakistan. In October he declared martial law, dismissed the central and provincial governments, abolished political parties and appointed the army commander, General Ayub Khan, chief martial law administrator. Mirza might despise the politicians, but he had been highly political himself. General Ayub Khan determined to get him out; one month later Mirza was summarily put into a plane and Ayub took over the presidency, declaring 'My authority is revolution; I have no sanction in law or constitution'.

He did not imply that a new social order was proposed; yet it was revolutionary not just to suspend but to abolish parliamentary government. At first, military officers were drafted in to 'clean up the mess'. Looking further ahead, Ayub sought to build a new power base among the pillars of rural society: the squires, the prosperous peasantry, the sturdy yeomen beloved of British district officers and familiar to the general as the backbone of the army. A year after taking over he announced a new system of Basic Democracy: 'of the type that people can understand and work'. The new Basic Democracies were councils for an area which might comprise a large village and surrounding hamlets or the wards of a city. Most educated people dismissed the new scheme – they were merely village councils – and almost a quarter of the new members were returned unopposed. The first task of the Basic Democrats was to vote upon the presidency. There was no other candidate, and almost 96 per cent signified their approval of Ayub.

In its early days the new regime turned its back on religion. Ayub spoke of 'the cobwebs of superstition and stagnation', and instituted some important reforms; for example, giving wives rights in a suit for divorce and prohibiting polygamy. The whole system was given legitimacy by presidential order in March 1962. Brushing aside the preference of his own constitutional commission for a directly elected legislature he announced the introduction of Guided Democracy, declaring that parliamentary government was only suited to those with 'cool and phlegmatic temperament which only people in cold climates seem to have'. He established a 'pyramid' system whereby the Basic Democracies formed primary electoral colleges choosing councils for districts. There was an electoral chain culminating in a National Assembly. An attempt was made to appease the Bengalis by making Dacca the seat of this legislature (if so it can be called) with government functioning at a new capital, Islamabad in the Himalayan foothills, far from the frenzied atmosphere of Karachi.

The Basic Democracies remained the foundation of the system and when elections were again held in 1964 they were hotly contested. Their first major assignment was to vote in another presidential election. This time there was an opposition candidate, Fatima Jinnah, the highly respected sister of the Qaid-i-Azam. A frail old lady, she nonetheless campaigned vigorously. Ayub won nearly 64 per cent of the votes; this added up to 74 per cent in the West wing and 53 per cent in East Pakistan; only in Karachi was he denied a majority vote. Because the Ayub regime began to yield tangible economic benefits (assisted by generous American aid) it seemed to have inaugurated a new era.

In India the economic progress made in the early years of independence was slowing down. The emphasis on centralised planning and development was costly and slow. The huge new steel industry was overmanned, with low productivity. Nehru made planning his special concern and the majority of the Cabinet played no part. He was considered to listen too much to those who were his own 'courtiers'. One who shared his ideology and his intellectual interests was V. K. Krishna Menon who had been long resident in London promoting the cause of Indian independence. He now returned to assume Cabinet office; when he became Minister of Defence he began to politicise the supreme leadership of the army, previously right outside the arena of politics.

Nehru was virtually the promoter of the international policy of nonalignment. Whereas from the mid-1950s Pakistan went along with the Dulles doctrine of containment of international Communism (thereby receiving a steady supply of sophisticated military hardware) India ostentatiously stood apart from the Cold War line-up and made much of friendship with China. It was hoped that friendship between the two Asian giants would preserve Asia from the global power struggle. When the two countries signed an accord proclaiming peaceful co-existence this was heralded in India as putting international relations on a moral rather than a material basis. Yet unresolved differences remained concerning the Himalayan frontier. This frontier had come about through British imperial pressure upon a supine China, resulting in a treaty concluded in 1914 which was never ratified by China even in its weakness. In the early 1950s Communist China sought to get rid of the anomalies which (they insisted) arose from imperialism. Burma and Pakistan were also confronted by divergencies between Chinese claims and the border they had inherited. They entered into negotiations, which were protracted, but ended in agreement. India, despite the dream of peaceful co-existence stuck to the British claim – the 'McMahon Line'.

Early in 1962 India decided to end the long-standing dispute over Goa by military action: the Portuguese exasperated India further by making Goa a province of Portugal. After non-violent pressure failed, India sent troops in. The operation was not well managed – which should have supplied a warning – but Portuguese resistance was negligible and the territory was speedily occupied. This gave false encouragement for a forward policy in the Himalayas. In October 1962 the Indian Army moved forward to occupy the great Buddhist monastery, Towang. Ill-equipped troops encountered experienced Chinese mountain units, who rapidly pushed them back. There seemed no reason why the Chinese should not keep going until they reached the Assam valley; but when they reached the limit of the territory they claimed they halted and proclaimed a unilateral ceasefire. There was panic in Delhi; only Mrs Gandhi emerged with credit. She was the current president of the Congress and she flew to the zone where the army had been defeated to reassure the civil population.

Nehru had been showing signs of declining powers; this debacle virtually finished him. There was a public outcry against Krishna Menon, and he was dumped. Nehru appealed to the United States and Britain; military aid was promptly supplied. This looked like the end of non-alignment, but there was no kind of break. Ayub Khan promised help if India would carry out the long-postponed plebiscite in Kashmir; he received no response. Mrs Bandaranaike mobilised Burma and other Afro-Asian countries in a search for compromise. These Colombo Powers (as they were now labelled) were sympathetic to India, but some could not conceal their impatience with Nehru's inability to face realities. It was a sad end to a brilliant life of service. Worn out, Nehru died two years later.

For years the question had been posed. After Nehru, what? And who? He had refused to groom a successor. Nevertheless, Parliament made its choice through a group of powerful State leaders who became known as the Syndicate. Lal Bahadur Shastri was an experienced Minister. His style was a complete contrast to that of the aristocratic Nehru. He was all humility, saying on many occasions 'I am only a glorified clerk'. His premiership was marked by a good deal of hesitancy. To neutralise the personal antipathy displayed by Indira Gandhi and draw on her family name he invited her into the Cabinet. She entered Parliament at the same time she became a Minister, in August 1964, taking her seat in the Upper House, the *Rajya Sabha*, where she did not have to undergo an election campaign.

In 1962 in Burma, General Ne Win took over; arresting U Nu, all his Cabinet, the President, and most of the opposition leaders declaring that the country was on the verge of collapse. He governed under martial law, with the advice of a Revolutionary Council of Brigadiers and Colonels (his Foreign Minister was the only civilian). Seeking to consolidate his regime he launched the Burma Socialist Programme Party or *Lanzin*. The party's structure was not unlike that of the Communist Party in the Soviet Union – in theory, but in actuality it barely existed. The general had made the disintegration of Burma the reason for his intervention but security everywhere, except in the central area, deteriorated further with a massive increase in guerrilla activity and a loss of control throughout most of the Shan State, much of the Kachin state, and the Karen border country with Thailand, stretching to within striking distance of the port of Moulmein.

Finally, 1962 saw an attempted coup in Ceylon by the military. The army was small in number, and the rising scarcely affected more than a group of disgruntled officers. It was claimed that the former Governor-General, Goonetillike was implicated. Hard evidence was lacking but he was known to dislike Mrs Bandaranaike's Cabinet, in particular her Marxist colleagues. The affair left an uneasy atmosphere.

Probably it was the Indian Army's doleful performance against China which gave the Ayub regime the idea of starting a border revolt in Indian-occupied Kashmir. This was the brainchild of Zulfikar Ali Bhutto, the son of a mighty Sindhi landlord. He received a polished education in Western universities and became Ayub's Foreign Minister. Maybe this would reactivate and internationalise the dormant Kashmir issue. Soldiers of the so-called Azad Kashmir force (actually a part of the Pakistan Army) would be infiltrated through the cease-fire line and encourage the population to revolt. Then Pakistan would intervene to 'liberate' the oppressed Kashmiris and the UN would have to take action.

Nothing went as planned; the infiltrators were all arrested; there was no rising. If the Pakistan Army advanced in the Mirpur sector they could sever the Indian lines of communication and force a showdown. On 6 September 1965 the Indian Army retaliated with a three-prong attack towards Lahore. In the ensuing fighting, honours were about even. The Pakistan Air Force with its Sidewinder missiles knocked out most of their adversaries on the ground. The attack by their division of Patton tanks 'The Shield of Pakistan' was shattered in a tank battle in which most of the Pattons were knocked out. The big powers came forward and on 22 September a general cease-fire came into effect.

Both sides met at Tashkent with Kosygyin as their chairman. They agreed to return to the prewar boundary (though India had made most territorial gains in the brief conflict). Lal Bahadur Shastri died at this Tashkent conference, thus hallowing the agreement. India was left to find another prime minister, with no prior warning. In Pakistan the agreement was accepted though bitterly resented. It had been an article of faith that the Muslims of the north could vanquish the Hindus, even against the odds. They had not been beaten; but they certainly had not won. Ayub's prestige dwindled, and from being an outgoing, benevolent leader he was transformed into a solitary, withdrawn figure. Those who had been his critics became boldly vocal. The originator of this disastrous scheme, Z. A. Bhutto escaped censure. Somehow he was able to project the idea that if only he had been in charge it would all have been different. The political stage was ready for changes among the leading actors.

In India, Kamaraj, who had orchestrated the shake-up among the states' leaders now brought together the fixers known as the Syndicate to choose the new prime minister. Morarji Desai of Gujarat was a strong candidate; a thoroughgoing Gandhian, he was also a capable manager. Perhaps he might prove too domineering. The choice of the Kamaraj clique fell on Indira Gandhi. With her lack of experience she must surely do what her sponsors wanted. And so her name went forward.

While these momentous events were rocking the sub-continent, Ceylon was about to make another electoral choice. During her years in office, 1960–65, the policy of Sirimavo Bandaranaike is best described as one of drift. Nothing was done to conciliate the Tamils; the welfare policy which entailed ever-rising subventions to keep the price of rice low (it was mainly imported) could not be met by the sagging export prices of tea. Mrs Bandaranaike was defeated in 1965, not because she had failed but because she had not succeeded. Meanwhile, Burma seemed to have withdrawn into isolation from the world. The deportation of thousands of Indians and other foreigners in 1962 deprived the country of its more enterprising entrepreneurs. Perhaps the only success for Burma in these years was the appointment of U Thant as Secretary General of the UN (1962–71) and he was known as a close associate of U Nu who languished in gaol (1962–6).

Altogether, South Asia in the mid-1960s seemed to be groping, looking for courses which would revive the burnt-out epic of the Freedom Struggle, awaiting an unknown future.

CHRONOLOGY OF EVENTS, 1948–1987

1948: Gandhi assassinated, January; Burma, civil war starts with Communists; tribal invasion of Kashmir, accession to India; death of Jinnah.

1949: Ceasefire in Kashmir; Karens join in civil war in Burma, capture Mandalay; Indian Tamils in Ceylon disfranchised; Pakistan, 'Objectives Resolution'; India, constitution finalised.

1950: India's National Planning Commission initiates first Five Year Plan.

1951: Colombo Plan inaugurated; AFPFL score heavy majority in Burma election; Liaqat Ali Khan assassinated in Pakistan.

1952: Overwhelming victory for Congress in first Indian election; first post-independence election in Ceylon, UNP victory; death of Senanayake; Burma's *Pyidawtha* welfare plan announced.

1953: West Pakistan, anti-Ahmadiyyah riots, Nizamuddin removed from premiership.

1954: Pakistan adheres to SEATO.

1955: Amalgamation of West Pakistan; Potti Sriramalu fasts to death for Andhra state.

1956: Pakistan constitution inaugurates Islamic Republic; Ceylon's second election – Bandaranaike and SLFP oust UNP; Sinhalese becomes sole national language; India – reorganisation of southern states following recommendations of Commission; Burma, AFPFL win reduced majority.

1957: Second Indian election sees massive Congress majority but in Kerala Communist government elected.

1958: Premier of West Pakistan, Dr Khan Sahib assassinated: Burma – handover to General Ne Win; Ceylon – inter-communal rioting leads to imposition of Emergency; Pakistan – President Iskander Mirza suspends parliament and parties; General

Ayub Khan, chief martial law administrator, ousts Mirza after one month.

1959: Ceylon – Emergency lifted; Bandaranaike assassinated; Basic Democracies established in Pakistan.

1960: Ceylon, two elections – first inconclusive, second won by Mrs Bandaranaike and SLFP; in Burma U Nu's handsome win in third election with newly-named party; Border agreement, Burma–China; Gujarat separated from Maharashtra.

1961: Nehru visits USA.

1962: Annexation of Goa by India; third election with handsome Congress majority; Indian troops driven back in retreat on NE Frontier by Chinese; Ayub announces Guided Democracy in Pakistan; Attempted military coup in Ceylon; General Ne Win arrests Nu and all leading politicians, forms military government.

1963: India – Official Language Act permits continued use of English.

1964: Presidential election in Pakistan – Ayub defeats Miss Jinnah; India – death of Nehru, Shastri becomes premier, Mrs Gandhi becomes Minister.

1965: Indo-Pak war ends in stalemate; death of Shastri – Mrs Gandhi becomes prime minister.

1966: Anti-Chinese riots in Rangoon; China severs relations with Burma.

1967: India, fourth General Election – Indira gets bare majority.

1968: Soviet arms supplied to Pakistan.

1969: Indira expelled from Congress by 'the Syndicate'; Indira endorsed by majority in All-India Congress Committee; Ayub Khan resigns from presidency after disorders in Pakistan; Yahya Khan succeeds.

1970: Ceylon's sixth election gives Mrs Bandaranaike convincing majority; Pakistan – Legal Framework Order lays down rules for national election; in West Wing, Bhutto's PPP gets majority; in East Wing Sheikh Mujib's Awami League scores overwhelming majority.

1971: After failure of Yahya Khan–Mujib talks in Dacca, massive military action; Mujib arrested and deported; underground resistance in East, claimed as Bangladesh; fifth Indian election – massive majority for Indira; Leftist insurrection in Ceylon; Indian Army invades East Pakistan; Pakistan Army capitulates.

1972: Ceylon's new constitution and new name – Sri Lanka; state elections in India confirm Indira's hold; Bangladesh independent, and enacts new constitution.

1973: Bangladesh – elections give Mujib and Awami League large majority.

1974: Burma – constitution of People's Socialist Republic; Famine in Bangladesh.

1975: Third Pakistan or 'New' Pakistan. Elections confirm Bhutto as leader; Mujib assassinated in Bangladesh; Indira's own election in 1971 declared invalid; she replies with National Emergency and mass arrests.

1976: Ceylon Tamils organise as Tamil United Liberation Front, demand *Tamil Eelam*.

1977: Bangladesh – General Ziaur Rahman takes over as President; Indira calls sixth election – defeated by Janata coalition with Morarji Desai as premier; Bhutto's PPP win election in Pakistan; result disputed, riots; General Zia-ul-Huq takes over as martial law administrator; Mrs Bandaranaike and SLFP defeated in seventh Ceylon election – new UNP leader J. R. Jayawardene.

1978: New constitution for Ceylon; President Jayawardene as head of government; in Pakistan Bhutto condemned to death by High Court; Indira returns to parliament – expelled; Bangladesh gives General Zia massive majority in presidential election; Burma expels thousands of illegal Bangladeshi immigrants.

1979: Bangladesh election gives Zia's Bangladesh National Party majority; Pakistan Supreme Court confirms verdict on Bhutto; hanged; Morarji resigns as premier; Charan Singh takes over, unable to secure majority, asks President to dissolve parliament; Soviet Union occupies Afghanistan; massive influx into Pakistan.

1980: Seventh election in India gives Indira substantial majority; Sanjay Gandhi dies in plane crash.

1981: Bangladesh, President Ziaur Rahman assassinated; presidential election votes for ailing Abdus Sattar.

1982: General Ershad becomes martial law administrator in Bangladesh; Presidential election in Ceylon gives Jayawardene massive majority.

1983: Ershad becomes President of Bangladesh; Ceylon, army clashes with Tamil Tigers followed by anti-Tamil pogrom in

Colombo; in India, disorder in Punjab leads to President's rule; in Burma, explosion at Martyrs' Memorial kills South Korean dignitaries.

1984: Pakistan – referendum confirms Zia as President; in India, army attack Golden Temple, Amritsar, thousand Sikh militants killed; Sikh guard assassinates Indira Gandhi; pogrom of Delhi Sikhs; Indira's son Rajiv becomes premier, calls election; eighth election gives Rajiv largest majority ever in parliament.

1985: In Pakistan, Bhutto's daughter Benazir returns to revive PPP.

1986: Political parties permitted in Pakistan; autonomy for Tamil north promised in Ceylon by Jayawardene; in Bangladesh, Ershad's Jatiya party wins parliamentary election; in presidential election Ershad defeats Mujib's daughter.

1987: Defeats for Congress in Indian state elections; siege of Tamils in Jaffna (north Ceylon) by army; India sends food supplies, turned back; accord signed by Jayawardene and Rajiv; Indian peace-keeping force takes over in north; Indian Army's battle with Tigers in Jaffna; attempt to assassinate Jayawardene by Sinhalese extremists; bombing campaign in Colombo.

11 Independence: the Long Hot Summer

The uncertain note of the mid-1960s was personified by Indira Gandhi. Did she have the strength of character to give leadership to a country increasingly riven by regional and local grievances, while Morarji Desai and others stood by, waiting for her to falter? In Pakistan, Ayub Khan had lost his appeal, and regional voices were clamorous, especially those of the Bengalis who recalled that during the Indo-Pak war their province was left undefended. Burma was marking time under Ne Win and increasingly turned inwards. Only in Ceylon did the situation seem more promising with the return of a UNP centrist government having a stable majority in 1965. This should assure better international support (especially from America) and the promise of prosperity.

Mrs Gandhi's first general election did little to offer reassurance. The year 1966 witnessed economic stagnation and devaluation of the Indian rupee. Many thought the 1967 election would be the last exercise in Indian democracy. Despite these gloomy forecasts Mrs Gandhi retained 270 seats in a total of 520 in the *Lok Sabha* though receiving less than 40 per cent of the popular vote. It was by far the narrowest post-independence result. The worst result among the States was in Madras (renamed Tamilnadu in 1968) from where only three Congress MPs were elected alongside 36 for the Dravidian populist movement, Dravida Munnetra Kazhagam (DMK). All the states except Andhra showed significant losses. Jan Sangh numbers went up from 14 to 35 while Swatantra was up from 22 to 44.

In the State Assemblies results were even more dismal. Madras saw a DMK victory with 138 seats to 49 for Congress and in Kerala the Communists won 71 seats and Congress retained only nine. Orissa also went against Congress and in Punjab (half the former undivided state) the Sikh Akali Dal made substantial gains with 24 seats. When all the post-election deals were completed, there remained only six Congress State governments with ten formed by the opposition. Many were opportunistic combinations but in Tamilnadu the DMK was to prove impregnable.

245

The political commentators had a great time prophesying the end of Congress Raj and the break-up of India. Mrs Gandhi's future was on the line: she won the first tussle. Morarji Desai wanted to contest the Congress leadership in the wake of the election. He was dissuaded, though appeased by receiving the post of Deputy Prime Minister: he was given no real increase of power. Her increasing contempt for the old guard, the Syndicate included, was challenged over the choice of a new President in 1969. The old guard put up Sanjiva Reddy (whom she had removed from office) as official Congress candidate. Her supporters nominated the Vice-President, V. V. Giri. The contest symbolised the machine confronting a dominant personality. Giri won by the narrowest margin; the old guard seethed with resentment. On 12 November 1969 the Syndicate formally expelled the prime minister from Congress for her arbitrary actions. Forming a majority in the Working Committee, the High Command, they became known as Congress (O), representing Organisation.

She fought back, and first she secured endorsement from 310 of the 429 Congressmen in both Houses of Parliament. Then the All-India Congress – the party's national convention – was called together and 446 of its 705 members gave support. The MPs of Congress (O) now moved over to the opposition benches, but Mrs Gandhi survived with the help of the Communists, Socialists and DMK. Apart from the veteran Untouchable leader, Jagjivan Ram, all the old guard – her father's generation, had departed.

The country was not able to return its verdict until March 1971. Mrs Gandhi had decided to abolish the privileges of the Princes, entrenched in the Constitution. She needed a two-thirds majority, which she received in the Lower House but not in the Upper House. She announced an election; the first to be held out of the regular five-year sequence. Most political analysts predicted she would not gain a majority: 230 to 270 seats was their forecast. The totally unexpected happened: her Congress (R), for Ruling, won 350 seats in the *Lok Sabha* out of 520. Congress (O) retained a paltry 16 seats: even the mighty Kamaraj was defeated. It was a personal triumph and the pundits hastened to describe this as 'New Wave' politics: more important was the calculation of big business that she meant stability and pumped in their largesse. Mrs Gandhi had changed the game of Indian politics: Gandhi and Nehru had sought consensus; she delighted in confrontation. The mystique of *ahimsa*, non-violence was exhausted.

In Burma the military regime assumed wide economic powers, establishing unwieldy quasi-military establishments to handle all imports. They disappointed public expectations, however diminished these were by years of austerity. The two South Asian military regimes were at sea, though the two civilian governments were not doing much better.

It may appear fanciful to suggest that de Gaulle has provided the model for systems of government during the 1970s and 1980s, yet it did seem agreed that either as General de Gaulle or President de Gaulle he provided an alternative which seemed more effective than Cabinet government. As the General, he stepped into the breach in the first post-war years and provided the stability which the frequent changes under the Third Republic had sadly lacked. He headed two successive provisional governments before giving way to the politicians and retiring into rural solitude. In May 1958 when armed insurrection had broken out in Algeria, threatening to engulf metropolitan France, he was again asked to be prime minister. Six months later he became President and in 1962 inaugurated a constitution (endorsed by popular referendum) in which the supremacy of the President over prime minister and Cabinet was clearly defined.

The suggestion that the Gaullist system is relevant to South Asia is not intended literally. Mrs Gandhi functioned through the office of prime minister with a tame president, and it was left to J R Jayawardene in Ceylon to replicate the Gaullist system in every detail. But certainly the presidential style has prevailed, and the example set by Nehru and Nu of accepting shared responsibility with Cabinet colleagues has disappeared, perhaps for ever.

Ayub Khan's presidency came to an ignominious end in 1969. He had sacked Bhutto in 1966 for his disastrous advice on Kashmir and that wily politician turned against his erstwhile chief. In East Pakistan Sheikh Mujibur Rahman emerged as leader of the Awami League. His rise was largely due to no rivals of any stature remaining: Suhrawardy had died. Mujib came from a landed family and became Secretary of the Awami League in 1956. He was an orator rather than a statesman. Soon after the 1965 war he issued the so-called Six Point Demand: demanding full autonomy for East Pakistan only just short of independence. In 1967 there was an attempt on Ayub's life and soon after it was announced that there had been a plot with Indian backing to launch an armed rising in East Pakistan to force secession. Twenty-eight persons were arrested and Mujib was said to be involved in this 'Agartala Conspiracy'. Soon after, Ayub's health seriously deteriorated. Discontent came into the open, boosted by the displaced Bhutto. He claimed that he had all along opposed the Tashkent agreement. Zulfi, as his admirers called him was arrested, and widespread student protest shook the big towns. Ayub turned this way and that. In desperation he announced the restoration of parliament, and when this fell flat he turned to the Chief of Staff, General Yahya Khan, to introduce martial law, just as Ayub himself had been instructed to, eleven years earlier.

Yahya Khan was a Pathan – like Ayub and most of the generals. He was known for his thoroughly non-partisan outlook. He was not going to prop up a discredited regime: Ayub was required to resign. Within 24 hours of taking over Yahya announced that he had no intention of being any but an interim president; this was greeted with scepticism. It was what had been promised in every other *coup d'état*. But in this case there was no deception. Mujib was released and returned to Dacca where the students hailed him as *Bangalabandhu* (Unifier of Bengal). The President began a dialogue. Mujib's main demand was for recognition that East Pakistan must be represented in a new legislature on the 'one man one vote principle', thus conceding most votes to Bengal. Yahya's response was issued as the Legal Framework Order of March 1970. This conceded the Bengali demand. The election took place on 7 December 1970, soon after a disastrous cyclone had devastated Bengal.

The election was totally divisive. Bhutto launched his Pakistan People's Party (PPP) one week before the election. The PPP did not dare run a single candidate in the east, though it dominated the West wing. The PPP won 81 seats out of a total of 138 in West Pakistan; in the east, the Awami League won 160 of the total 162. The Awami League had a clear majority in the whole of Pakistan. In his speeches in the weeks that followed Mujib showed no disposition to modify his Six Point Programme. Meeting no compromise there, Yahya turned to Bhutto who was confident of breaking the deadlock with the aid of the hard-line generals (all, of course, Pathans and Punjabis). Yahya still continued to negotiate with Mujib whose declared goal was now Bangladesh, an independent nation-state.

Yahya visited Dacca in mid-March 1971 to parley with Mujib. The Sheikh insisted on the substance of independence with concessions only over foreign affairs and defence. Yahya departed, and a new governor, General Tikka Khan, persuaded the President that he could topple the Bengali politicians as Mirza had done in 1954. On 26 March the military moved in with their tanks and guns. They bombarded the halls of the Dacca University students who were butchered. Dacca was subjugated, but elsewhere resistance flared up. In Chittagong, the major port, the Second in Command of the East Bengal Regiment, Major Ziaur Rahman made a radio broadcast announcing the formation of the provisional government of Bangladesh. Mujib was sent as a prisoner to the west. An underground army, the Mukti Bahini, supplied with arms from India began operating: among its leaders 'Tiger' Kader Siddiqi acquired a reputation for ferocity, but in general the Bahini were limited to hit-and-run raids from the Indian border. Caught in the crossfire, crowds of civilians, mainly Hindus, poured into India as refugees, totalling 10 million at the peak.

Mrs Gandhi toured Western capitals, hoping to secure intervention, but to no avail. Despite the logistical problems involved in shifting troops from west to east Pakistan when denied the use of Indian air space the military occupation force was steadily strengthened and unleashed on the civilian population.

A military confrontation between India and Pakistan looked increasingly inevitable. The great powers were taking sides. India had a military alliance with the Soviet Union; Pakistan was assured of the support of China and Richard Nixon's America. Would they allow the quarrel which was in international law an internal problem for Pakistan to escalate out of control? The question became urgent when on 3 December 1971 an Indian thrust at Dacca opened up. The Pakistan army had decided to adopt a 'stay put' strategy, hanging on in their frontier bunkers. In the West the Pakistan Air Force tried to repeat its 1965 success by launching a preemptive strike; but this time the Indians were ready for them. Mrs Gandhi gave total support to 'fighting' General Manekshaw, designated commander of all three services. The advance on Dacca continued relentlessly. By 14 December the Indians were in the outskirts of the city; the Pakistan Eastern Command under General Niazi capitulated unconditionally to Lieutenant-General J. S. Aurora, and the troops who had sat tight had to hand in their arms; 90,000 passed into captivity. It was unrelieved humiliation for Pakistan. Reeling from the blow, Yahya resigned; handing over as President and Chief Martial Law Administrator to Bhutto on the evening of 20 December when he returned from pleading their cause before the UN.

Ceylon did not experience full-scale war in 1971, yet that once tranquil island was shaken by insurrection. The periodic seesaw of elections had brought Mrs Bandaranaike back into power in 1970 with an enhanced majority. In her election campaign she made lavish promises of better conditions for the underprivileged. Among her motley supporters was a revolutionary group, Janatha Vimukthi Peramune (JVP) or 'People's United Front'. They represented youth, especially the ex-students, now numerous and largely unemployed. During the previous twelve years the numbers enrolled in university had expanded from 3,000 to 15,000 while employment in the bureaucracy, the law and other white-collar occupations had not increased. The new SLFP-led United Front Government was no more successful than the UNP in manufacturing jobs. The dynamic JVP leader, Rohana Wijeweera planned a rising, hoping that total surprise would ensure success for a 'one-day revolution'.

The revolt was launched in April 1971 and nearly succeeded. However, some JVP activists were prematurely mobilised and surprise was not total, although several police stations in the centre of the island were captured and arms were seized. The Ceylon army numbered only 6,600: the previous military plot had discouraged expansion. Mrs Bandaranaike appealed for international aid and military equipment was supplied by India, Pakistan, the USA, Britain, the Soviet Union and Yugoslavia. In addition, Indian and Pakistani naval vessels patrolled the coastline (for it was expected aid from China and North Vietnam would be landed). Indian troops stood guard over Colombo's airport. In the subsequent repression, 14,000 fighters – all in their early twenties or their teens, and all Sinhalese – were captured and detained.

Unable to introduce economic reforms, Mrs Bandaranaike produced an impression of reform by introducing constitutional changes: for now she had an adequate majority (60 per cent) for that purpose. Ceylon was at last declared a republic under the new name of Sri I anka. The Senate was abolished and the lower house renamed the National State Assembly. The exiguous rights of the Tamils were further eroded, the judiciary was declared subordinate to the legislature and Buddhism was given 'the foremost place' in religion. The divisions within Ceylon society were becoming irreparable.

Meanwhile, Bhutto was also engineering a new constitution in Pakistan. He made it clear that he preferred the presidential system, but his PPP included democratic elements who believed that Ayub's methods would only be eliminated by returning to federal, parliamentary institutions. Bhutto acquiesced, and in the third constitution, promulgated in August 1975 there was a parliament for the 'New Pakistan' in which the Lower House was dominant under a

Prime Minister whose removal was constitutionally complicated. Bhutto moved from the presidency into the premiership with no change of role.

He tackled the two institutions which had menaced the politicians previously, the army and the civil service. The Civil Service of Pakistan as a *corps d'élite* was liquidated and a powerful injection of new bureaucrats was inserted by recruiting political appointees. Between 1973 and 1977, 1,374 new officers were accepted: three times the previous recruitment rate. Bhutto intended that the army should never again be able to intervene in government. Military authority was divided between a Chief of Staff, a Secretary of Defence, and a Defence Adviser to the Prime Minister, responsible for internal security. Tikka Khan was removed; Bhutto was determined that no Pathan power bloc should be able to undermine his authority. He selected Zia-ul-Huq as Chief of Staff. Zia came from what was now Indian Punjab; he had no territorial power base. He had been serving with the army of King Hussain of Jordan so was a relative stranger to other senior officers. Finally, unlike most of the military, he was known for his personal piety and must therefore be unworldly. As an additional precaution Bhutto established a para-military Federal Security Force so that in cases of urban disaster it would not be necessary to call in the army.

Within this institutional framework, Bhutto had to evolve policies and programmes to realise the 'New Pakistan'. His slogan was Islamic Socialism. His critics retorted that it was neither Islamic nor Socialist. A man of wealth, a bon viveur, he was also not a believer (his mother had been a Hindu). A number of economic and social policies were initiated, but none made real progress. One cause was the dismantling of the elite civil service which left him with no administrative machinery to implement the reforms. Another cause was the steady exodus of professional people from a country where rhetoric was substituted for progress (Map 12). Thus, one tangible improvement was the expansion of medical training, with 6,000 new doctors being qualified in five years. This should have increased the supply of trained doctors from 13,000 to 19,000: instead during that period, 1972–7, the total fell to 11,000 as many emigrated overseas.

The emigration phenomenon applied to India and Bangladesh also. During the early 1960s the great majority went to Britain and the better qualified to Canada. Then the United States became the mecca of the professional man from South Asia, with its 'Green Card' system admitting huge numbers of relatives. The unqualified – and

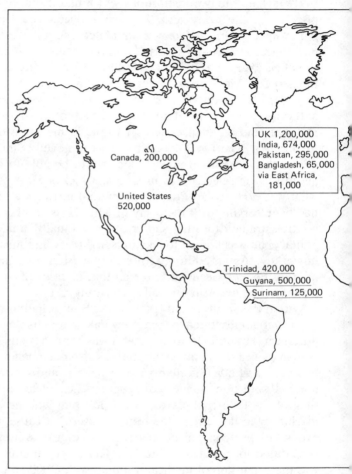

UK 1,200,000
India, 674,000
Pakistan, 295,000
Bangladesh, 65,000
via East Africa,
181,000

Canada, 200,000

United States
520,000

Trinidad, 420,000
Guyana, 500,000
Surinam, 125,000

Map 12. The South Asian exodus. Where underlined, from the old emigration,
1830–1939, e.g. *Mauritius, 700,000*

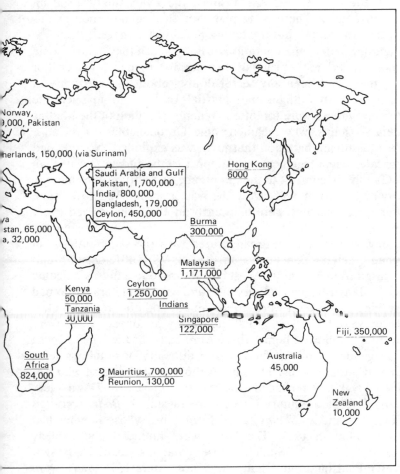

Norway,
9,000, Pakistan

herlands, 150,000 (via Surinam)

Saudi Arabia and Gulf
Pakistan, 1,700,000
India, 800,000
Bangladesh, 179,000
Ceylon, 450,000

Hong Kong
6000

va
stan, 65,000
a, 32,000

Burma
300,000

Malaysia
1,171,000

Kenya
50,000
Tanzania
30,000

Ceylon
1,250,000

Indians

Singapore
122,000

Fiji, 350,000

South
Africa
824,000

Mauritius, 700,000
Reunion, 130,00

Australia
45,000

New
Zealand
10,000

All others, mainly since 1960. Note emigration to Burma and Ceylon from India.
In every case numbers are approximate as methods of enumeration are so varied.

that included most leaving Bangladesh – continued to find the loopholes in British immigration laws. Finally, the oil boom of the 1970s attracted thousands from unskilled labourers to trained professionals to the Gulf states. As Muslims, the Pakistanis were at an obvious advantage. There is no place for this phenomenon in this book, which the author has treated more fully elsewhere.[1]

In the aftermath of the liberation of Bangladesh the Indian people were more united, more proud of their country than ever before – or after. If there had been any secret doubts about the capability of Indian soldiers to outfight the 'martial races' who manned the Pakistan army these were forgotten. When a battalion of the Madras Regiment – Tamils, who included some Untouchables – overran a Punjabi Mussulman battalion that myth was exploded. Nobody had given greater encouragement and support to the Indian *jawans* than Indira Gandhi, in contrast to the impotence of Nehru in 1962 and the passivity of Shastri in 1965. Now she was supreme. Wherever state elections were due they were held early in 1972; she carried every state.

The new Bangladesh was inaugurated with the same enthusiasm which had greeted independence in 1947–8. With little delay, Mujib was released from gaol in the West and returned to a hero's welcome in Dacca. Many Bengali civil servants, and some army units who had been serving in the West were still detained, and only returned after months or years. The 90,000 Pakistan army prisoners of war were also eventually allowed home: there were calls for the trial of those guilty of genocide, but in the end the difficulty of obtaining legal proof ruled out any trials. The fate of those in Bangladesh who had remained loyal to Pakistan during the fateful year 1971 was very different. Two para-military forces were raised, *Al-Badr*, recruited from Bengalis and *Al-Shams* raised from some whose families had fled from Bihar in 1947. The latter were hounded and publicly executed by Tiger Kader Siddiqi. Those remaining pleaded to be sent to (West) Pakistan, but Bhutto was not interested. Many were casually slaughtered; years later most were still in refugee camps.

In the wake of the war, India found the resources to fund a massive aid programme to Bangladesh. A Treaty of Friendship was signed, to run for 25 years from 1972. A Constituent Assembly adopted a new constitution for Bangladesh in December 1972 and a general election

[1] See the author's *The Banyan Tree; Overseas Emigrants from India, Pakistan and Bangladesh*, Oxford, 1976.

held next year gave Mujib's Awami League a landslide majority. He formed his Cabinet mainly from the politicians who had functioned as a government in exile in Calcutta. The underground fighters, all more radical than these lawyer politicians, resented their exclusion. Although all Mujib's Ministers were Muslims he proclaimed a secular state: the new national anthem was a poem by Rabindranath Tagore (as the composer of India's national anthem, *Jana Gana Mana*, he is almost certainly the only man to whom two nations have turned).

There was a famine in 1974 which claimed 50,000 victims. The euphoria evaporated. Mujib was pushing his family members into important jobs and lining his own pocket. His regime became ever more dictatorial. On 14 August 1975 he was gunned down, along with numerous members of his family. The assassins were two Lieutenant-Colonels, Farukh Rahman and Abdur Rashid. The new army was divided into factions. Those who had organised resistance against the Pakistanis were favoured by Mujib, to the resentment of the 1,000 officers who had been interned in the West during the war and were alleged to be still pro-Pakistan. The assassins came from this group. A third group were those who had actually assisted the Pakistanis in the task of repression, and all except those especially identified crept back into position. The senior officers in each category gave preference to those with a similar background.

After Mujib's death, the former Commerce Minister, Khandakar Mushtaq Ahmed, assumed the presidency, banned all political parties and declared martial law. Zia, the hero of the Chittagong rising was now a Major-General. As Chief of Staff he carried out the martial law regulations. In November, Brigadier Khalid Musharaf led a counter coup and arrested Zia; only four days elapsed before he was overthrown and Zia was back as Chief of Staff. The Chief Justice formally assumed the presidency but Zia played the leading role in the government. Not until April 1977 did he take over as president. His action received overwhelming support in a popular referendum.

Pakistan had set aside military leadership; Bangladesh had fallen back into the pattern. Burma showed no disposition to discard the apparently immovable General Ne Win. Bids to shift him among senior army officers collapsed: the dissidents were despatched to distant capitals as ambassadors. Neither was he unsettled by public disorders. Following the Cultural Revolution in China in 1966 the Rangoon Chinese community paraded the streets, chanting and flourishing the Little Red Book. The display of Maoist emblems was forbidden, leading to further Chinese demonstrations in which numbers of students joined. Anti-Chinese riots followed in which much property, including the Embassy was damaged and destroyed. Relations between Burma and China were severed and the great neighbour supplied increased aid to the rebels, especially to the Kachins in the north. Diplomatic relations were restored in October 1970.

At last, in 1974 the new constitution of the People's Socialist Republic (called *Pyidaungsu Socialist Thammada Myanma* in Burmese) came into being. In its pyramid structure it was not unlike Ayub's Basic Democracies. People's Councils were set up at the local level and they acted as electoral bodies for the higher echelons which in turn elected a People's Assembly of 450 members. All the functions of government are exercised by a 28-Member Council of State, headed by a Prime Minister. In addition to the Assembly there are People's Courts and People's Inspectors who are supposed to act as a check on the administration. None of this made much difference to the daily life of the people who remained a nation of rice farmers. Production rose slowly, subject to frequent variations. Burma's principal trading partners were Japan (11 per cent of exports), Singapore (12 per cent) and Indonesia (15 per cent). The former massive export of rice to India virtually ceased.

This was partly a reflection of India's growing self-sufficiency in foodgrains. Being almost a sub-continent, India's economy showed extreme divergencies. The much publicised 'Green Revolution' was almost entirely confined to Punjab and Haryana: some other states, notably Gujarat and Maharashtra were areas of economic growth because of industrialisation. All this was arrested by widespread drought in 1972 and 1974 with an industrial downturn accompanied by industrial unrest. Amid these discontents the much-respected Jayaprakash Narayan stood up to call upon the students – especially those in his native Bihar – to give a year of their lives to the regeneration of their country. This was the background to an unexpected event which, however irrelevant to the country's problems, served as a catalyst.

Mrs Gandhi's opponent in the 1971 election had filed a petition alleging that her election was irregular, citing the use of government jeeps for political purposes. The Allahabad High Court mulled the election petition over for four years and then pronounced that there had been irregularities and her election was therefore invalid. This verdict need not have been a disaster; under the constitution she could continue six months as Prime Minister without being an MP.

By then she could have fought and won a by-election elsewhere or alternatively referred the question to the Supreme Court. Instead she acted in a manner characteristic of her forceful, some would say overbearing personality. The opposition gave her an excuse by announcing a campaign to remove her from office. On the night of 25–26 June 1975, armed with a Declaration of Emergency from the President, she moved against her enemies. It was August 1942 all over again! There were numerous arrests of opposition leaders and even some Congressmen. The press was placed under total censorship. Parliament still functioned, as a rump and as her instrument. Emergency legislation validated her election, and other measures consolidated her hold over the country.

Many believed that her precipitate action owed much to the urging of Sanjay, her younger son, who was being groomed as heir apparent. If Indira displayed a harshness alien to the Indian democratic tradition, Sanjay was even more ruthless: some accused him of gangster methods. Among his priorities in the Emergency was a programme of resettlement of the thousands of squatters who camped out in central Delhi. They were piled into trucks and dumped in outlying districts. Their shanties were bulldozed and the central area was tidied up. Even more arbitrary was the campaign of male sterilisation. For years there had been a birth control programme, expensive to run and devoid of results. Now, throughout northern India, fathers of families of three or more were taken away for sterilisation, being rewarded with a transistor apiece.

All this was accepted surprisingly passively by the public. It was important to Mrs Gandhi to secure the approval of 'the intellectuals', and many were induced to issue supportive statements. Most surprising was endorsement by the aged Vinoba Bhave for preventing the disintegration of India. Whatever the value of these testimonials, the business world certainly approved of Mrs Gandhi's measures, and also the actions of Sanjay as restoring momentum to economic development while strikes were outlawed.

Then quite unexpectedly she announced that fresh elections would be held. There are different explanations, all speculative, but in any event the election was fixed for March 1977 and proved entirely free from government manipulation.[1]

---

[1] Among the reasons advanced as to why Indira took this sudden decision, three seem possibilities. It is said that her father appeared to her in dreams, rebuking her for betraying his democratic beliefs. It is said that when Michael Foot visited her in Delhi and stressed how shocked the British Labour Party was at her behaviour she

The opposition leaders stumbled out of confinement (the older detainees complained that their treatment was worse than in 1942). They hastily patched up a common front, aligning extreme Left with extreme Right. This Janata (People's Party) as it was named was shortly joined by Jagjivan Ram, the principal leader of the Untouchables who had remained at Indira's side during the Emergency. He now headed the Congress for Democracy (CFD). Her sudden decision took her own supporters by surprise. Sanjay had planned to nominate a cohort of his Youth Congress lieutenants as candidates but at such short notice they could not elbow aside sitting MPs: hence some of Mrs Gandhi's most committed supporters lost an important incentive to work for her. Perhaps sensing that Sanjay had become a liability his mother told him to stick to his own constituency while she boldly set out on another campaign marathon.

When all the votes were counted Janata had won 270 seats together with 29 wins for the CFD; a clear majority. Indira's support in parliament numbered 153 of whom 92 came from the southern states. She lost her seat by 50,000 votes and Sanjay's defeat was worse. Not waiting to face parliament, Indira lifted the remains of the Emergency and retired into private life after a last tearful farewell with her faithful supporters. The Indian intelligentsia was delighted. Not so much that Janata was in power but because Indian politics had demonstrated that the opposition could become the elected government. Jayaprakash led the Janata MPs to Gandhi's shrine at Rajghat (he had not been a candidate). He made them swear that they would eschew all personal interest, all corruption, and govern solely for the nation's good.

While Indira Gandhi was tasting defeat, Sirimavo Bandaranaike was swallowing the same medicine. Because of the introduction of the new constitution in 1972 the five-year cycle came round in 1977. Dudley Senanayake had died in 1973 and the leadership of the UNP passed to J. R. Jayawardene, then seventy years old. He was not related to the Senanayakes though he belonged to an upper middle-class lawyer family. After seven years in power, Mrs Bandaranaike had incurred the antipathy of many of the public. The Tamils were totally alienated from the SLFP while the Sinhalese clergy and out-of-work middle class were disenchanted. For the first time in a

---

impulsively assured him that there would shortly be an election. Most probable seems the theory that, as an ardent devotee of astrology she was informed that the stars were moving into a hostile figuration and she tried to move beforehand.

Ceylon election the UNP received over 50 per cent of the vote on an unprecedentedly high turnout (over 86 per cent). The quirks of First Past the Post gave them over 84 per cent of the seats in parliament. The SLFP obtained less than 5 per cent of the seats. Most of the remainder were won by the Tamil United Front representing all Tamils. They demanded an autonomous state of their own, *Eelam*. This is the Tamil rendering of Ceylon or *Silan*, Tamil not having a sibilant. The Tamil Tigers now began to take up arms, receiving supplies from Tamilnadu.

Although Jayawardene was conciliatory the legacy of inter-communal hatred was now bitter. In August 1977 there were severe inter-communal riots. The Tigers attacked police and also civilians in the north and tit-for-tat attacks on Tamils followed in the south: over 100 were killed. The following year the constitution was substantially amended (indeed it was a new constitution). Tamil was recognised as the second national language and facilities for Tamils in the Courts and universities were improved. There were moves towards decentralisation by extending the powers of district councils in which, in the north, the Tamils would take control. The First Past the Post system was replaced by proportional representation whereby seats won would more accurately reflect the votes counted. Some asserted that under the new system the Tamils could have a decisive role in choosing which party governed.

The greatest innovation in the 1978 constitution was the reproduction in full detail of the Gaullist system. The President was now the Executive head of government and the prime minister and Cabinet were responsible to him. The presidential candidate of the UNP, J. R. Jayawardene was automatically assured of election by virtue of his party's overwhelming majority.

The crises in India and Ceylon coincided with the collapse of the Bhutto regime in Pakistan. The PPP had produced no tangible changes; the landlords remained over-powerful, the middle classes were worse off; only certain newly promoted elements, such as individual workers had more economic muscle. Elections were due in 1977 and were announced for March. They were preceded by the introduction of land reforms designed to win peasant support. Also, there was an apparent upturn in the economy, largely due to the injection of foreign exchange remitted by Pakistani workers in the Gulf: in 1976 these amounted to one-third of the country's earnings of hard currency. Bhutto wooed the oil rich rulers of the Gulf, trying to attract money by promising to manufacture the Islamic H-Bomb.

The United States reacted swiftly and adversely; Saudi Arabia was urged to withhold aid while France was told not to supply fissile materials. Bhutto turned to Libya, but this was counter-productive. When the election was called, Saudi money was given to the opposition.

All this activity was no substitute for genuine development, and the year 1976–7 proved to be one of standstill or even decline. However, Bhutto was supremely confident and in his pre-election speeches he gave indications that the constitution would be amended to grant him greater power. Many of his opponents and critics were in gaol and the press was bridled but the opposition sought to maximise support by forming a National Alliance which Bhutto dismissed as 'a cat with nine tails'; for some were strongly Islamic and some were secular. The result seemed to vindicate Bhutto. Out of a total of 200 seats in the National Assembly the PPP won 155, based on 77 per cent of the popular vote with an even higher percentage in all-important Punjab. The National Alliance captured only 36 seats and polled significantly only in Sind and the Frontier Province. There were also nine independents from the tribal areas.

At once, the opposition claimed that the result was fraudulent; Bhutto would only concede minor irregularities. Agitation mounted and even flared up in Lahore where the PPP was supposed to have triumphed. The Federal Security Force created for just such an emergency was unable to contain the increasing violence. After six weeks of struggle Bhutto imposed 'limited' martial law and the army came in to restore order. Early in July it was rumoured that PPP thugs were preparing to crush the demonstrators. On 5 July, General Zia staged a bloodless coup; there was imminent danger of chaos he told the country.

At first Bhutto was only confined to his own home. Out of power, many of his misdeeds began to come to light. A case was lodged in the Lahore High Court in which Bhutto was accused of conspiracy to murder a political adversary back in November 1974. The judges did not announce their verdict until March 1978, finding him the 'arch culprit' in the ambush of his opponent. The Court condemned him to death. The former prime minister had been removed to prison where he remained until in March 1979 the Supreme Court confirmed the earlier verdict. Bhutto was hanged in Rawalpindi gaol on 4 April 1979. It was a kind of rough justice.

In the first phase of martial law, Zia-ul-Huq promised an early return to civilian government. Thereafter he informed the nation that it had been revealed to him in a dream that elections were un-Islamic. Those who had dismissed him as a simpleton, the front men for a clique of powerful generals, were to find that he was a shrewd political operator. Zia's position was strengthened internally and internationally when in December 1979 thousands of Russian troops entered Afghanistan to occupy the country. Afghan refugees began to pour over the border. If the Russian invasion brought dangers it also brought renewed large-scale American aid, both economic and military. The CIA saw in Afghanistan the opportunity to manufacture a Vietnam in reverse, with the Russians acting out the former American role. Zia became valuable as a sound anti-Communist. His regime which at first appeared tenuous was consolidated.

The Indian scene, 1977–9, was one of confusion. Morarji Desai at last achieved his ambition to be prime minister, but his undoubted abilities did not outweigh his defects. Though an experienced politician he could not hold together his contradictory Cabinet in which George Fernandez, the Marxist labour leader had to co-exist with Jan Sangh zealots. The Cabinet could not even agree what to do about Mrs Gandhi. A commission was set up under a senior judge, J. C. Shah, and uncovered a mass of evidence concerning the harsh conduct of 'The Gang of Four' (Indira, Sanjay, and their hatchet men R. K. Dhawan and Bansi Lal). What should be done? Fernandez and the Home Minister Charan Singh pressed for her impeachment; others advised against making her a martyr. Early in October 1977 she was arrested. She told the arresting officer 'Where are the handcuffs? I am not going without handcuffs'. Taken before a magistrate, the evidence produced was meagre. She was discharged and returned home in triumph.

Her next move took a little time. The Congress survivors seemed reluctant to commit themselves. She carved out a faction loyal to her, the Chief Minister of Karnatika provided her with a by-election in his state; she was elected with a majority of 77,000. She took her seat in Parliament in November 1978 and then was charged with breach of privilege. She chose to make a defiant speech; she was expelled from parliament and sent to gaol for the remainder of the session (which turned out to be one week). She started on her journey to a Delhi gaol singing a verse of the song popular in wartime Britain: 'Wish me luck as you wave me goodbye'.

Meanwhile the Janata leadership was busy tearing itself apart. On 15 July 1979, Desai submitted his resignation, unable to govern with a Cabinet which had lost its more important members, notably Charan

Singh. After other moves had failed, the President called in Charan Singh who undertook the formation of a ministry. He was encouraged by Indira's vague promises, but she backed off. On 20 August the transitory premier resigned, advising the President to notify a dissolution.

The election was delayed until January 1980. Jagjivan Ram attempted to make his way back into the Indira Congress but was rebuffed: even though he had always been able to deliver millions of Untouchable votes. When the election came, the result almost replicated that of 1971: Mrs Gandhi won 351 of the 525 seats in the Lok Sabha. Janata was reduced to 31 seats while Charan Singh's faction of Janata, named Lok Dal, won 41 seats. Mrs Gandhi ensured her own return by standing in Karnatika again as well as in her old seat, Rae Bareli. She won both seats handsomely, and Sanjay – whose unpopularity had been assumed by all – won in a neighbouring constituency with a 120,000 majority. Her new Cabinet was more notable for those she omitted rather than those she included.

In the aftermath of her triumph Indira suffered a personal tragedy. Sanjay was a keen amateur pilot, and he liked to show off. While performing aerobatics in the Delhi sky in June 1980 his plane stalled and he was killed. Where, now, would she find her successor? Her elder son, Rajiv (born 1943) had shown no interest in politics. Not being an intellectual he had joined Indian Airways as a pilot, and later a company executive. Although lacking all political experience he was appointed a General Secretary in the Congress and began to deliver rather halting speeches.

In the following year, Bangladesh lost another leader. President Zia had survived numerous attempted coups by army officers. The would-be assassins came from the radical faction of former Freedom Fighters. Because in 1971 it had been patriotic to repudiate the military oath and rebel they still considered this legitimate. Although Zia had been an outstanding resistance leader he relied more and more on the 'repatriates', thus incurring even more enmity from the politically activist officers. Zia formerly retired from the army; he was given a resounding victory in 1978. In the following year his Bangladesh National Party secured a two-thirds majority in the legislature, vanquishing the erstwhile victorious Awami League.

Zia made efforts to strengthen the vulnerable agricultural economy, described by Dr Kissinger as a 'Basket Case'. He concentrated on rural development, birth control, mass literacy and canal building, giving the peasants his own personal aid and encouragement. Like all ex-military leaders he promoted local level councils, Gram Sarkar, as well as Village Defence Parties to preserve law and order and to form a guerrilla army in the event of invasion. For after the first brief period in which friendship with India was the keynote (probably the Indians expected Bangladesh to rejoin Mother India) relations with the big neighbour were, if anything, worse than when it was East Pakistan.

Zia had demonstrated that he was a survivor, but in Chittagong where he had first raised the banner of resistance in 1971 he was assassinated on 30 May 1981. The Chief of Staff, Lieutenant-General H. M. Ershad at once sped to the hospital in Dacca Cantonment where the ageing Vice-President, Abdus Sattar was convalescing. He was taken to the President's house, *Banga Bhaban*, where he took the oath as Acting President. Sattar had already suffered three strokes and was not really a credible leader. Ershad's motive was probably to block Major-General Nurul Islam known to entertain presidential ambitions.

The country then went through the motions of conducting a presidential election. There were eight candidates, but the front runners were Abdus Sattar and Kamal Hossain for a revived Awami League. The former won easily (November 1981). Although Ershad was assiduous in proclaiming the non-political stance of the army, the feeble Sattar was obviously a stopgap. In March 1982 Ershad took over as chief martial law administrator; in December 1983 he assumed the position of President.

After the constitutional changes in Ceylon–Sri Lanka in 1978 the country appeared to be entering a period of growing prosperity. Agricultural production was up; tourism was booming; remittances from the 60,000 islanders working in the Middle East made a big contribution. Only the attempt to attract industry and capital by establishing tax-free zones for exports was a mixed success (too many Third World countries were offering similar facilities). In mid-1982 the political scene was startled by the news that a presidential election would take place that year. It was generally agreed that Jayawardene's popularity was greater than that of his party. The opposition hastily chose their candidates. The most likely choice of the SLFP would have been Sirimavo Bandaranaike, but she was debarred from office for alleged offences when in power (doubtless the example of Mrs Gandhi was not overlooked). Instead the SLFP chose H. Kobbekaduwa, a close relation and a senior party member. Another important contender was Rohana Wijeweera, leader of the JVP insurrection in 1971, for the JVP was now a constitutional body. The Tamil Congress also fielded a candidate, as did the long-established Marxist parties.

When election day came in October 1982, Jayawardene scored a major victory with 3,450,811 votes, almost 53 per cent of the total (higher than the UNP share in 1977). Kobbekawduwa did very respectably with 2,548,438 votes (39 per cent) and the next best candidate, Wijeweera only received 4 per cent of the total vote. Encouraged by this turnout, the UNP announced that a referendum would take place in December to extend the life of parliament until August 1989. This time there would be a straightforward *Yes* or *No* vote, which should have simplified the task for the opposition. Yet again strong support was given to the government with 3,141,223 *Yes* votes and *No* 2,605,983. Those who hoped that the introduction of proportional representation would benefit the party system must have been dismayed at this version of the manipulation of the popular will.

Unexpectedly, the Jayawardene regime was threatened by a different form of politics, that of extremism on the streets. The Tamil Tigers had been steadily gaining strength and acquiring experience in guerrilla combat. In mid-July 1983 they ambushed an army patrol, killing thirteen soldiers (virtually the whole army was Sinhalese in composition). These army–guerrilla encounters were openly communal. The soldiers' bodies were paraded through the centre of Colombo and retaliation was immediate. Tamil shops were looted and shopkeepers killed. Even more disgraceful was the slaughter of 52 Tamil prisoners in a Colombo gaol by Sinhalese convicts with the connivance and perhaps participation of the prison staff. Jayawardene seemed loath to act; his main preoccupation was to reassure the Sinhalese that he would not grant concessions to the Tamils. Not until 26 July was a curfew imposed, and this did not stem the terrorist attacks which continued throughout August. Sinhalese psychology assumed a *minority* complex. There are at least 30 million Tamils living just across the Palk Strait on the Indian side and they were seen (not unjustly) as active advocates of Tamil separatism in Ceylon. Fantastic rumours that Tamil hordes were about to descend on Colombo were circulated, and fed the flames of violence. Communal hatred even spread to the Catholic minority (mainly Sinhalese around Colombo) who were accused of giving aid and comfort to the Tamils.

The nightmare eventually abated, leaving a terrible sense of insecurity and a loss of confidence in Jayawardene in both communities. The beneficiaries were the Tamil Tigers who seemed to provide the only hope of protection to their people. A similar sequence of violence and counter-violence now erupted in north India.

When Mrs Gandhi returned to power in 1980, many hoped – and believed – that she would now have a much stronger concern for constitutional proprieties. Her inclination to solve critical situations by invoking President's rule had caused her downfall. Nobody could pretend that the task facing her was straightforward, for northern and eastern India was plagued by the rise of local chauvinism: the claim of those who called themselves *Bhumi-putra*, 'Sons of the Soil'. They and only they were entitled to political and economic rights in their native places. Some of these 'nativist' movements had been astir for twenty years – or even since independence. The Nagas, the tribal people of the eastern borderland claimed they were not Indians at all and demanded their own, separate independence. Nagaland, despite its poverty and backwardness, was granted concessions beyond those offered to other states (including the remarkable provision that English would be the language of government; the same concession was later given to the other eastern frontier mini-states – Arunachal, Mizoram and Meghalya). All were situated in a sensitive area near the China frontier. Kashmir – another border state – was not satisfied with the same status as other Indian states. All these restive peoples were now joined by the Sikhs, whose claims were even more outrageous.

Mrs Gandhi attempted to deal with the most difficult of these claims by destabilising their governments. 'To destabilise' has become a cliché of political science; for Indira it was a vital element in political strategy. In Kashmir she brought down the Abdullah administration by suborning the governing party, inducing representatives to cross the floor in the State Assembly, cobbling together an alternative administration. When this did not succeed, President's rule was imposed on the grounds that no leader could command a stable majority.

Her technique was applied with dire consequences in Punjab where the Sikh community formed a bare majority – some 52 per cent. In their holy city, Amritsar, the Sikhs were 35 per cent of the population; in Jullundur their next most important centre they were 34 per cent. In Chandigarh, joint capital with Haryana, they numbered 22 per cent. However, if numbers were not their strong feature they enjoyed other important advantages. In the army, although forming only 2 per cent of the total population of India, into the 1970s they provided

20 per cent of the soldiers. Because they were favoured by the British, and this policy continued for many years after, their representation among the officers – especially senior ranks – was even higher. Sikhs were pioneers in overseas emigration; they acquired wealth in Britain, North America and even the Middle East, and a considerable proportion was remitted to Punjab: some to support Sikh separatist politics. Hence they had a fine sense of their own importance and made large demands on the central government.

Their political strategy had two prongs: they had taken over the Congress in Punjab, and if this did not provide adequate dividends they could push their own organisation, the Akali Dal, originally created to safeguard the management of Sikh temples.

Mrs Gandhi also used a dual strategy. She rewarded Congress Sikhs; Giani Zail Singh became a Home Minister in the central government and subsequently President. He had no particular political skills; his role was representational. Alternatively she might try to manipulate the Akali Sikhs. A new leader emerged, Sant Jarnail Singh Bhindranwale, an obscure village preacher with fanatical appeal. Mrs Gandhi decided to encourage his faction to outbid the major leaders. This was a fatal move. Bhindranwale adopted methods similar to those of the IRA. He was allowed to make his headquarters in the Golden Temple itself. The overseas Sikhs supported his militancy and funnelled arms to him. How did they reach their destination? Many concluded that they were imported via Pakistan where weapon training was permitted.

Realising that the situation was getting out of hand, Mrs Gandhi imposed President's rule in Punjab in October 1983. This did not hinder Bhindranwale's activities. His assassins emerged from the temple complex on their murder missions, riding motor-cycles to gun down their victims. Besides their political opponents, they chose as victims the police, Hindus of all sorts, even men who had mixed marriages with Sikh or Hindu wives, such as a young Sikh journalist and a Hindu professor. The parallel with the IRA was hideously close.

At last it was agreed that only military action would end the reign of terror. In an operation code-named Blue Star the army moved into Amritsar on 1 June 1984. Fierce fighting ensued in which 200 troops and 1,000 Sikhs were killed, among them Bhindranwale. Extensive damage was inflicted on the Golden Temple and its surroundings which passed under military occupation. The destruction was resented by all Sikhs including the most moderate. Khushwant Singh the eminent writer who had assailed Bhindranwale's murderous activities was moved to return the high decoration awarded by the President. Bhindranwale became a martyr and the massacre of 1984 was compared to that of 1919 (which it far exceeded). A great impetus was given to the movement for Khalistan, a separate Sikh state, which had been germinating since independence. The overseas Sikhs were especially vocal in calling for Khalistan.

The Prime Minister's personal guard included Sikhs; they were sent off on leave to allow passions to cool but about four months after the attack they returned to duty. On 31 October 1984 one of them shot Indira in her own home. The country was plunged into a state of shock. In Delhi and its suburbs there was a pogrom. The Sikh men were killed (many burnt to death) and Sikh women degraded. Over 2,700 were killed. Perhaps it was this breakdown in control which induced Indira's principal colleagues to press Rajiv to assume the premiership. This young man (for in Indian politics anyone under 60 – or 70 – is young) had never held any position in government, but he accepted the challenge and his first moves gave reassurance: he dismissed those who had permitted the massacre and brought in the army to restore order.

He called a general election for 24 December. The campaign was unusually subdued: Rajiv spoke generally of unity. The result was sensational. The Lok Sabha now numbered 508; Congress won 401 seats. Nehru had never attained such success. The opposition was fragmented. Janata was down to 10 MPs and Jagjivan Ram's following to four. Total support: but what was his policy? His slogan was 'Taking India into the 21st Century'. Did this mean anything? The first priority was to appease the Sikhs. Khalistan was excluded from consideration; maybe they could be satisfied by receiving Chandigarh in return for transferring a pocket of Hindi villages to Haryana.

While these momentous events were happening, little seemed to change in Burma. Leopold von Ranke sketched out a history of the world; this was entirely Eurocentric, and Asia was dismissed as 'the Land of Eternal Standstill'. This sweeping judgement did seem applicable to Ne Win's Burma.

One issue created a diversion. Land-hungry peasants from Bang-ladesh filtered through the borderland of meandering creeks and low hills north of Arakan. Ever since independence there had been spasmodic attempts to set up a separate Muslim state in this area with its separate connections going back to Mughal times. In the mid-1970s this influx reached mass proportions (a similar exodus was invading Assam). Only in 1978 did the Rangoon government grasp the situation, which was sharpened by the efforts of the Bangladesh military attaché in Rangoon. He was expelled, and so were more than 130,000 squatters who became pathetic refugees back in their own country.

In November 1981 the office of President was conferred on Brigadier San Yu, a somewhat colourless officer in indifferent health. Ne Win also gave up the chairmanship of *Lanzin*, appointing Brigadier Tin Oo, head of military intelligence. Anywhere else this might have been a dangerous dispersion of supreme authority, but Ne Win knew what he was doing. He watched Tin Oo carefully and decided he was accumulating illegal wealth. He was ousted from the post of Chairman and tried for corruption, being sentenced to life imprisonment. Ne Win returned to the Chair with every appearance of vigour. However, it would seem that Tin Oo's disappearance from military intelligence left a vacuum. In October 1983 there was a ceremonial visit from the leaders of the military government of South Korea (Burma recognised the South and the North equally, in conformity with the policy of strict neutrality in international affairs). Every official visit always included a wreath-laying ceremony at the 'Martyrs' Memorial' commemorating Aung San and those who died with him. On 9 October, while they were inside the Memorial a bomb placed in the ceiling exploded, killing 21; mainly South Koreans with some Burmese officials. The crime was traced to two members of the North Korean Embassy and on 4 November Burma broke off diplomatic relations. Thereafter, Burma faded behind the accustomed news blackout. The news which emerged came mainly via Thailand, and was of the growing guerrilla activities along Burma's western border. The best funded tribal army was the Shan United Army, funded from the international demand for narcotics grown in 'the Golden Triangle'. The most effective was the Karen Independence Army which in one form or another had been fighting in the jungle since 1948. The Burma Army waged a continuous, bitter war against the guerrillas without ever bringing them to a decisive action.

The regime in Pakistan began to shed its overwhelmingly military character though President Zia took care to remain Commander-in-Chief. Various attempts were made to kill him, the first as early as 1979 and the most dangerous the launching of a SAM missile at his plane. In December 1984, the General sought to legitimise his presidency by holding a referendum on a limited basis. Officially, 60 per cent of those eligible voted (the opposition claimed the turnout was 30 per cent). Of those voting 98 per cent gave Zia a *Yes* vote. This was the signal for martial law to be lifted in December 1985. A civilian prime minister, Mohammad Khan Junejo was installed.

Zulfikar Bhutto's daughter returned to Pakistan in April 1985 (his son had died, supposedly of a drugs overdose). Benazir Bhutto had her father's magnetism; she made a triumphal progress through the big cities. She was detained, briefly, from August to September 1985. In June 1986 political parties were permitted once more. Zia's supporters reconstituted the Pakistan Muslim League. Benazir Bhutto reawakened the popular appeal of the PPP. Despite her personal dynamism it was difficult to discern the substance of a programme, aside from a strident affirmation of the rights of the poor.

Zia's zeal for Islam was extended from his personal to his public life. He began to apply portions of the Islamic code of punishment, including public floggings for certain crimes and even corporal punishment for adulterous women. The revolution in Iran and the international appeal exercised by Ayatollah Khomeini offered a warning; Khomeini had dealt harshly with the Iranian generals, and although Iran is Shia and only about 5 per cent of Pakistani Muslims are Shia, Zia sensed danger, as well as the disapproval of his American patrons, for whom a particularly sensitive issue was the Islamic H-Bomb. This had reached the point where production of the Bomb was feasible. In 1986 the US Congress approved aid to Pakistan for the five years 1987–92 totalling $4.2 Billion (the largest foreign aid grant outside Israel). Certain members of Congress made discontinuance of the nuclear programme a condition of aid. By now there was a stockpile of fissile material and the compromise was to delay the start of actual manufacture.

Bangladesh also moved cautiously from military to civilian government. Parliamentary elections were held in May 1986 in which President Ershad headed the Jatiya Party. The main opposition came from a revived Awami League whose leader was Mujib's daughter, Hasina Wajed. The new parliament, *Jatiya Sangsad* was composed of 300 members. The Jatiya Party won 153 seats, increased to 208 by the adherence of independents and the 30 women members. The Awami League won 76, and the Communist Party 5; the revived Muslim League won in four seats only. Ershad retired from the army command on 31 August 1986, indicating his confidence that there could be no military coup. A presidential election was called for 15 October. Mujib's daughter was the principal challenger though a macabre candidate emerged: Faruk Rahman, Mujib's murderer who had been living in exile. The result gave Ershad an overwhelming victory with 84 per cent support; Hasina Wajed obtained 6 per cent and Faruk Rahman 4 per cent of the votes. Ershad appeared to be unassailable.

These public performances had no relevance to the country's underlying problem: a backward economy. At the 1951 Census the East Pakistan population numbered 42 million (about 22 per cent being Hindu). In 1981 this had risen to more than 90 million, despite the exodus of the Hindus and the migration of about 300,000 Muslims to Britain. The bulk of the population still depended on agriculture, vulnerable to the vagaries of the season as in 1987 when the worst floods ever were experienced. Ershad, like Ziaur Rahman attempted to modernise the rural economy – with no more success.

While Burma and Bangladesh experienced internal stress, India and Ceylon – Sri Lanka – found their internal problems becoming the source of international tension. The alienation of the Ceylon Tamils moved inexorably towards crisis point. Tamil demands clashed with a constitutional amendment passed in 1983 requiring all candidates for parliament to take an oath renouncing any claim that would divide the country. The UNP and the miniscule SLFP group of MPs passed this amendment over the opposition of the Tamil United Liberation Front who thereafter forfeited their seats in parliament. Jayawardene was considerably more willing to accommodate Tamil demands than his Cabinet, but these demands only intensified. In June 1986 a plan was unveiled for autonomy for the northern and eastern provinces where the Tamils were in strength; but a demand that the two provinces be united as *Tamil Eelam* was rejected (the eastern province had a Tamil component of only 40 per cent). The Tigers were emerging as the arbiters in the north and there was something like civil war. The Sinhalese military forces were under constant attack, and they responded by increasingly heavy-handed repression. Support from Tamilnadu grew in strength with a regular traffic in arms across the Palk strait.

Rajiv was beset by similar defiant responses from almost all India's border states. Amongst new regional demands, one was for a new state to be called Gorkhaland centred upon the hill station, Darjeeling. A Gurkha National Liberation Front orchestrated the demand. They could be stalled. The Sikhs were increasingly turbulent. Punjab had become a no man's land where indiscriminate murder was an accepted part of life. The terrorists could operate also in Delhi at will.

The Prime Minister himself was under siege. His family dare not leave home, and he only moved around under the most elaborate security. In 1987 his difficulties reached crisis point. Elections were due in several states and in one after another Congress suffered defeat; in Kerala and West Bengal in March, and in Haryana in June. There, Bansi Lal, Indira's hatchet man, lost his seat. Rajiv's solitary success came in the Presidential election of July 1987. Zail Singh had imagined he could exploit Rajiv's difficulties and began to demand that the prime minister ask the president's advice on a range of problems. His term came to an end in July 1987 and he indicated that he intended to stand again. All this came at a delicate time when Rajiv was trying to purge his Cabinet. He had already expelled his Defence Minister V. P. Singh who wanted to dig into the circumstances of bribery in massive defence contracts. Now, three more ministers were expelled. All four belonged to Uttar Pradesh, the largest state in the Union, and they could count on the support of the MPs belonging to their state. Refusing to give away to either the retiring president or the ex-ministers Rajiv threw his weight behind the alternative candidate, the Vice-President, R. Venkataraman. When the MPs came to make their choice he won by a small margin. Rajiv had survived that contest: not unimportant if he wanted to invoke president's rule in any other state.

However, domestic difficulties counted for little beside the crisis brewing in Sri Lanka. The Tigers, growing ever bolder, attacked army units and Sinhalese civilians. The army mounted a major operation against Jaffna, supported by air power. The Tigers, and also the non-combatants, were bottled up, and began to run out of food and fuel. Feeling in Tamilnadu rose to boiling point. The first response from Delhi was mild. A flotilla of small civilian craft approached Jaffna with relief supplies. The Sri Lanka navy turned them back. On 4 June India sent over military transport planes to drop supplies. The Sinhalese expressed outrage at this infringement of sovereignty. It had become clear that India would have to employ muscle if anything was to be achieved.

Jayawardene was shrewd. He could see they were on collision course. After preliminaries, an accord was signed with India on 29 July 1987 promising an immediate grant of autonomy to the Tamils. More far-reaching concessions were made allowing India to send in a peacekeeping force with the task of disarming the Tigers. The Sri Lankan forces would pull back. Additionally, there was an undertaking that facilities in the Trincomalee naval base would not be granted to a third power (this was aimed at the United States) while the

Indian navy would patrol off the Jaffna coastline to prevent further arms imports.

Rajiv flew into Colombo to sign the accord on 20 July. Next day, the first Indian army units began to disembark. That same day, as Rajiv inspected a naval guard of honour on his departure from Colombo one sailor tried to strike him down with a rifle butt. He was not the only dissentient. Mrs Bandaranaike led a sit-down protest and even Jayawardene's prime minister, Ranasingha Premadas made no secret of his dissatisfaction. Nevertheless, Indian troops were now occupying Jaffna and the Indian navy was running Trincomalee. Negotiations to persuade the Tigers to lay down their arms were protracted; but on paper agreement was secured, and some arms were handed in. It soon became obvious that this was only a cover for further operations once the Sri Lanka army had withdrawn. In Jaffna and its environs, the Tamils were the overwhelming majority; but Trincomalee had a mixed population. The Tamils began a campaign of terror against their Sinhalese neighbours to make them depart and thus transform Trincomalee into a Tamil stronghold.

The Indian Army was not there to implement the Tigers' strategy. Within a few weeks there was a complete change in their priorities. They began to undertake the systematic reduction of the Tigers' position in Jaffna, for it was now clear that the arms handover had merely been a token gesture. The Indians were determined to end the Tigers' power. But they were not waging war on an enemy; they had to conduct operations with the least harm to non-combatants and their property, so it all took time. It was many weeks before Jaffna could be considered even tolerably free of armed guerrillas. Meanwhile, in Tamilnadu public opinion was on the Tigers' side and there was renewed talk of a Tamil state separate from India.

The state of war over the Ceylon Tamils' claims had no effect on the campaign for Khalistan: even though many of those at risk in Jaffna were Sikhs trying to implement the policy of Delhi and Colombo. Nor did Jayawardene flinch before the bombing which Sinhalese extremists were inflicting on Colombo. He survived an assassination attempt when his MPs were debating the award: a grenade was thrown at him in the Parliament building. Later, on 9 November when the Sri Lanka parliament considered the Bill to enable the Tamils to hold elections for the northern and eastern autonomous authorities there was an immediate bombing campaign in Colombo. Parliament went ahead and passed the Bill.

Rajiv's dilemmas seemed to defy solution: as did those of Jayawardene. Ending amid a sea of uncertainties this study certainly cannot presume to make predictions, or even speculations. South Asia today provides many clues to the historian; but not to the prophet.

POSTSCRIPT (August 1988)

Two leaders who had appeared unassailable suddenly disappeared from the political stage in the summer of 1988. Student protest in Burma, never far below the surface, erupted in July and was answered with increased brutality. Over forty students made prisoner were crammed into a police van: on arrival at the police station, most had been suffocated. This event apparently shook General Ne Win: he promptly stepped down as Chairman of *Lanzin*, proposing that a referendum be held in September to decide whether the country wished to return to a multi-party system. A special congress of *Lanzin* rejected this proposal and nominated another military man, San Lwin, as President. Popular protest in Rangoon and other towns became violent. Many were killed by the military, who lost some soldiers in confused fighting. After only eighteen days San Lwin withdrew from the Presidency. His successor was named as U Maung Maung, jurist and writer, the grey eminence behind Ne Win and intellectual apologist for his regime. This failed to satisfy the demonstrators, who, led by the students, disrupted the life of the country even further. Law and order collapsed. It seemed only a matter of time before the government made some sort of compromise. The crowd called for Aung Gyi, a former Brigadier and one-time henchman of Ne Win: though the goal remained a general election with multiple political parties in the contest.

The change of direction in Pakistan was even more abrupt. General Zia, with leading military officers, was killed when his Hercules transport crashed without warning. Inevitably, sabotage was suspected with the finger pointing at the Kabul government who had most to gain from his removal. The new chief of the army, General Beg, announced that a general election would be held in November 1988, as previously announced. The army would take no further part in the political process: 'Politics should be left to the politicians.' All eyes turned to Benazir Bhutto, the only leader with a mass party, the PPP, who has inherited much of her father's appeal to the populace. Whether the United States would accept her, or whether despite their protestations the army would accept her, was not beyond doubt.

Further Reading

This reading list seeks to provide a cross-section of the vast literature of the history of this area. For India, this literature is so extensive that a selective list will necessarily omit many works of merit. For Burma and Ceylon (Sri Lanka) the choice is more limited.

General

S. Arasaratnam, *Ceylon*, Prentice-Hall, Englewood Cliffs, 1964.

W. T. de Bary (ed.) *Sources of Indian Tradition*, Columbia University Press, New York, 1958.

Judith Brown, *Modern India: the Origins of an Asian Democracy*, Oxford University Press, Delhi, 1985.

J. F. Cady, *A History of Modern Burma*, Cornell University Press Ithaca, 1958.

B. H. Farmer, *An Introduction to South Asia*, Methuen, London, 1983.

Htin Aung, *A History of Burma*, Columbia University Press, New York, 1967.

E. F. C. Ludowyk, *The Story of Ceylon*, Faber, London, 1962.

R. C. Majumdar, N. C. Raychaudhuri and K. Datta, *An Advanced History of India*, Macmillan, London, 3 vols, 2nd edn, 1958.

W. H. Moreland and A. C. Chatterjee, *A Short History of India*, Longmans, London 4th edn, 1957.

K. M. de Silva, *A History of Sri Lanka*, C. Hurst, London, 1981.

D. P. Singhal, *A History of the Indian People*, Methuen, London, 1983.

T. G. P. Spear, *India: a Modern History*, University of Michigan Press, Ann Arbor, 1961.

Stanley Wolpert, *A New History of India*, Oxford University Press, New York, 1977.

Ancient and Medieval History: Chapter 1

Michael Aung Thwin, *Pagan: the Origins of Modern Burma*, University of Hawaii Press, Honolulu.

A. L. Basham, *The Wonder That Was India*, Sidgwick & Jackson, London, 1954.

G. E. Harvey, *History of Burma*, Longmans, London, 1925.

D. D. Kosambi, *Culture and Civilisation of Ancient India in Historical Outline*, Routledge & Kegan Paul, London, 1963.

G. C. Mendis, *The Early History of Ceylon*, YMCA, Calcutta, 9th imp., 1948.

274

H. G. Rawlinson, *India: a Short Cultural History*, Cresset Press, London, 4th rev. edn, 1952.
D. P. Singhal, *India and World Civilisation*, Michigan State University, East Lansing, 2 vols, 1969.

Traditional Society and Economic Life: Chapter 2

J. Auboyer, *Daily Life in Ancient India*, Weidenfeld & Nicolson, London, 1965.
J. S. Furnivall, *An Introduction to the Political Economy of Burma*, People's Literature Committee and House, Rangoon, 3rd edn, 1957.
U. N. Goshal, *The Agrarian System in Ancient India*, University of Calcutta, Calcutta, 1930.
D. D. Kosambi, *An Introduction to the Study of Indian History*, Popular Book Depot, Bombay, 1956.
W. H. Moreland, *India at the Death of Akbar; an Economic Study*, Macmillan, 1920.
R. Pieris, *Sinhalese Social Organisation*, University of Ceylon Press, Colombo, 1956.

Traditional Religion and Politics, Chapters 3 and 4

These themes are so interwoven it seems best to put them together.

Sir Olaf Caroe, *The Pathans, 550 BC–AD 1957*, Macmillan, London, 1958.
E. Conze, *Buddhism: its Essence and Development*, Faber, London, 1951.
D. Devahuti, *Harsha; a Political Study*, Oxford University Press, London, 1970.
W. Geiger, *Mahavamsa, or the Greater Chronicle of Ceylon*, Ceylon Government Information Department, Colombo, new imp., 1950.
Htin Aung, *Burmese Law Tales*, Oxford University Press, London, 1962.
Khushwant Singh, *History of the Sikhs*, Princeton University Press, Princeton, Vol. I, 1963, Vol. II, 1966.
Victor Lieberman, *Burmese Administrative Cycles: anarchy and conquest, c. 1580–1760*, Princeton University Press, Princeton, 1984.
Pe Maung Tin and G. H. Luce, *The Glass Palace Chronicle of the Kings of Burma*, Oxford University Press, London, 1925.
I. H. Qureshi, *The Administration of the Sultanate of Delhi*, Muhammad Ashraf, Lahore, 1942.
Louis Renou, *Religions of Ancient India*, Athlone Press, University of London, 1953.
Sir Jadunath Sarkar, *Mughal Administration*, M. C. Sarkar & Sons, Calcutta, 1935.
R. Shamasastry, *Kautilya's Arthasastra*, Wesleyan University Press, Mysore, 3rd edn, 1929.
Melford Spiro, *Buddhism and Society: a Great Tradition and its Burmese Vicissitudes*, Harper & Row, New York, 1972.
Romola Thapar, *Asoka and the Decline of the Mauryas*, Oxford University

Press, London, 1961.
Tara Chand, *The Influence of Islam on Indian Culture*, The Indian Press, Allahabad, 1936.

The West and Asia: Chapter 5

C. R. Boxer, *Race Relations in the Portuguese Colonial Empire, 1415–1825*, Clarendon Press, Oxford, 1963.
Holden Furber, *John Company at Work: a Study of European Expansion in India in the Late Eighteenth Century*, Harvard University Press, Cambridge, 1951.
K. W. Goonewardena, *The Foundation of Dutch Power in Ceylon, 1638–1658*, Netherlands Institute for International Cultural Relations, The Hague, 1958.
K. M. Panikkar, *Asia and Western Dominance*, Allen & Unwin, London, 1953.
C. R. de Silva, *The Portuguese in Ceylon, 1617–1638*, Ceylon University Press, Colombo, 1972.
T. G. P. Spear, *The Nabobs: a Study of the Social Life of the English in Eighteenth Century India*, Oxford University Press, London, 1932.
T. G. P. Spear, *Twilight of the Mughals: Studies in Late Mughal Delhi*, Cambridge University Press, Cambridge, 1951.
Guy Wint, *The British in Asia*, Faber, London, 1947.

Economic Development, Chapter 6

J. R. Andrus, *Burmese Economic Life*, Stanford University Press, Stanford, 1947.
Vera Anstey, *The Economic Development of India*, Longmans Green, London, 5th edn, 1952.
D. H. Buchanan, *The Development of Capitalist Enterprise in India*, Macmillan, 1934.
Cambridge Economic History of India, Vol. i, ed. Tapan Raychaudhuri and Irfan Habib, Cambridge University Press, 1982, Vol. ii, ed. Dharma Kumar, 1983.
S. J. Catanach, *Rural Credit in Western India, 1875–1930*, California University Press, Berkeley, 1970.
Cheng Siok-Hwa, *The Rice Industry of Burma, 1852–1940*, University of Malaya Press, Singapore, 1968.
M. L. Darling, *The Punjab Peasant in Prosperity and Debt*, Oxford University Press, Bombay, 4th edn, 1947.
R. E. Frykenberg, ed. *Land Control and Social Structure in Indian History*, Wisconsin University Press, Madison, 1969.
J. S. Furnivall, *Colonial Policy and Practice*, Cambridge University Press, Cambridge, 1948.
W. W. Hunter, *Annals of Rural Bengal*, Smith, Elder & Co., London, 1868.
J. C. Jack, *The Economic Life of a Bengal District*, Clarendon Press, Oxford, 1916.

Sir Ivor Jennings, *The Economy of Ceylon*, Oxford University Press, Bombay, 2nd edn, 1951.

Eric Stokes, *The Peasant and the Raj: Studies in Agrarian Society and Peasant Rebellion*, Cambridge University Press, Cambridge, 1978.

Hugh Tinker, *A New System of Slavery: the Export of Indian Labour Overseas, 1830–1920*, Oxford University Press, London, 1974.

Government of the British: Chapter 7

Kenneth Ballhatchet, *Race, Sex and Class Under the Raj: Imperial Attitudes and Policies and their Critics, 1793–1905*, Weidenfeld & Nicolson, London, 1980.

Cambridge History of India, ed. H. H. Dodwell, Cambridge University Press, Vol. v, 1929 Vol. vi, 1932.

F. S. V. Donnison, *Public Administration in Burma*, Oxford University Press, London, 1953.

Ainslie Embree, *Charles Grant and British Rule in India*, Allen & Unwin, 1962.

R. E. Frykenberg, *Guntur District, 1788–1848: a History of Local Influence and Central Authority in South India*, Clarendon Press, Oxford, 1965.

S. Gopal, *British Policy in India, 1858–1905*, Cambridge University Press, 1966.

A. B. Keith, *A Constitutional History of India, 1600–1935*, Methuen, London, 1936.

Stephen Koss, *John Morley at the India Office, 1905–1910*, Yale University Press, New Haven, 1969.

G. C. Mendis, *Ceylon Under the British*, Colombo Apothecaries, Colombo, 3rd edn, 1952.

L. A. Mills, *Ceylon Under British Rule, 1795–1932*, Oxford University Press, London, 1933.

B. B. Misra, *District Administration and Rural Development: Policy Objectives and Administration Changes in Historical Perspective*, Oxford University Press, Delhi, 1983.

Hugh Tinker, *The Foundations of Local Self-Government in India, Pakistan and Burma*, Athlone Press, University of London, 1954.

Philip Woodruff [Philip Mason], *The Men Who Ruled India*, Cape, London, Vol. i, *The Founders*, 1953, Vol. ii. *The Guardians*, 1954.

Lewis Wurgaft, *The Imperial Image: Magic and Myth in Kipling's India*, Wesleyan University Press, Middletown, 1983.

Social, Religious and Political Movements: Chapter 8

A. R. Desai, *The Social Background of Indian Nationalism*, Popular Book Depot, Bombay, 3rd edn, 1959.

C. H. Heimsath, *Indian Nationalism and Hindu Social Reform*, Princeton University Press, 1964.

S. Abid Husain, *The Destiny of Indian Muslims*, Asia Publishing House, London, 1966.

J. T. F. Jordens, *Swami Sharddhananda: his Life and Causes*, Oxford University Press, Delhi, 1981.

D. D. Karve, *The New Brahmans: Five Maharashtrian Families*, University of California Press, Berkeley, 1963.

R. P. Masani, *Dadabhia Naoroji: the Grand Old Man of India*, Allen & Unwin, London, 1939.

S. R. Mehrotra, *The Emergence of the Indian National Congress*, Vikas, Delhi, 1971.

B. R. Nanda, *Gokhale: the Indian Moderates and the British Raj*, Oxford University Press, Delhi, 1977.

Rosalind O'Hanlon, *Caste, Conflict and Ideology: Jotirao Phule and Low Caste Protest in Nineteenth Century India*, Cambridge University Press, 1985.

Michael Roberts, *Caste Conflict and Elite Formation: the Rise of the Karava Elite in Sri Lanka, 1500–1931*, Cambridge University Press, 1980.

Bruce Ryan, *Caste in Modern Ceylon*, Rutgers University Press, New Brunswick, 1953.

Anil Seal, *The Emergence of Indian Nationalism: Competition and Collaboration in the Later Nineteenth Century*, Cambridge University Press, 1968.

K. M. de Silva, *Social Policy and Missionary Organizations in Ceylon, 1840–1855*, Longmans, London, 1965.

W. Cantwell Smith, *Modern Islam in India*, Gollancz, London, 1965.

Hugh Tinker, *The Ordeal of Love: C. F. Andrews and India*, Oxford University Press, Delhi, 1979.

Stanley Wolpert, *Tilak and Gokhale: Revolution and Reform in the Making of Modern India*, University of California Press, Berkeley, 1962.

Movements for Independence: Chapter 9

C. F. Andrews and G. Mookerji, *The Rise and Growth of the Congress in India*, Allen & Unwin, London, 1938.

Abul Kalam Azed, *India Wins Freedom*, Orient Longmans, Calcutta, 1959.

Azim Husain, *Fazl-i-Husain: a Political Biography*, Orient Longmans, Bombay, 1946.

Joan Bondurant, *The Conquest of Violence: the Gandhian Philosophy of Conflict*, Princeton University Press, 1958.

N. R. Chakravarti, *The Indian Minority in Burma: the Rise and Decline of an Immigrant Community*, Oxford University Press, London, 1971.

J. L. Christian, *Modern Burma*, University of California Press, Berkeley, 1942.

Gandhi, M. K., *An Autobiography: the Story of my Experiments with Truth*, Phoenix Press, London, 1949.

S. Gopal, *Jawaharlal Nehru: a Biography*, Cape, London, Vol. i, *1889–1947*, 1975; Vol. ii, *1947–1956*, 1979; Vol. iii, *1956–1964*, 1984.

Anita Inder Singh, *The Origins of the Partition of India, 1936–1947*, Oxford University Press, Delhi, 1987.

Ayesha Jalal, *Jinnah: the Sole Spokesman*, Cambridge University Press, 1985.

Sir Charles Jeffries, *Ceylon, the Path to Independence*, Pall Mall Press, London, 1962.

Khalid Bin Sayeed, *Pakistan: the Formative Phase*, Pakistan Publishing House, Karachi, 1960.

V. P. Menon, *The Transfer of Power in India*, Longmans, London, 1957.

Maung Maung, *Burma's Constitution*, Nijhoff, The Hague, 2nd edn, 1961.

B. B. Misra, *The Indian Political Parties: an Historical Analysis of Political Behaviour up to 1947*, Oxford University Press, Delhi, 1976.

Penderel Moon, *Divide and Quit*, Chatto & Windus, London, 1961.

R. J. Moore, *The Crisis of Indian Unity, 1917–1940*, Clarendon Press, Oxford, 1974.

R. J. Moore, *Escape from Empire: the Attlee Government and the Indian Problem*, Clarendon Press, Oxford, 1983.

Jawaharlal Nehru, *An Autobiography*, Bodley Head, London, 20th imp., 1953.

Thakin Nu, *Burma Under the Japanese: Pictures and Portraits*, Macmillan, London, 1954.

B. N. Pandey, *Nehru*, Macmillan, London, 1976.

R. Suntharalingam, *Indian Nationalism: an historical Analysis*, Vikas, Delhi, 1983.

J. R. S. Weerawardena, *Government and Politics in Ceylon, 1931–1946*, Ceylon Economic Research Association, Colombo, 1951.

After Independence: Chapters 10 and 11

A. Jeyaratnam Wilson and Dennis Dalton, *The States of South Asia*, C. Hurst, 1982.

Gunnar Myrdal, *Asian Drama: an Inquiry into the Poverty of Nations*, Allen Lane, London, 3 vols, 1968.

Saul Rose, *Socialism in Southern Asia*, Oxford University Press, London, 1959.

Saul Rose (ed.), *Politics in Southern Asia*, Macmillan, London, 1963.

Burma

U Nu, *U Nu- Saturday's Son*, Yale University Press, New Haven, 1975.

Josef Silverstein, *Burma: Military Rule and the Politics of Stagnation*, Cornell University Press, Ithaca, 1977.

David Steinberg, *Burma: a Socialist Nation of Southeast Asia*, Westview Press, Boulder, 1982.

Hugh Tinker, *Burma: the First Years of Independence*, Oxford University Press, 4th edn, 1967.

Ceylon/Sri Lanka

James Manor (ed.), *Sri Lanka in Change and Crisis*, Croom Helm, London, 1984.

S. A. Pakeman, *Ceylon*, Benn, London, 1964.
Tarzie Vittachi, *Emergency '58*, Deutsch, London, 1958.
A. Jeyaratnam Wilson, *Politics in Sri Lanka, 1947–1979*, Macmillan, 2nd edn, 1979.
A. Jeyaratnam Wilson, *The Gaullist System in Asia: the Constitution of Sri Lanka, 1978*, Macmillan, 1980.
Howard Wriggins, *Ceylon: Dilemmas of a New Nation*, Princeton University Press, 2nd edn, 1960.

India
Paul Brass, *Factional Politics in an Indian State: the Congress Party in Uttar Pradesh*, University of California Press, Berkeley, 1965.
Paul Brass, *Religion and Politics in North India*, Cambridge University Press, Cambridge, 1974.
A. R. Desai (ed.), *Peasant Struggles in India*, Oxford University Press, Delhi, 1979.
Francine Frankel, *India's Political Economy, 1947–1977*, Princeton University Press, 1978.
A. H. Hanson, *The Process of Planning: a Study of India's Five Year Plans, 1950–1964*, Oxford University Press, London, 1966.
Selig Harrison, *India: the Most Dangerous Decades*, Princeton University Press, 1960.
Jayaprakash Narayan, *Socialism, Sarvodaya and Democracy*, Asia Publishing House, 1964.
Rajiv Kapur, *Sikh Separatism: the Politics of Faith*, Allen & Unwin, 1986.
W. H. Morris-Jones, *Parliament in India*, Longmans, London, 1957.
Lloyd and Suzanne Rudolph, *The Modernity of Tradition: Political Development in India*, University of Chicago Press, Chicago, 1967.
Donald E. Smith, *India as a Secular State*, Princeton University Press, 1963.
M. N. Srinivas, *Social Change in Modern India*, University of California Press, Berkeley, 1966.
Myron Weiner, *Party Building in a New Nation: the Indian National Congress*, University of Chicago Press, 1967.
Myron Weiner (ed.), *State Politics in India*, Princeton University Press, 1968.

Pakistan
Craig Baxter (ed.), *Zia's Pakistan: Politics and Stability in a frontline State*, Westview Press, Boulder 1986.
Leonard Binder, *Religion and Politics in Pakistan*, University of California Press, 1961.
Shahid Javed Burki, *Pakistan Under Bhutto, 1971–1977*, Macmillan, 1980.
G. W. Choudhury, *Democracy in Pakistan*, Green Book House, Dacca, 1963.
Herbert Feldman, *From Crisis to Crisis, Pakistan in 1962–69*, Oxford University Press, London, 1973.
Mohammad Ayub Khan, *Friends Not Masters: a Political Autobiography*, Oxford University Press, London, 1967.
Gustav Papanek, *Pakistan's Development: Socialist Goals and Private Incentives*, Harvard University Press, Cambridge, 1967.

Lawrence Ziring (ed.), *Pakistan: the Long View*, Duke University Press, Durham, 1971.

Bangladesh
G. W. Choudhury, *The Last Days of United Pakistan*, C. Hurst, London, 1974.
Marcus Franda (ed.), *Bangladesh: the First Decade*, Vikas, Delhi, 1982.

Index

Asian names are listed under the first name (Ayub Khan, Aung San) except when an individual is better known by his last name (Gandhi, Nehru). Where there may be doubt, the entry is cross-referenced.